Benjamin Franklin's Intellectual World

Benjamin Franklin's Intellectual World

Paul E. Kerry and Matthew S. Holland

FAIRLEIGH DICKINSON UNIVERSITY PRESS
Madison • Teaneck

Published by Fairleigh Dickinson University Press
Co-published with The Rowman & Littlefield Publishing Group, Inc.
4501 Forbes Boulevard, Suite 200, Lanham, Maryland 20706
www.rowman.com

10 Thornbury Road, Plymouth PL6 7PP, United Kingdom

British Library Cataloguing in Publication Information Available

Library of Congress Cataloging-in-Publication Data

Paul E. Kerry and Matthew S. Holland.
Benjamin Franklin's intellectual world / edited by Paul E. Kerry and Matthew S. Holland.
p. cm.
Includes bibliographical references and index.
ISBN 978-1-61147-028-4 (cloth : alk. paper) -- ISBN ISBN 978-1-61147-029-1 (electronic)
1. Franklin, Benjamin, 1706-1790--Knowledge and learning. 2. Franklin, Benjamin, 1706-1790--Political and social views. 3. United States--Intellectual life--18th century. I. Kerry, Paul E. II. Holland, Matthew Scott, 1966-
E302.6.F8B494 2012
973.3092--dc23
2012029446

Printed in the United States of America

Contents

Acknowledgments

Many of the papers featured in this volume developed out of the only major Benjamin Franklin conference held in the United Kingdom, amid the various tercentenary celebrations of Franklin's birth held in 2006–2007. The conference was hosted by the University of Cambridge at the Centre for Research in the Arts, Social Sciences and Humanities (CRASSH)—a fitting location given Franklin's British friendships and his array of interdisciplinary interests.

We wish to express our thanks to those who participated in the conference:

- Patricia Fara, Clare College, Cambridge
- Paul Giles, Linacre College, Oxford
- Roy Goodman, American Philosophical Society
- Alan Houston, University of California, San Diego
- Mary Jacobus, Churchill College, Cambridge
- E. Philip Krider, University of Arizona
- Carla Mulford, Pennsylvania State University
- Simon Newman, University of Glasgow
- Michael O'Brien, Jesus College, Cambridge
- Jürgen Overhoff, University of Hamburg/University of Regensburg
- Finn Pollard, University of Glasgow
- Lady Joan Reid, Benjamin Franklin House, London
- Mark Skousen, Grantham University
- Sir John Meurig Thomas, University of Cambridge
- Jerry Weinberger, Michigan State University
- Michael Zuckerman, University of Pennsylvania

We were also delighted to see a few of our former Brigham Young University students, who were at the time postgraduate students in the United Kingdom, helping at the conference, including Jacob Lybbert (University College London), and Andrew Reed and Alexandra Zirkle (Woolf Institute, Centre for Jewish-Christian Relations, Cambridge).

We owe Roy Goodman, assistant librarian and curator of printed materials at the American Philosophical Society and a past president of Friends of Franklin, a special debt of gratitude for his encouragement, enthusiastic support, and extraordinarily helpful suggestions during the planning stages of the conference. A couple of short-term resident research fellowships at the American Philosophical Society and the David Library of the American Revolution provided the context for the fruitful collaboration between Roy and Paul. Thanks to the research seminars held at the McNeil Center for Early American Studies at the University of Pennsylvania, where Paul was a research associate, he was able to meet and learn from other scholars. Paul wishes to express his particular thanks to Professor Daniel K. Richter, director of the McNeil Center and professor of history at the University of Pennsylvania, for his continued support over the years.

Institutional and transatlantic cooperation were the hallmark of this project. We are grateful to the following institutions for their support of the Benjamin Franklin Conference held at the University of Cambridge in March 2007: the Centre for Research in the Arts, Social Sciences and Humanities at the University of Cambridge; History and Political Science Departments and the Kennedy Center for International Studies at Brigham Young University; American Philosophical Society; Friends of Franklin, Philadelphia; Association for the Study of Free Institutions; Benjamin Franklin House, London (36 Craven Street); FORA.tv; Lawrence Ventures; Mark Skousen (Franklin descendant); Tocqueville Institute; Wolfson College, Cambridge; King's College, Cambridge. Not least, we acknowledge gratefully the research support of the Woolf Institute, Cambridge; Utah Valley University; and the Wheatley Institution at Brigham Young University.

The key stages of the editing of this volume took place at Corpus Christi College, Cambridge, and Villanova University. Paul wishes to express his warmest thanks to Christopher Andrew, former president of Corpus and professor of history and to David Ibbetson, Regius Professor of Civil Law, chairman of the Law Faculty, and warden of Leckhampton. Their boundless hospitality and wit as they presided over dinner and combination were models of Cambridge conviviality. Similarly, we are grateful to Professor Colleen Sheehan, director of the Matthew J. Ryan Center, and Professor R. Emmett McLaughlin, History Department, for extending the hand of cooperation and kindness at Villanova.

We express our gratitude to Professor Harry Keyishian, director of Fairleigh Dickinson University Press, who gave this project his full attention at a critical time as the Press entered into a partnership with Rowman & Littlefield publishers to expand its reach. It has been a pleasure to associate with a gentleman and scholar of such wisdom and warmth over the years. A number of peer reviewers gave of their time to evaluate articles—a scholarly service that often goes unrecognized. Ruth Eldredge was enormously helpful as the preliminary copy editor and Doug Thomas brought his usual creativity to the cover's design and typographical look.

Thomas notes that the font design for the cover of this volume is similar to one that Franklin often used. The typefaces are based on William Caslon's London types that were employed with great frequency during the late eighteenth century, including for printings of the Declaration of Independence and the United States Constitution. The title on the front cover is Caslon redrawn by the type designer Matthew Carter. The technical name for the font is Carter & Cone Big Caslon Italic Medium. The smaller text on the back cover is Adobe Caslon, by Carol Twombly. The cover images feature several of Franklin's well-known publications such as the *Pennsylvania Gazette, Way to Wealth, Poor Richard's Almanack*, as well as the American founding documents he signed: the Declaration of Independence and the United States Constitution. The playful paper boats signify not only Franklin's personality, but allude to his transatlantic assignments in London and Paris as they sail across a 1793 French navigational map.

Our contributors were patient through the vicissitudes of the peer review and publishing process, even when the project appeared to languish. In fact, a couple of journals preempted us in publishing two pieces that we have here brought back to their origins. Professor Simon P. Newman's chapter was published in the *Journal of American Studies* 43 (2009):161–75. It is reprinted here by permission of Cambridge University Press. Professor Jürgen Overhoff's chapter was published in *German Studies Review* 34, no. 2 (2011): 277–86 © 2011 The German Studies Association. It is reprinted by permission of The Johns Hopkins University Press.

I would like to thank my colleague and friend Professor Matthew S. Holland for his continued active interest in this project even after he left Brigham Young University to become president of Utah Valley University. Without his support it would not have been possible to bring this volume to a successful conclusion; indeed, the conference would not have occurred in the first place. A truly collaborative spirit animated us as we envisioned a Benjamin Franklin conference at Cambridge, and another conference at the University of Edinburgh, Institute for Advanced Studies in the Humanities, on Transatlantic Ideas of the American Founding. The cover of this volume is based on the poster for the Edinburgh conference. We have always had a strong interest in bringing together political thought and intellectual history and in connecting American and European ideas—this book represents one fruit of those endeavors.

We were able to discuss the Franklin conference and other projects thanks in large part to Professor Holland having been awarded a visiting fellowship at Princeton University's James Madison Program in American Ideals and Institutions at a time when I was researching in archives in the area and affiliated with the McNeil Center. We would meet regularly, often at the Madison Program breakfast discussions in Bobst Hall generously hosted by the James Madison Program's founding director, Professor Robert P. George, who holds the McCormick Chair in Jurisprudence at Princeton University. Sometimes we would simply stroll through the beautiful Princeton environs and converse about ideas. When we have occasion to walk and talk about ideas now, it remains the best of times.

Preface

Lady Joan Reid

"Ideas will string themselves like Ropes of Onions."[1] Benjamin Franklin wrote this in a letter to an academic friend when he was consumed with excitement about the nature of electrical fire, and many other natural phenomena. This all-encompassing curiosity was the hallmark of his intellectual contribution throughout his life. There was simply nothing that he was not interested in and wanted to know more about, investigate, and also share with whoever would respond.

His few years of serious research took place in Philadelphia, mainly during the years 1748 to 1757. But because his reputation preceded him to London, he was able to fit in immediately to the Philosophical Societies that represented the English Enlightenment: The Royal Society and the Society of Arts.

His diplomatic life in London precluded active research, but enabled him to communicate with most of the likeminded philosophers of Europe, and made him one of the most prolific correspondents in an age of letter writers.

His intellectual contribution was startling. The combination of Observation, Experiment, and Intuition set the pattern of research into, and revelation of, the natural world, until the more systematic accuracy of the nineteenth century took over. It was said that he drove a wedge into the "congeries de bizarreries" and struck a shaft of lightning into the cloud of superstition.

Furthermore, his scientific discoveries rapidly became enmeshed in the political upheavals of the late eighteenth century as the Master of Lightning also became the figurehead of an Enlightened Republic. This dual role has catapulted Franklin into becoming one of the most researched and discussed of all the eighteenth-century figures. In the papers reproduced in this volume, we have a new contribution to this genre, and hope that a wide audience will find nuggets of originality and interest in the essays contained in the collection.

Long may the study of Franklin continue, and match his curiosity, clarity of style, and flow of innovative ideas. He created huge relevance to his own era and continuing fascination and inspiration for our own.

NOTE

1. Franklin to Jared Eliot, 17 July 1747, in *Papers: Digital Edition;* print edition in *Papers* 4:147.

Introduction: "Once more unto the breach, dear friends, once more ..."[1]

Paul E. Kerry and Matthew S. Holland

The recent Franklin tercentenary has produced a welcome spur to Franklin scholarship and any gaps in research are bound to attract learned tomes to fill them, even as they at times challenge established views and sometimes create new breaches. This volume represents an effort to bring together historians and political philosophers to explore elements of Franklin's self-fashioning and intellectual world in fresh ways.

The question of who was B. Franklin, which for decades in American history seemed self-evident,[2] has become increasingly prominent, especially in light of his self-fashioning strategies. Thankfully, there are differences of opinion on this subject, even in this volume. Simon Newman gives one view: "A true master of spin, Franklin enjoyed an enviable ability to construct and popularize certain public faces and images for himself while yet contriving to obscure others. As his autobiography makes abundantly clear, Franklin was enormously sensitive to the ways in which his contemporaries and posterity might regard him." On the other hand, Jerry Weinberger "disputes the prevailing view of Franklin as a mysterious, many faceted and ultimately unfathomable character."

Does the way we choose to refer to him, "Ben" or "Benjamin," say something about our views on the kind of man he was or the kind we believe he wanted us to see? Is "Ben" the man who Walter Isaacson charmingly calls "the founding father who winks at us," or is "Benjamin" more akin to the 1789 Francesco Lazzarini sculpture of Franklin in a Roman toga?[3] H. W. Brands calls him "The First American," but Gordon Wood perhaps would have him be the last.[4] Eliga Gould writes: "Before Franklin became the quintessential American, however, he was the quintessential British American."[5]

Stacy Schiff points out that Franklin's life was full of "protean transformations," some out of his control, in particular in the wake of his diplomatic mission to France.[6] She describes vividly how he was seen as a "British traitor," a "French saint," an "expatriate patriot," the "ur-American" who was "un-American," the man who could mingle in the salons and royal court of Versailles and yet be despised by the American gentry as a lowborn upstart.[7] Here, Michael Zuckerman considers how Franklin could fit into the courtly worlds of both London and Paris, the former requiring an aristocratic sensibility and the latter an almost pietistic one. He observes that Franklin's public career was a succession of performances: "As he admitted in his autobiography, which was in many ways a memoir of his mastery of disingenuousness and disguise, he perfected his technique in the provinces. By the time he came to act on the grandest stage in the Western world, with the fate of the American Revolution in his hands as surely as it was in Washington's, he was ready." Thus, Zuckerman gives weight to Franklin's escape from the religious homogeneity and narrow intellectual establishment of the Puritan capital of Boston and links the release of Franklin's creative powers to the religious, ethnic, and cultural diversity of Philadelphia and the Delaware Valley. In the words of Philip Dray, one could say that Franklin was "Made at Philadelphia."[8]

As Carl Van Doren opines of Franklin, "The death of a great man begins another history, of his continuing influence, his changing renown, the legend which takes the place of fact."[9] Wood acknowledges that Americans do not remember the historical significance of Franklin "that made him second only to Washington in importance" during the Revolution, but rather the "symbolic Franklin . . . who personifies the American dream."[10] Franklin was acutely aware of his legacy, and it is of course in the *Autobiography* that Franklin's self-fashioning occurs, both subtly and spectacularly. Jerry Weinberger avers here that although Franklin's thinking has been cast as elusive, it is nevertheless possible "for us to see the philosophical man beneath the masks he creates—to see his deepest and unified thinking about the big questions of life: morality, God, the good life, and the ends and best forms of government. And when the real Franklin emerges, he turns out to be a more disturbing and unconventional and radical thinker than is compatible with the complicated but deistic hero of public service of the fashionable biographies and recent scholarship."

Edmund Morgan is not alone in having called Franklin's attitude toward politics "pragmatic" and concentrated "on doing what was possible, what would work."[11] This has sometimes led to Franklin being seen more as a doer than a thinker, although it was his successes in natural philosophy that opened the door of his diplomatic mission in France, as E. Philip Krider indicates.[12] Franklin's writing style and effort to communicate broadly have contributed to the misperception of his intellectual vapidity: "Franklin's very simplicity of expression was taken as a representation of presumed shallow thinking. His rhetorical goal of writing in a plain style so as to be understood by many rather than a few was entirely disregarded."[13] Franklin was a master stylist, as attested to in his voluminous correspondence, and is considered "the most effective satirist publishing in the English-speaking world during the Revolutionary era."[14]

Carla Mulford points out in her chapter that Franklin has been accused of inconsistency in his colonial policies and proposals toward the British Empire. She insists, however, that one consistent strand in Franklin's long life is the position Franklin held regarding the ends of empire. These ends "ought to be the creation, material support, and protection of the best possible living circumstances for the greatest number of people living within the borders of territories putatively held as British territory, whether on the mainland or in colonies geographically dispersed." Yet, Franklin experienced time and again inconsistencies in British policies and thinking that led him, she argues, to criticize a Great Britain that had created "a system that yoked colonialism to liberalism and called it freedom." Similarly, Edmund Morgan considers that Franklin envisioned a "reconstructed empire . . . a union of equals."[15]

Neil York captured Franklin's conception of such an empire, more akin to a Commonwealth: "For so many years Franklin, the proud citizen of empire, had believed that he could be both—that he could think of Pennsylvania as his country, that as an agent he could talk to his employers of Massachusetts as 'our' country and not see such identities as irreconcilable with loyalty to empire." Franklin's humiliation in the "cockpit" at Whitehall in 1774 effectively caused him to recognize the true nature of the imperial relationship from the perspective of the Crown.[16] York here illuminates, however, why Britain failed to coax revolutionary Americans back into the empire through the microcosm of a shadowy episode in which Franklin, while on his diplomatic mission in France, is enticed to reconsider the colonial break with Britain. This episode, asserts York, is a "reminder that many people knew then, as scholars emphasize now, that identities and boundaries were fluid in the British Atlantic world, that most Americans who turned to revolution did so reluctantly, and that many did not embrace it at all."

Simon Newman's piece focuses on Franklin in Philadelphia. He limns a powerful portrait associating Franklin, more than any one of his illustrious colleagues, with the leather apron and craftsmanship, one who rose from Boston apprentice to successful journeyman and master craftsman in Philadelphia. Very few of the founding generation's leaders could claim this kind of background of both obscurity and manual labor. Newman observes that although Franklin was constantly drawing attention to his own achievements

(Joyce Chaplin describes his self-promotion as careful and relentless),[17] he also never tired of celebrating similar successes by others: "He revelled in the life that commercial success and financial independence afforded him, writing, conducting scientific experiments and exchanging ideas with some of the greatest minds of his generation, and he told all who would listen that he had succeeded. Yet throughout his life Franklin never looked down upon honest and capable workers, identifying with them and affording them a remarkable status and level of respect." There is a comprehensive logic to Franklin's approach to both the macrocosm and microcosm of his life; in other words, if the ends of empire are, as Mulford argues, a mutually beneficial relationship no matter the kind of colony, then for Franklin the ends of human relationships are mutual respect and recognition of merit, no matter the origin of the person.

The vision that Franklin opened up in the new American Republic was one of a vast array of areas in which one could excel. Although opportunities differed, the qualities of mind between those of high birth or inherited wealth with those who had neither were not inherent—Franklin, himself "a commoner and colonist," had through science won recognition and reward.[18] Franklin believed not only that self-improvement was possible but that an entire community could improve,[19] as Alan Houston so effectively argues.[20] This self- and community-improvement could be assisted through education, of which Franklin was a life-long and innovative proponent. Indeed, Zuckerman observes that among the Founding Fathers Franklin had no equal as an educational thinker save perhaps Benjamin Rush: "[Franklin] wrestled conscientiously and creatively with educational issues that perplex and preoccupy us to this day, issues of class, gender, and race."[21] Franklin's lifelong development of voluntary associations, private enterprise, and community-based solutions are a strong testament to a political philosophy that fostered institutions and activities that would allow structured liberty to flourish and that resisted intrusive policies that would attempt to occupy completely the social and creative spaces of its citizens.[22]

Franklin worked through voluntary associations, such as the forerunner to the Library Company of Philadelphia he helped to found, to level the playing field of opportunity. It follows that Franklin's own academic foundation, which would eventually become the University of Pennsylvania, placed commerce on an equal footing with traditional subjects. Walter Isaacson proposes that Franklin's university vision encouraged all "'aspiring' young men" whereas Thomas Jefferson's University of Virginia favored a "'natural aristocracy'" and filtered for a "new leadership elite."[23]

David Shields voices the view that "Franklin's contemporary reputation as a member of the international community of thinkers and writers known as the 'republic of letters' has received less attention" than other areas of his life.[24] Recent exemplary books by Joyce Chaplin and Stacy Schiff are rectifying this imbalance, as does Jürgen Overhoff's chapter in this volume.[25] Certainly Franklin has become accepted as one who represents and is associated with Enlightenment ideas and institutions.[26] He valued and learned from his associations in London (especially The Royal Society), Paris, and Göttingen and helped to found a similar association in colonial Philadelphia, the American Philosophical Society.

Overhoff mines a neglected area of research—Franklin's 1766 journey to Germany—to get at Franklin's intellectual world. He provides key evidence that in this crucial year Franklin was doing more than taking a holiday along the Rhine and enjoying the mineral water (Mulford also notes that this period was critical to Franklin's thinking about empire). Overhoff describes how Franklin did more than pay mere social calls to some of the greatest political thinkers in the Germanic lands. He focuses on Franklin's interest in understanding the governing principles of the complicated structure of the Holy Roman Empire. Overhoff demonstrates how Franklin's questions were aimed in particular at the empire's federal constitution—a subject that would of course be of especial interest to the writers of the Federalist Papers in their evaluation of different forms of government. In this thinking, Overhoff is in sync with a recrudescence of interest in the Holy Roman Empire in connection with Great Britain and the colonies argued by, among others, Brendan Simms.[27]

Benjamin Franklin caught the attention of and was celebrated by German luminaries outside of Göttingen as the knowledge of his publications and political actions fanned out across the patchwork quilt of Germanic kingdoms and principalities. The intellectual elite, including Lessing, Herder, and Schiller, were aware of his exploits and successes, and his humane and enlightened views. The most well-known German man of letters, Johann Wolfgang von Goethe, was also not immune to admiring Franklin. He devoured the *Autobiography* and as a man of science himself was drawn to Franklin's experiments in electricity. In some ways it is no surprise that one of Germany's foremost self-fashioners should be attracted to another.

Yet, Paul E. Kerry distills more from the influence of Franklin on Goethe. Goethe's views go beyond seeing Franklin as one consumed by controlling his image, legacy, and fame. Fame, as Richard Beeman postulates, had multivalent meanings: "The pursuit of fame, in the eighteenth-century meaning of that word, had a dynamic quality, encouraging one to make history, to leave the mark of one's deeds and ideals on the world."[28] Goethe saw that Franklin's commitment to self-creation allowed him to believe in this same possibility for others and to be tolerant toward those who followed their own paths of self-development. Franklin's "vision of America" was not dependent on wealth or social class but was "based on [one's] willingness to be industrious and cultivate their virtues."[29] This resonated with Goethe's own ideal of *Bildung*, a concept of self-cultivation and the creation of personal meaning that would become an ideal for others, including Emerson and Carlyle.

Franklin, unlike some of the *philosophes* with whom he associated in Paris, was (like Goethe) open to others choosing religion as a pathway to such development. Kerry S. Walters captures the underlying assumptions at work in this broad acceptance: "For Franklin, the essence of religious belief was its ability to enhance personal meaning and promote virtue."[30] Franklin understood that successful existence in a community as diverse as Philadelphia required patience, tolerance, and cooperation. The city's commitment to a variety of religions was brought home to Goethe through reports sent back to Weimar by a royal who had journeyed to America to observe the young country.[31] Philadelphia features in one of Goethe's major works as a place of "Religionsfreiheit" (religious freedom).[32]

For all of Franklin's emphasis on personal self-development, it is remarkable that he invested so much of his life in public service and community improvement. Alan Houston shows that Franklin considered earnestly the deeper philosophical questions behind the politics of improvement, such as: "At any given point in time, what options are available? Which has the greatest advantages, or the fewest disadvantages? Can men and women be brought to support it? Using what means? And with what consequences?"[33] Indeed, as the Roy E. Goodman collection of Frankliniana plainly illustrated when it was recently exhibited as "Cents and Sensibility: Benjamin Franklin and Popular Culture" at the Phillips Museum of Art in the Dana and Rothman Galleries of Franklin and Marshall College, Franklin's name and image have come to be associated with civic service in the worlds of commerce, philanthropy, and government, and in American popular culture generally.[34]

Franklin struggled with a central paradox: "knowledge was sociable and collaborative, but not everyone could contribute to it."[35] Yet, as John Pollack's recent collection of essays brings to light, as many as possible should have the opportunity to benefit from learning.[36] Shields propounds that it is necessary to go beyond the institution of the press to account for Franklin's role in the Republic of Letters and to investigate "domains upon which the republic's communication depended: libraries, clubs, learned societies, and associations. Franklin cultivated models of communication and persuasion favored by the republic of letters—conversation, wit, and the familiar letter."[37] Of course, Franklin was a printer, bookseller, and publisher, the latter being "the most entrepreneurial of all the members of the book trade."[38] Douglas B. Thomas notes a new direction in Franklin scholarship to take seriously these roles, in particular the "primacy of printing to any interpretation of Franklin's life, writings, and intellectual world."[39] Thomas draws in particular on the work of James Green and Peter Stallybrass to highlight the new trend.[40]

Although Franklin was undoubtedly a self-fashioner, one should avoid the temptation to see in this merely self-promotion. His life itself stands against such a narrow interpretation. This seems to be a central tension of the *Autobiography*: that certain virtues keep in balance self-improvement and and community development. Michael Zuckerman has put forward the idea that Franklin "did not set any sharp distinction between private pursuits and a self-conscious consideration of the public welfare," and hence so many of Franklin's civic contributions were genuinely conceived of from the start as "cooperative ventures."[41]

The drive in Franklin to improve himself and his community, to be of genuine service, springs from a blend of sources, including Enlightenment thought[42] and his Judeo-Christian inheritance.[43] He famously stated that he looked to both Socrates and Jesus as moral and ethical models, thus suggesting that the wisdom of Athens and Jerusalem should contribute to full human flourishing.[44] There is something almost Pauline in the way Franklin lived his life. It is not too difficult to imagine Franklin penning words similar to these: "For though I be free from all men, yet have I made myself servant unto all, that I might gain the more" (1 Corinthians 9:19).[45] Saint Paul sought to evangelize Jews and non-Jews to the Christian faith. But for what cause did Franklin seek to gain? It can be described pithily through what is often attributed as a Hindu proverb: "Help thy brother's boat across, and Lo! Thine own has reached the shore." Franklin perceived that communities, whether his local one in Philadelphia, the transatlantic one that failed, or the new national one he had helped to inaugurate, required an ethic of reciprocity to flourish. This central civic ethic of reciprocity could bind a nation of disparate beliefs together. Perhaps this is a little of what Franklin had in mind when he referred to "the necessity of a publick religion."[46] Others of the founding generation, such as Jefferson, also understood that political liberty could not stand alone without other virtues that would allow communities to thrive.[47] Franklin's life of public service and certainly his portrayal of that life conveyed the sense that we are all in this together. Surely this is a sentiment worth reviving in our current civic culture, for following from that proposition are the concepts of mutual respect and cooperation and, perhaps, finding ways to serve one another.

One example from Franklin's life illustrates this point. The challenge and fragility of everyday living and the choices we make no matter our beliefs are thrown into vivid relief in the *Autobiography*. Franklin reveals a deeply personal event with a touch that manages to be at once poignant and yet detached, but also gently prescriptive, so that his life, including his regrets, might be profitable to others. He gives us a window on what one scholar calls a "very private tragedy":[48] "In 1736 I lost one of my Sons, a fine Boy of 4 Years old, by the Small Pox taken in the common way. I long regretted bitterly and still regret that I had not given it to him by Inoculation; This I mention for the Sake of Parents, who omit that Operation on the Supposition that they should never forgive themselves if a Child died under it; my Example showing that Regret may be the same either way, and therefore the safer should be chosen."[49] This seems less a self-fashioning strategy and more a sharing of self, as Franklin sought to do in so many areas, practical and philosophical.

NOTES

1. *Henry V*, act 3, scene 1, in *The Riverside Shakespeare: The Complete Works*, 2nd ed. (Boston: Houghton Mifflin, 1997), 991.
2. George Bancroft on Franklin: "He was a man of the best understanding, never disturbed by recollections or fears, with none of the capricious anxieties of diseased minds, or the susceptibilities of disturbed self-love. Free from the illusions of poetic natures, he loved truth for its own sake, and looked upon things just as they were. As a consequence he had no eloquence but that of clearness. He computed that the inheritor of a noble title in the ninth generation represents at most but the five hundred and twelfth part of the ancestor; nor was he awed by a crosier or dazzled by a crown. He knew the moral world to be subjected to laws like the natural world; in conducting affairs he remembered the necessary relation of cause and effect, aiming only at what was possible; and with a tranquil mind he signed the treaty with France, just as with a tranquil eye he had contemplated the dangers of his country. In regard to money he was frugal, that he might be independent, and that he might be generous. He owed good health to his exemplary temperance. Habitually gay, employment was his resource against weariness and sorrow, and contentment came from his superiority to ambition, interest, or vanity. There was about him more of moral greatness than appeared on the surface; and while he made no boast of unselfish benevolence, there never lived a man who would have met martyrdom in the course of duty more surely or more unmoved." In *History of the United States from the Discovery of the American Continent* (Boston: Little, Brown and Company, 1866), 9:490–91.
3. Walter Isaacson, *Benjamin Franklin: An American Life* (New York: Simon & Schuster, 2003), 2.
4. H. W. Brands, *The First American. The Life and Times of Benjamin Franklin* (New York: Doubleday, 2000), and Gordon S. Wood, *The Americanization of Benjamin Franklin* (New York: Penguin, 2004). Konstantin Dierks: "Gordon Wood stands as something of an exception among the ranks of new Franklin biographers, since he postpones Franklin's becoming an American until after his death in 1790," in "Benjamin Franklin and Colonial Society," in *A Companion to Benjamin Franklin*, ed. David Waldstreicher (Malden, MA: Wiley-Blackwell, 2011), 89.
5. Eliga Gould's "Empire and Nation," in *A Companion to Benjamin Franklin*, ed. David Waldstreicher (Malden, MA: Wiley-Blackwell, 2011), 359.
6. Franklin, of course, had the intellectual resources to understand how to adapt rapidly in so many settings, not least through his wide reading. See Edwin Wolf 2nd and Kevin J. Hayes, *The Library of Benjamin Franklin* (Philadelphia: American Philosophical Society and Library Company of Philadelphia, 2006). See also Kevin J. Hayes, "Benjamin Franklin's Library," in *The Cambridge Companion to Benjamin Franklin*, ed. Carla Mulford (Cambridge: Cambridge University Press, 2008), 11–23.
7. Stacy Schiff, *A Great Improvisation: Franklin, France, and the Birth of America* (New York: Henry Holt and Company, 2005), 404. David Waldstreicher questions just how far such transformations went on the issue of Franklin and slavery in *Runaway America: Benjamin Franklin, Slavery, and the American Revolution* (New York: Hill and Wang, 2004).
8. This phrase is the title to chapter 2 of Philip Dray's *Stealing God's Thunder: Benjamin Franklin's Lightning Rod and the Invention of America* (New York: Random House, 2005), 23.
9. Carl Van Doren, *Benjamin Franklin* (New York: Viking Press, 1938), 781.

10. Wood, *Americanization of Benjamin Franklin*, 246.

11. Edmund S. Morgan, *Benjamin Franklin* (New Haven, CT: Yale University Press, 2002), 181.

12. E. Philip Krider, "Benjamin Franklin's Science," in *Benjamin Franklin: In Search of a Better World*, ed. Page Talbott (New Haven, CT: Yale University Press, 2005), 196–97.

13. Nian-Sheng Huang and Carla Mulford, "Benjamin Franklin and the American Dream," in *The Cambridge Companion to Benjamin Franklin*, ed. Carla Mulford (Cambridge: Cambridge University Press, 2008), 156.

14. David S. Shields, "Franklin in the Republic of Letters," in *The Cambridge Companion to Benjamin Franklin*, ed. Carla Mulford (Cambridge: Cambridge University Press), 61; see also Paul E. Kerry, "Franklin's Satiric Vein," in ibid., 37–49.

15. Morgan, *Benjamin Franklin*, 182.

16. Neil Longley York, *Turning the World Upside Down: The War of American Independence and the Problem of Empire* (Westport, CT: Praeger, 2003), 113.

17. Joyce Chaplin, *The First Scientific American: Benjamin Franklin and the Pursuit of Genius* (New York: Basic Books, 2006), 132.

18. Ibid., 132.

19. Jürgen Overhoff suggests that Franklin's citizens' initiatives model engines of reform, namely, bottom-up movement (rather than top-down) and a use of civic liberty to influence and foster good government. (*Benjamin Franklin: Erfinder, Freigeist, Staatenlenker* [Stuttgart: Klett-Cotta, 2006], 304.)

20. Alan Houston, *Benjamin Franklin and the Politics of Improvement* (New Haven, CT: Yale University Press, 2008). See Albrecht Koschnik's "Benjamin Franklin, Associations, and Civil Society," in *A Companion to Benjamin Franklin*, ed. David Waldstreicher (Malden, MA: Wiley-Blackwell, 2011), 335–58. Koschnik's historiographical discussion is especially enlightening.

21. Michael Zuckerman, "Founding Fathers: Franklin, Jefferson, and the Educability of Americans," in *"The Good Education of Youth": Worlds of Learning in the Age of Franklin*, ed. John Pollack (New Castle, DE, and Philadelphia: Oak Knoll Press and University of Pennsylvania Libraries, 2009), 36–53; see also Carla Mulford, "Benjamin Franklin, Traditions of Liberalism, and Women's Learning in Eighteenth-Century Philadelphia," in ibid., 100–121.

22. For arguments on the importance of these principles, see Jean Bethke Elshtain, *Sovereignty: God, State, and Self* (New York: Basic Books, 2008); and Peter Berger and Richard John Neuhaus, "Mediating Structures and the Dilemmas of the Modern Welfare State," in *To Empower People: From State to Civil Society* (Washington, DC: American Enterprise Institute, 1996), 157–64.

23. Isaacson, *Benjamin Franklin: An American Life*, 149.

24. David Shields, "Franklin in the Republic of Letters," in *Cambridge Companion to Benjamin Franklin*, ed. Carla Mulford (Cambridge: Cambridge University Press, 2008), 50.

25. Schiff, *Great Improvisation*; Chaplin, *The First Scientific American*. See also Jack Fruchtman Jr., *Atlantic Cousins: Benjamin Franklin and His Visionary Friends* (New York: Basic Books, 2005).

26. See the Franklin entries in these volumes: *Encyclopedia of the Enlightenment*, ed. Alan Charles Kors (Oxford: Oxford University Press, 2003), vol. 2; *Encyclopedia of the Enlightenment*, ed. Peter Hanns Reill and Ellen Judy Wilson (New York: Facts on File, 1996); *The Blackwell Companion to the Enlightenment*, ed. John W. Yolton, Roy Porter, Pat Rogers, and Barbara Maria Stafford (Oxford: Blackwell, 1995). See also Frank Kelleter's "Franklin and the Enlightenment," in *The Cambridge Companion to Benjamin Franklin*, ed. Carla Mulford (Cambridge: Cambridge University Press, 2008), 77–90.

27. Brendan Simms, *Three Victories and a Defeat: The Rise and Fall of the British Empire, 1714–1783* (London: Allen Lane, 2007).

28. Richard Beeman, "Benjamin Franklin and the American Enlightenment," The Benjamin Franklin Tercentary, www.benfranklin300.org/_etc_pdf/Enlightenment_Richard_Beeman.pdf .

29. Isaacson, *American Life*, 149.

30. Kerry S. Walters, *Benjamin Franklin and His Gods* (Urbana: University of Illinois Press, 1999), 145.

31. Prince Carl Bernhard von Sachsen-Weimar-Eisenach, *Reise Sr. Hoheit des Herzogs Bernhard zu Sachsen-Weimar-Eisenach durch Nord-Amerika in den Jahren 1825 und 1826*, ed. Heinrich Luden (Weimar: Wilhelm Hoffman, 1828).

32. Paul E. Kerry, *Enlightenment Thought in the Writings of Goethe: A Contribution to the History of Ideas* (Rochester, NY: Camden House, 2009), 156–76.

33. Houston, *Politics of Improvement*, 16.

34. See the catalog for the exhibition at http://books.google.com/books. Also see Andrew M. Schocket's "Benjamin Franklin in Memory and Popular Culture," in *A Companion to Benjamin Franklin*, ed. David Waldstreicher (Malden, MA: Wiley-Blackwell, 2011), 479–98.

35. Ibid., 55.

36. John H. Pollack, ed., *"The Good Education of Youth": Worlds of Learning in the Age of Franklin* (New Castle, DE, and Philadelphia: Oak Knoll Press and the University of Pennsylvania Libraries, 2009).

37. Shields, "Republic of Letters," 51.

38. James N. Green, "Benjamin Franklin, Printer," in *Benjamin Franklin: In Search of a Better World*, ed. Page Talbott (New Haven, CT: Yale University Press, 2005), 76.

39. See also J. A. Leo Lemay, *Life of Benjamin Franklin: Volume 1, Journalist, 1706–1730*, and *Volume 2, Printer and Publisher* (Philadelphia: University of Pennsylvania Press, 2005–8).

40. James N. Green and Peter Stallybrass, *Benjamin Franklin, Writer and Printer* (New Castle, DE: Oak Knoll Press, 2006).

41. Michael Zuckerman, "Doing Good While Doing Well: Benevolence and Self-Interest in Franklin's *Autobiography*," in *Reappraising Benjamin Franklin: A Bicentennial Perspective*, ed. J. A. Leo Lemay (Newark, DE: University of Delaware Press, 1993), 441–51.

42. See Douglas Anderson, *The Radical Enlightenments of Benjamin Franklin* (Baltimore: Johns Hopkins University Press, 1998). Anderson sees Franklin participating in the educational and moral discourse of the Enlightenment, in particular with Franklin's commitment to a "gradual, tutorial strategy" as embodied in his almanac (106).

43. See John C. Van Horne, "Collective Benevolence and the Common Good in Franklin's Philanthropy," in *Reappraising Benjamin Franklin: A Bicentennial Perspective*, ed. J. A. Leo Lemay (Newark, DE: University of Delaware Press, 1993), 425–40. Van Horne argues that although Franklin drew on Christian ideas, he secularized them so that a civic institution such as the Library Company that served the common good could be considered "divine" (430–31).

44. *Autobiography*, 150.

45. See John Fea's "Benjamin Franklin and Religion," in *A Companion to Benjamin Franklin*, ed. David Waldstreicher (Malden, MA: Wiley-Blackwell, 2011), 129–45.

46. As quoted in Martin E. Marty with Jonathon Moore, *Politics, Religion, and the Common Good: Advancing a Distinctly American Conversation about Religion's Role in our Shared Life* (San Francisco, CA: Jossey-Bass, 2000), 14. The quotation is found in the pamphlet *Proposals Relating to the Education of Youth in Philadelphia*, in *Papers* 3:413.

47. See Matthew S. Holland, *Bonds of Affection: Civic Charity and the Making of America—Winthrop, Jefferson, and Lincoln* (Washington, DC: Georgetown University Press, 2007). See also Douglas Anderson's "The Art of Virtue," in *The Cambridge Companion to Benjamin Franklin*, ed. Carla Mulford (Cambridge: Cambridge University Press, 2008), 24–36.

48. See George W. Boudreau's "The Philadelphia Years, 1723–1757," in *A Companion to Benjamin Franklin*, ed. David Waldstreicher (Malden, MA: Wiley-Blackwell, 2011), 25–45, esp. 35 where Boudreau discusses the context of this tragedy.

49. *Autobiography*, 170.

Abbreviations

The following works are cited with the following abbreviations throughout this volume:

Autobiography

Franklin, Benjamin. *The Autobiography of Benjamin Franklin*. Edited by Leonard W. Labaree, Ralph L. Ketcham, Helen C. Boatfield, and Helene H. Fineman. New Haven, CT: Yale University Press, 1964. [First published in Paris: Buisson 1791 (French edition); first English publication in London: J. Parsons, 1793.]

Papers

Franklin, Benjamin. *The Papers of Benjamin Franklin*. 39 volumes to date. Edited by Leonard W. Labaree, et al. New Haven: Yale University Press, 1959–.

Papers: Digital Edition

Franklin, Benjamin. *The Papers of Benjamin Franklin*. Edited by Leonard W. Labaree, et al. Digital edition, including forthcoming print volumes, published by the Packard Humanities Institute. http://franklinpapers.org/franklin/framedVolumes.jsp.

Chapter One

Franklin's Masks

A Play upon Possibility

Michael Zuckerman

America was always a place of possibility. The soaring visionaries saw it. So did the adventurous and the avaricious.

They sailed with Columbus and conquered with Cortes. They searched for El Dorado and the Seven Cities of Cibola. They burned with avidity for mineral treasure and, some of them, for something more. They meant to be ravishingly rich and, some of them, to explore wider horizons and wilder lusts, for power and for perpetuity. They did not just search for gold. They enslaved Aztecs and Incas, and they imported Africans when they ran out of natives. They scoured the New World for the fountain of youth.

The English came later than the conquistadors, but they came with a comparable conviction that marvels were possible in the New World that were not possible in the Old. In Guiana, Sir Walter Raleigh did not doubt the stories he heard of men whose heads hung below their shoulders. He even averred that he had seen such wonders for himself. In Roanoke, John White did not hesitate to draw the natives as noble savages. He even imagined them as men who might redeem a ruined Europe and return it to an innocent primitivity in which it could begin anew.

William Penn put it best. On the day after he received his royal charter for Pennsylvania, he imagined his unborn colony "the seed of a nation." A few months later, before he had even seen the first voyagers off from England, he confided his hope that there would "be room there, though not here," for the "holy experiment" he envisioned. [1]

Others less eloquent felt the same sense that what could only be conceived at home might be achieved in America. Half a century before Penn, Puritans who despaired of reforming the Church of England set sail for a new

England across the Atlantic. What could not be done under King James, King Charles, and Archbishop Laud might be accomplished in a remote wilderness, where God's ordinances could be made manifest and the dream of repressive discipline made law.

The founders of Pennsylvania and Massachusetts began with blueprints. They prepared frames of government and prized charters. They had a notion of what their ideal society would look like before they laid eyes on it. America was to them only an arena where their fabulous plans could be put into practice.

Others were more open to a fuller play of possibility. They had no ambition of instituting God's will, nor any aspiration to establish a utopian community. They were driven by greed and go-getting, and they went where opportunity offered.

From the first, Virginia aroused a passion for outlandish wealth. The early Virginians expected to find precious metals, to discover the Northwest Passage, to cultivate silk, and to grow every exotic tropical commodity in demand in the mother country.

The pamphlets they published to attract immigrants to the infant settlement expressed their unbounded optimism, and something else as well. Those promotions promised luxurious living without effort. They offered a life of ease. They told of streams teeming with fish, where a single dip of the net would bring up more of the finny creatures than a man could eat in a day. They told of skies alive with game birds, where a single pull of the trigger would bring down a half-dozen or more. They told of a virgin soil grateful for seed, where a single sowing would bring up grain in an abundance unknown to the weary fields of Europe. They told of riches, but they intimated Eden.

All of those dreams were European dreams. Fabulous wealth, fountains of youth, Quakerism, Puritanism, a world turned upside down, redemption, and a paradisal prospect of surcease from labor were all notions born and nourished in the Old World.

And those European dreams did not end with the end of the colonial connection to the Old World. If anything, they grew more vivid. They drove a continuing migration to an America whose streets were reliably reported to be paved with gold.

America was always, for Europeans susceptible to its allure, the possibility of a larger life. In time, Americans themselves came to embrace those European aspirations. And no American pointed the way to the domestication of European dreams as evocatively as Benjamin Franklin.

Franklin was hardly the first colonist to achieve affluence in the New World. But those who preceded him dealt with it differently. Some, primarily the sugar planters of the West Indies, acquired extravagant wealth and used it to return to England, acquire vast estates, and live like lords. Others, on the mainland, made more modest fortunes from tobacco and tried to separate themselves from lesser planters as a creole gentry.

Franklin was the first to live the dream and boast that he had done so. He did not deny his humble past. He did not try to leave it behind him. At the end of his days, he was a more committed democrat than he had ever been in his youth. He even came full circle to manual laboring once more, on the working press he outfitted at Passy. In his last will and testament, he referred to himself as "Benjamin Franklin, printer."

The very point of his autobiography was his emphatic insistence on his humble origins. He recalled in pungent detail his father's inability to afford him more than a couple of years of inconsequential schooling, his own penniless entry into Philadelphia with those three puffy rolls, and his struggles to shed his leather apron. The salience of his story, as he chose to tell it, was that such a youth could look with pride on "the poverty and obscurity in which [he] was born and bred," after he came "to a state of affluence and some degree of reputation in the world." A low-born American son could glory in fulfilling his humble father's prophesy that he would one day "stand before kings."[2]

If, to this day, Americans still identify their character with the possibility of rising wondrously in the world, it is in no small measure because Ben Franklin taught them to do so. If, to this day, they still imagine themselves inhabitants of a land of opportunity and cherish their American dream as a democratic dream, it is in substantial part because he coached them in such self-congratulation and such self-construction. It is not for nothing that his recent biographers have hailed him as the first American and even as the veritable inventor of America.[3]

But such invention is more than a little equivocal. It conjures consideration of facades and phantasms rather than facts on the ground. And well it should. Franklin was nothing if not a master of the management of impressions.

He was, after all, a man who could wear wigs and waistcoats for the British, when he was provincial Pennsylvania's agent at Whitehall, and then put on that cockamamie coonskin cap for the French, when he was America's minister plenipotentiary in Paris. Acutely alert to images as he was, Franklin figured out fast that the British would ignore anyone who did not exhibit an aristocratic bearing and figured out even faster that the French would ignore any imposter who did. The court of George III was full of arrivistes. The more glittering entourage of Louis XVI teemed with real noblemen who would recognize and resent aristocratic affectation. At Versailles and in the salons of Paris, Franklin abandoned the pretense of calculated homage that he had paid to the nouveaux riches of London. He presented himself not as a gentleman, whom the British gentry could accept as one of their own, but as a backwoods Quaker, whom the French elite could patronize.

Knowing that Montesquieu, Voltaire, Raynal, and other French men of letters admired the Quakers, Franklin let Parisians think him a follower of the Friends, though he had no discernible gift for spirituality and no aptitude for the Inner Light at all. Knowing that Rousseau and his followers were infatuated with fantasies of noble savages, he posed as a frontier *philosophe*, though he had always made his home in the leading cities of the land.

In playing to French sensibilities, Franklin was doing what he had done all his life. His public career was a succession of performances. As he admitted in his autobiography, which was in many ways a memoir of his mastery of disingenuousness and disguise, he perfected his technique in the provinces. By the time he came to act on the grandest stage in the Western world, with the fate of the American Revolution in his hands as surely as it was in Washington's, he was ready.

From his first appearance in public life, Franklin showed his instinct for the theatrical. Rather than attempting to find his own voice, he assumed another's. Walter Isaacson caught his audacity exactly. "Silence Dogood was a slightly prudish widowed woman from a rural area." Franklin himself was "a spunky unmarried Boston teenager who had never spent a night outside of the city."[4]

Such an impersonation must have delighted Franklin. He found pleasure in deception for its own sake. He found special pleasure in duplicity that embarrassed the editor of the *The New England Courant*, James Franklin, who would not have published the essays if he had known that they were written by his precocious younger brother. But Franklin's imagination of himself as different and distant from his actual condition was more than sweet subterfuge, more than a satisfying embarrassment of his brother, more even than the commencement of a lifelong habit of anonymity and pseudonymity. It was also a necessity, to evade the authority of his brother and the much more imposing authority of Boston orthodoxy. It was the only way he could "change the joke and slip the yoke," as Ralph Ellison put it in an extraordinary essay that actually invokes Franklin.[5]

Franklin could never have been Franklin in Boston. Sooner or later, its religious and intellectual establishment would have driven him to self-destruction, either by acquiescence or by ineffectual defiance. Even as an adolescent, he understood that much. In a society that insisted on uniformity, there were but two alternatives, compliance and opposition. Again and again in his autobiography, Franklin recalled his reluctance to comply and his awareness of the perils of opposition. He knew that he could not hold his tongue and that his outspoken alienation from local norms was "productive of disgusts and perhaps enmities." Proper Bostonians already viewed him "in an unfavorable light," as one who "had a turn for libeling and satire." He could see that he was bound to "bring [him]self into scrapes," by the "rubs" he gave to "rulers" and by the "indiscreet disputations about religion" from which he refused to refrain. He knew that he would have to escape the Puritan metropolis. People there were already pointing at him "with horror."[6]

Franklin could only have flourished in a pluralistic place like Philadelphia, where the choices were not the debilitating ones of conformity or resistance but the vitalizing ones of an open society.

In Boston, he learned about integrity. One way and another, it was the only thing the town had to teach. But he fled Boston, and he never again lived in a place of such coercive homogeneity. In Philadelphia, he discovered a religious, ethnic, and national diversity undesired and unimaginable in the Puritan capital, and he realized as if intuitively that, though he had left his native land behind, he had arrived in his native element. He was, in more ways than not, born in Philadelphia, at the age of seventeen.

Amid the multitudinous cultures on the Delaware, he grasped from the first the one essential thing. If he meant to make his way in a community where no religion ruled and where all men and all creeds were welcome, he would have to disabuse himself of any ideals of integrity brought from Boston. If he wished to advance himself among people of so many faiths, he would have to talk to them each on their own terms. If he wished to promote his plans among people of so many nations, he would have to master the management of impressions and the presentation of self. In Philadelphia, he learned about style.

In politics, he had a genius for catching the views and values of others. He represented the artisans to the gentry and the gentry to the artisans, and the skill and fidelity with which he did made him the most powerful man in Pennsylvania.

In his prose, he ranged even more widely and wandered even more daringly from his own presumptive person. He took the part of rich people when he was poor and of poor people when he was richer. He played old folks when he was young and young ones when he was older. He did female impersonations. He did escape artistry. He did ventriloquism. Like the one American who would ever rival him, P. T. Barnum, he was always in the show business.

Franklin crafted characters effortlessly, and almost every one was strikingly unlike the Franklin we think we know. Silence Dogood forecast Alice Addertongue, Anthony Afterwit, Polly Baker, Celia Single, Jethro Standfast, Abigail Twitterfield, and dozens of others. From his first writings to his last, Franklin was fearless in assuming identities distant from his own.

He made his initial appearance in print as a woman and his valedictory as Sidi Mehemet Ibrahim, an African defender of the enslavement of Christians. He wrote as an Indian chief and, twice, as an African American slave. Indeed, his Dingo was the first "slave" voice in American letters, and his Blackamore the second.

His dying declamation as a devout Muslim was no more a fictive reach, for Franklin, than his earlier affectations of other religious personae and prose styles. He passed for a Jesuit and for a Jewish patriarch. He played both parts in a debate between two Presbyterians. More than once, he masqueraded as a Quaker lady. He composed parables in the idiom of the Old Testament and the New. And he outdid himself in his counterfeit of an orthodox New England clergyman.

His secular range was wider still. He was the dirty old man of "Old Mistresses Apologue"—written before he turned forty—and the daft old man Father Abraham of *The Way to Wealth*. He was the lying shopkeeper Betty Diligent and the self-deluding merchant Mercator. He was Ned Type, the poet of the burning of the Virginia capitol, and Fart-Hing, the promoter of a natural science of flatulence. He was Obadiah Plainman and the Count de Schaumberg, Homespun and the King of Prussia. He enunciated the reply of a colonial governor's council and promulgated an Act of Parliament.

He was an incorrigible masquerader, and his appetite for imposture went beyond individuals and their institutions. He took the perspective of a left hand, a handsome and a deformed leg, the flies in his apartment, the letter *Z*, and insects that perished in a single day. He even wrote as his own gout.

His most imperishable persona, Richard Saunders—the Poor Richard who allegedly put out the almanacs—has often been mistaken for Franklin's alter ego. He was nothing of the sort. Franklin made fun of him at every turn, and with both reason and passion. Poor Richard was a henpecked husband and an incompetent provider, and his creator had no patience with such men. Poor Richard was an astrologer, and his creator had a very genuine contempt for astrological study of the stars. Yet Franklin kept Richard Saunders alive for a quarter of a century, mocking him, improving him, always allowing him his own voice.

In his brilliant meditation on African American masking, Ralph Ellison insisted that such facework was "motivated not so much by fear as by a profound rejection of the image created to usurp [the Negro's] identity." Some of it, Ellison went on, was "for the sheer joy of the joke," and some "to challenge those who presume . . . to know [the black man's] identity."[7]

Ellison understood masking in the context of race relations in America. But he never misunderstood it as merely an African American maneuver. "The 'darky' act" was, he said, "in the American grain." It made "brothers of us all." In his select company of America's profoundest champions of charade, its deepest deceivers, Ellison counted Hemingway, Faulkner, Abe Lincoln, and, first in the splendid succession, Ben Franklin.[8]

Ellison did not develop or elaborate his shrewd intuition about Franklin. That is the work that falls to pedantry such as this. But he did survey the terrain within which what he called the "American virtuoso of identity" worked. His reconnaissance was marvelously apt.[9]

Take the two letters, by Abel James and Benjamin Vaughan, that Franklin set so oddly between the 1771 and 1784 parts of his memoir. Both letters begged him to resume his reminiscences and to publish them. James applauded their "power" to "promote a greater spirit of industry and early attention to business, frugality and temperance with the American youth." Vaughan thought them "a pattern for all youth" in the cultivation of "private character" and "happiness both public and domestic."[10]

This epistolary interlude was as bizarre in its matter as it was bound to be in its manner. The letters invaded the voice of the autobiography and fatuously misread its substance. They made Franklin a bourgeois paragon on the basis of the 1771 segment, which simply did not sustain the moral message James and Vaughan saw in it. That first part was a saga of scheming, scamming, and self-seeking. It was, from start almost to finish, a tale of tricks and betrayals, duplicity and disappointment, thieving and conniving. It was a narrative of its author's expensive education in human nature and an evocation of the moral milieu of America. It was the confession of the first juvenile delinquent in American literature.

Franklin must surely have incorporated those letters for what, as stated above, Ellison called the sheer joy of the joke and, more, for the fun of challenging those who presumed to know his identity. James and Vaughan thought Franklin an epitome of the Protestant ethic and an embodiment of benevolence. He would give them the slip. They would not imprison him, not even in the most congratulatory confinement. He was an inveterate masker, and masking is, as Ellison said, "a play upon possibility."[11]

Franklin doubled the joy of the joke in the second part of his memoir. There he assumed the role that he had never played in the first part, the role on which his correspondents wanted to empedestal him, as ethical and economic exemplar to the youth of the new nation. There he set out his project for moral perfection.

But the project was a spoof, an extravagant jest, almost a shaggy dog story. It subverted itself in a mocking myriad of paradoxes and preposterous pomposities. And as it did, it made fools of James and Vaughan, who stood for all those, then and since, who hoped to hold Franklin hostage to middle-class morality.

Some of the subtlest, sweetest humor in the autobiography lurked in the byplay between the letters that prefaced the project and Franklin's ironic account of the project itself. Vaughan, for example, went out of his way to praise Franklin for his modesty. Franklin went out of his way to admit that he added humility to his original list of twelve virtues because a friend "kindly informed" him that he was "generally thought proud . . . and rather insolent." Yet Franklin undermined his resolution to achieve humility as swiftly as he enunciated it. He "annexed" to each virtue "a short precept, which fully expressed the extent [he] gave to its meaning." For humility, the precept which gave that meaning was "Imitate Jesus and Socrates." There was only the most modest humility in an ambition to subdue pride by emulating the two most famous men in the history of Western civilization. [12]

Similarly, there was scant silence in an injunction to speak solely "what may benefit others or yourself." There was not much frugality in the avoidance of all expenses but those that "do good to others or yourself." There was slender sincerity in abstinence only from "hurtful deceit." There was little more than a mockery of chastity in a resolution to refrain from "venery" except for "health or offspring." [13]

Putting such conundrums at the very heart of his project, Franklin dismantled it in the very act of describing it. His playful send-ups of his virtues implied the incoherence of his endeavor itself. And he did not stop there. He framed his enterprise in episodes that aspersed its authenticity even more explicitly.

He set two stories before his recounting of the project and another after. None of these tales seemed to have anything to do with the project or with one another. But they were far from the aimless anecdotes of a garrulous old man.

In the first of the two that preceded the project, he marked "how luxury will enter families." All his married life, he had eaten from an earthen bowl with a pewter spoon. Then, one morning, he came to breakfast to find in their place a china bowl and a silver spoon. His hitherto-frugal wife Deborah had bought them for "the enormous sum" of twenty-three shillings. Asked why, she had "no other excuse or apology" than that she thought he deserved such service "as well as any of his neighbors." But Franklin did not scorn her paltry justifications for her petty extravagance. He accepted them and far exceeded them. All on his own, he accrued "several hundred pounds" worth of "plate and china." [14]

In the second story, Franklin recalled his resentment of a minister of the Presbyterian church to which he belonged. The man put Franklin off by preaching "the peculiar doctrines of our sect" rather than any more general "moral principle." He sought "rather to make us Presbyterians than good citizens." Finding such sermons "unedifying," Franklin rarely attended them, despite the minister's admonitions "to attend to his administrations." The men's differences came to a head when the minister promised a sermon on a verse that Franklin thought "could not miss of having some morality." Giving up his "studying-day," Franklin went to church, only to hear the minister confine himself to five points of Presbyterian dogma. "Disgusted," Franklin "attended [the minister's] preaching no more." [15]

In the last story, the one which followed his account of the project, Franklin made even plainer his disdain for doctrinal purity and his preference for goodness over perfection. In an offhand fable, he told of a simpleton who bought an ax and "desired to have the whole of its surface as bright as the edge." The blacksmith from whom he purchased the ax, seeing a prospect of sport, promised "to grind it bright for [the simpleton] if he would turn the wheel." The poor simpleton turned and turned, though the labor was "very fatiguing." Finally, he stopped and said he would take his new ax "as it was." Reluctant to give up the game, the blacksmith pressed him to continue. "We shall have it bright by and by; as yet 'tis only speckled." "The simpleton, seeing at last that he'd been played for a fool, spurned his tormentor's importunity. "I think I like a speckled ax best."[16]

And then, in case all his paradoxes of virtue and parables of resignation to imperfection were too subtle, Franklin spelled out their significance in so many words. The project was a hoax. He had never meant to master the virtues in which his admirers meant to enclose him. He had never been so fondly foolish as to seek the moral perfection that they thought they saw in him. He had known all along that "such extreme nicety" was nothing but "a kind of foppery in morals, which if it were known would make [him] ridiculous." Indeed, he had understood from the first that "a perfect character" would have made him "envied and hated." He would, he concluded, keep his "faults" in order to "keep his friends in countenance." And the cream of the jest, the perfection of the paradox, was that the very friends for whose sake he resigned himself to imperfection included those like James and Vaughan who saw in him a figure of the perfection he repudiated.[17]

Exactly as Ellison said, American virtuosi of theatricality such as Franklin maintained "an ironic awareness of the joke that always lies between appearance and reality." They caught the comedy "at the center of American identity." Their country was, and was bound to be, "a land of masking jokesters."[18]

In fact, Franklin was as open and articulate about all this as Ellison. When he abandoned "abrupt confrontation and positive argumentation" and took up the Socratic method, he did not suddenly turn to truth seeking or a concern to learn from those with whom he argued. He merely discovered that he could embarrass his enemies as well as vanquish them if he "put on the humble inquirer." He admitted frankly that he "took a delight" in debasing as well as defeating them by his "diffidence."[19]

Even as a youth, Franklin apprehended what the Andre Agassi commercials for Canon would tell us 250 years later, that image is everything. We will never know whether he worked hard with any regularity, but we do know that he worked assiduously at being seen working hard. He did not clank his paper-laden wheelbarrow along the cobblestone streets of the city at midday, when it would hardly have been heard in the hubbub. He went much earlier or much later, when the neighbors would notice. As he advised a young tradesman, "the sound of your hammer at five in the morning or nine at night, heard by a creditor, makes him easy six months longer."[20]

To the end of his days, he recognized that he could not conquer pride. "Mortify it as much as one pleases, it is still alive." But the persistence of vanity did not disturb him much. Though he had never had "success in acquiring the *reality*" of humility, he "had a good deal with regard to the *appearance* of it."[21]

Max Weber thought Franklin the ultimate embodiment of the Protestant ethic, and the project for moral perfection the ultimate expression of Franklin's outlook on life. But Weber never understood Franklin. Weber did not notice the American masks and did not get the American jokes. Franklin's father was a believing Puritan. His youngest son was an unbeliever who could never have practiced the Protestant ethic. His priority on appearances took for granted a world without the God of his father. That God could see beneath the surface.

For Franklin, there was nothing beneath the surface to see. His life, in the *Autobiography*, was "an incessant act of staging a self." He never invited his readers to penetrate the veil of appearances that he presented from his youth to his dying days. On the contrary, as Mitchell Breitweiser said, he "scrupulously blocked" the curiosity that his account of his successive fronts was bound to arouse. It was not the man behind the veil that he thought would be of use to posterity. It was the veil itself, and "the strategic decisions governing [its] manufacture," that were "the gist of what he considered worth preserving" in his memoir. Surfaces were his depth, and dissembling the closest he could come to truth. An unrepentant relativist from his first writings to his last, he was always at home in Philadelphia and the truly new American world that it anticipated. Such a society was an unending masquerade ball, and masking was its only essence.[22]

In that sense, even Ellison missed Franklin. Ellison held that, "out of the counterfeiting of the black American's identity there arises a profound doubt in the white man's mind as to the authenticity of his own image of himself."[23] But no profound doubt arose in Franklin's mind. Once he left Boston behind, he cared no more for authenticity than he did for integrity. In the plural society of his adopted city, such qualities were nothing more than impediments and impossibilities.

Over the years, a multitude of writers have seen in Franklin the ultimate embodiment of the self-made man. But they never understood Franklin either. Franklin never claimed, as they claimed for him, that he had hoisted himself by his bootstraps. Quite the contrary. In his autobiography he made very clear that he had risen by enlisting the mutual assistance that the members of the Junto pledged to one another and, especially, by cultivating the patronage of wealthy merchants.

But Franklin was a self-made man in a deeper and indeed a more literal sense. He made and remade his identity, in an incessant succession of sympathetic triumphs. He had an uncanny knack for imagining himself as another, for feeling himself into another, for becoming another. He lived his life and made his career in such creations and re-creations. They were, for him, his recreation, his play and his playground. In Clifford Geertz's sense of play, they were his deep play indeed. They were about the meaning of things.

NOTES

1. Jean Soderlund, ed., *William Penn and the Founding of Pennsylvania, 1680–1684: A Documentary History* (Philadelphia: University of Pennsylvania Press, 1983), 52–53, 77.
2. *Autobiography*, 43, 144.
3. H. W. Brands, *The First American: The Life and Times of Benjamin Franklin* (New York: Doubleday, 2000); Edwin Gaustad, *Benjamin Franklin: Inventing America* (New York: Oxford, 2004).
4. Walter Isaacson, *Benjamin Franklin: An American Life* (New York: Simon & Schuster, 2003), 29.
5. Ralph Ellison, "Change the Joke and Slip the Yoke," in *Shadow and Act* (New York: Random House, 1964), 45–59.
6. *Autobiography*, 60, 69, 71.
7. Ellison, "Change the Joke," 55.
8. Ibid.
9. Ibid., 56.
10. *Autobiography*, 134, 138, 135.
11. Ellison, "Change the Joke," 54.
12. *Autobiography*, 138, 158–59, 150.
13. Ibid., 148–50.
14. Ibid., 145.
15. Ibid., 146–48.
16. Ibid., 155–56.
17. Ibid., 156.
18. Ellison, "Change the Joke," 53–55.
19. *Autobiography*, 64–65.
20. Benjamin Franklin, "Advice to a Young Tradesman, Written by an Old One," in *Benjamin Franklin: Writings*; *Autobiography, Poor Richard's Almanack, Bagatelles, Pamphlets, Essays & Letters*, ed. J. A. Leo Lemay (New York: Library of America, 1987), 321.
21. *Autobiography*, 159, 160.
22. Mitchell Breitweiser, Review of *Becoming Benjamin Franklin: The Autobiography and the Life*, by Ormond Seavey, *William and Mary Quarterly*, 3rd ser., 46 (1989): 816–19; quotations at 816.
23. Ellison, "Change the Joke," 53.

Chapter Two

Benjamin Franklin Unmasked

Jerry Weinberger

This conference in Cambridge was organized to celebrate the tercentenary of Benjamin Franklin's birth, in the country that was arguably his second home, and to assess the current state of scholarship about Franklin. I am very happy to celebrate the tercentenary with you. Had it not been for a certain disagreement about taxation and representation in Parliament, we might be celebrating the birthday of a Benjamin Franklin who when he died was a distinguished servant of the British Crown and Empire. Franklin really did not want the American split with Britain and worked hard to prevent it. He signed on to the Revolutionary cause quite late in the game and, when the Americans won, thanks in great measure to his diplomatic efforts in France, he regretted that the war could not have been prevented and thought King George and the Parliament fools to have picked the fight and thus lost the vast promise America had held for the British Empire.[1]

I am also happy to celebrate the recent spate of books about Franklin, which in my own recent book (*Benjamin Franklin Unmasked: On the Unity of His Moral, Religious and Political Thought*) I described as a "Benjamin Franklin craze."[2] As more and more serious books about Franklin have appeared, the Franklin once thought such a simple and boring bourgeois soul has emerged as ever more complicated and difficult to know. That is certainly a good thing. But in my view it has been perhaps too much of a good thing.

My book disputes the prevailing view of Franklin as a mysterious, many-faceted, and ultimately unfathomable character. This view developed in American scholarship in reaction to the famous attacks on Franklin by the likes of Max Weber and D. H. Lawrence and others, who decried Franklin as the paragon of American materialism and philistinism. Contrary to the anti-bourgeois and ham-fisted readings that took the *Autobiography* to be a priggish and selfish primer on how to get rich and famous, American scholars such as John William Ward saw correctly that Franklin's most famous work is ironic and deceptive and multilayered, and that it reflects a similar mind and character.

Said Ward of the *Autobiography*: "Franklin contained in his own character so many divergent aspects that each observer can make the mistake of seeing one aspect as all and celebrate or despise Franklin accordingly." Far from being a one-dimensional flathead, Franklin, said Ward, gets under our skin; we admire him, "but at the same time we are uneasy with the man who wears so many masks that we are never sure who is there behind them."[3]

As the scholarship matured, to this picture of Franklin's unfathomable complexity has been added more recently a bedrock of simplicity: for all of his psychological elusiveness, Franklin was a freethinker who after a bout of youthful nihilism made his way pragmatically to rational religion and morality. He was in the end a Deist—and his mature faith and morality were the grounds of his life-long dedication to public service, to which he subordinated his many gifts. This account of Franklin was worked out in greatest detail by Alfred Owen Aldridge in the mid-1960s and is still the prevailing view in recent biographies of Franklin by popular writers like Walter Isaacson and academic historians like Edmund Morgan and Gordon Wood.[4]

I do not in my book dispute Franklin's elusiveness and complexity and propensity for wearing masks (the very first one, by the way, was his appearance in literary drag). If anything, I think I make the case that Franklin was more elusive than anyone has so far realized. But I do in my book argue that Franklin makes it possible for us to see the philosophical man beneath the masks—to see his deepest and unified thinking about the big questions of life: morality, God, the good life, and the ends and best forms of government. And when the real Franklin emerges, he turns out to be a more disturbing and unconventional and radical thinker than is compatible with the complicated but Deistic hero of public service of the fashionable biographies and recent scholarship.

I did not start out to dispute the picture of the unfathomable Franklin. Nor did I doubt Franklin's public-spirited morality and Deism. When I started reading Franklin for my book, I did not know what to think—I had never read a word of Franklin and started doing so in response to a request to do a proposal for a book in the University Press of Kansas series on American Political Thought. I was asked to do this project not because I knew anything about Franklin but because I had written a lot about Francis Bacon and the editor of the series, the late Carey McWilliams, thought for that reason I would be good for the project since, as he told me, Franklin was America's first full-blown Baconian.

So I read widely in Franklin and read and reread the *Autobiography*, which I immediately discovered was far from a materialistic story about rags to riches. It was, on the contrary, a saga of moral and spiritual fall caused by

Enlightenment freethinking and of subsequent redemption caused by the hard knocks of experience and by pragmatic introspection. And it was full of self-deprecating irony as well.

So I found myself generally in step with prevailing scholarly and biographical points of view: Franklin was a complicated and many-faceted and elusive character who, after a nihilistic crisis of faith, came back to morality and religion. But then, while engaged in my umpteenth reading of the *Autobiography*, I discovered something that caused me to drop the book on the floor.

I knew that Franklin was a slippery customer and writer: the story about the Reverend Whitefield's mistake of leaving his reputation hostage to the written word, and Franklin's warning that the "written word remains," made it clear that he did not always write (or speak) exactly as he really thought. But even knowing this fact did not prepare me for what I found.

According to the story related in the *Autobiography*, Franklin lost his faith in particular divine providence as the result of reading Enlightenment philosophy; this loss of faith was evidenced in his moral errata, one of which was his metaphysical pamphlet *A Dissertation on Liberty and Necessity, Pleasure and Pain*, written and published in London in 1725. This pamphlet denied free will and the existence of virtue and vice, and it contributed to Franklin's introduction to London intellectual society. But Franklin soon burned all the copies of it (well, not quite all, since we have it) because of its potential "ill tendency." And then, reflecting later on his moral corruption and the harms he did to others and suffered from them in return, Franklin had the moral epiphany that led him back to the moral straight and narrow and, later, also to belief in particular providence, and from all that to a life of business as the means to a life of public service as the best means of serving God.[5]

But in part two of the *Autobiography*, and at some textual distance from the account of his philosophical fall and his narrow escape from corruption and the clap, Franklin tells us almost offhandedly that, regarding his religious beliefs, he "never doubted" God's government of the world by "his Providence" and that "all crime will be punished and virtue rewarded either here or hereafter."[6] It is when I first saw the contradiction this statement entailed that I dropped the book on the floor: Franklin thus says: "My life story is about denying morality and particular providence, paying the moral price, and then coming back to morality and particular providence. Oh by the way, I never doubted particular providence."

This remarkable contradiction cannot be dismissed as an error on Franklin's part: first, because no normal human being could forget such an important spiritual event as having lost and then regained one's faith; second, because the moral saga of fall and redemption is *the* thematic frame for the *Autobiography*, and Franklin, as we know, revised the *Autobiography* over and over again with meticulous care. How could a writer of his massive intellect and seriousness make such a mistake? To think that he did is to make him not worth being taken seriously by anyone in this room. But the contradiction makes the *Autobiography's* moral saga in one way or another a big fat lie.

There is no way for me or anybody else to make this contradiction go away. And any attempt to explain it away, as I argue in my book, is at best speculative and with no substantial evidence. A critic accused me of arguing, in effect, that all who have written about Franklin have been "dunderheads."[7] I never say that, and I do not believe it (Mark Twain and John Updike boobs?). But it is not my fault that this contradiction has been unnoticed by those who have written about Franklin (which is not to say it has been unnoticed by those who simply read Franklin).

Once I saw the fundamental contradiction at the heart of the *Autobiography*, I could then begin to make out the ironic layers of the text and see how those layers reveal a series of conundrums that force us to think through the problems Franklin had in mind. It turns out, I argue, that the *Autobiography* and the writings to which Franklin points us in that book unfold to depict his remarkable path of thinking. That path did go from a conventional moral and religious education to Enlightenment freethinking, as the *Autobiography* makes clear and the scholarship rightly takes for granted. But it did not then go from there to nihilism and then to salvation in a practical moral and religious epiphany.

I argue that Franklin's real intellectual crisis involved his discovery that the Enlightenment atheists could not defend the reasonableness of their atheism—and so on Enlightenment grounds he could not defend the reasonableness of his own profound skepticism about religion. But what he could not find in Hobbes and Spinoza, he learned *how* to find from his intellectual saviors: Xenophon and the Socrates of Xenophon's *Memorabilia* (with some surprising help, I think, from Shaftesbury).

The scholarship in my view is right to say that Franklin gave up Enlightenment metaphysics as the ground for his radical, but dogmatic, theological skepticism. But he did not then turn to a practical morality and Deism that included particular providence. I argue rather that Franklin re-grounded his radical theological skepticism in a dialectical investigation of the commonsensical moral opinions and intuitions that serve as the background conditions for what people think are experiences of conscience and the spirit moving within.

Franklin worked this critique out in his aggressive, dialectical, Socratic refutations of his neighbors and acquaintances, described in the *Autobiography* and in the dialectical writings to which he points us in that book. I argue that Franklin stuck with the *Dissertation's* conclusion that "virtue and vice are empty distinctions, no such things existing." But he did not derive this conclusion from deductive, metaphysical arguments from the attributes of God; he rather came to it by working through the incoherence of our every-day notions of virtue and vice (and more specifically, dignity, righteousness, honesty, justice, and responsibility). Franklin's engaging in these refutations got him run out of Boston as an "infidel or atheist" and, though he continued his aggressive investigations in Philadelphia, he eventually abandoned them and never forgot the lesson of how dangerous they were. [8]

I thus conclude that the once-fallen but then Deistic Hero of Public Service is a myth, that Franklin rather did only what Franklin liked to do, and that Franklin was a serious thinker (perhaps the most serious America has ever had) who, though he wore a leather apron, philosophized not with a hammer but with a joke.

Franklin's profound doubts about the intellectual grounds of Enlightenment freethinking can be demonstrated from some of his comic writings. At the time of the Great Awakening (from the mid-1730s to the mid-1740s) Franklin made up and published some Ripley's Believe-It-or-Not-like stories about believers gone wild. He reported an absurd trial by water of witches accused by believers of having caused their neighbors' sheep to dance and hogs to speak and sing Psalms. [9]

And after this the hoaxes got even more bizarre. One made fun of the radical Quaker Abolitionist Benjamin Lay, whom Franklin calls "the Pythagorean-cynical-Christian-philosopher," who made a ridiculous spectacle of himself by staging a demonstration against the vice of drinking tea (and the issue was not so much tea as the slavery used to produce it). Lay tried in pious indignation to smash his dead wife's expensive china but was thwarted when the crowd knocked him down and made off with the teapots and cups and saucers. [10]

Another hoax told of a man who ordered his wife to put her tongue in his mouth and then, after biting off a big chunk, threw it in his fireplace as he said: "Let this be for a burnt offering." [11] And the zaniest of the lot deserves to be quoted in full:

"About two weeks ago, one John Leek, of Cohansie in West-New-Jersey, after twelve months of deliberation, made himself a eunuch (as it is said) for the Kingdom of Heaven's sake, having made such a construction upon Matt 19:12. He is now under Dr. Johnson's Hands, and in a fair way of doing well." [12]

It is hard to read these pieces without thinking that the believers, especially the enthusiastic ones, belong in Bedlam. But this same debunking Franklin in 1730 wrote another funny story, at first apparently at the expense of religion, that has an absolutely surprising twist that leads us to think that perhaps these believers are not so crazy after all and that their Enlightenment opponents may be on pretty shaky grounds. [13]

Franklin wrote and printed a letter to his own paper, the *Pennsylvania Gazette*, by a man who seeks some advice: The man was once convinced by impious writers like Hobbes and Spinoza not to believe in spirits and the devil. But then he came to believe in spirits by a perfectly sane and sober Reverend Gentleman, who told him a remarkable story. The Reverend met with some colleagues to discuss preventing the spread of atheism. After the meeting, they were at night, before midnight, in their hotel room visited by the devil, who terrified them by banging a drum unheard by others in the hotel and by pulling the toe of one colleague in the room who claimed he had not heard the drum.

Later, however, the new believer was "staggered" in his belief by a skeptic who said that according to the German divines the devil only bangs his drum after midnight. The same skeptic also pointed out that when a drunken preacher, who was pulled from a pub to serve at a funeral, said in the course of his prayers, "I heard a voice from heaven," his drinking pal, who had come along to the funeral said, "that's a damned lie, for I was drinking with you all day at the pub and should have heard it too since my ears are as good as yours." So given these staggering facts, the writer asks the editor, "should I still believe the Reverend?"

To this letter Franklin responded a few days latter in a letter-to-the-editor from one "Philoclerus."[14] The upshot of the first part of the reply is that this piece is a clear attempt to mock and debunk the clergy, and that the paper's editor should be careful about printing such things—even a nonbeliever should be prudent enough not to corrupt his fellow citizens by denying them the restraint of the clergy. (This was the first of many of Franklin's admonitions against speaking against religion.) And then Philoclerus makes an amazing move aimed directly at Hobbes.

Hobbes argues that the belief in spirits arises from our ignorance of the causes of things, especially of our good and bad fortune. Not knowing these causes, we dream up "invisible agents," and then imagine that these agents are of the same substance as the soul, and that the soul is the same substance as visions in dreams or in mirrors, which though they are apparitions, are taken to be real and external substances at once existing and yet not material—that is, spirits. But for Hobbes, the notion of an "incorporeal substance" is unintelligible speech, as much as to say "body" that is "not body."[15]

To this Philoclerus replies, regarding spirits, "besides, as far as we know there is nothing impossible in the thing itself: We cannot be certain that there are not spirits existing; it is rather highly probable that there are: But we are sure that if spirits do exist, we are very ignorant of their natures, and know neither their motives nor methods of acting, nor can we tell by what means they may render themselves perceptible to our senses."

Philoclerus then continues that: "Those who have contemplated the nature of animals seem to be convinced that spirit can act upon matter, for they ascribe the motion of the body to the will and power of the mind. Anatomists also tell us, that there are nerves of communication from all parts of the body to the brain: And philosophers assure us, that the vibrations of the air striking on the auditory nerves, give to the brain the sensation of what we call sound; and that the rays of light striking on the optic nerves, communicate a motion to the brain which forms there the image of that thing from which those rays were reflected."

Philoclerus goes on to point out that a blow upon our eyes produces a sense of light that no one else can see, and from this he concludes: "Now, how can we be assured that it is not in the power of a spirit without the body to operate in a like manner on the nerves of sight, and give them the same vibrations as when a certain object appears before the eye (though no such object is really present) and accordingly make a particular man see the apparition of any person or thing at pleasure, when no one else in company can see it?"

Philoclerus does not here refute Hobbes. That would take at least a book. But he does show with a stroke that Hobbes's argument may well cut very little ice because it may in fact turn out to depend on Hobbes's unproven and intransigent, almost hysterical, materialism. It could well be that all Hobbes really shows is that if one begins with materialistic presuppositions (that mind and spirit do not exist), one ends up with a materialistic conclusion (that there are no minds or spirits to act on the matter of our nerves and brains).

The notion of an incorporeal spirit cannot simply be dismissed. Philoclerus calmly argues that we really do at least experience the interactions of mind and matter, even if that interaction is beyond our capacity fully to understand. And if we grant that simple experience—or even better, unless we can prove that it does not really happen—then we cannot rule out the possibility that God and spirits are akin to mind, or even some kind of bodies akin to mind which in a manner akin to mind communicate with our nervous tissue and give to us apparitions and revelations, which are like the actions of our minds on our nerves, beyond our merely human powers to comprehend.

This, by the way, is pure Franklin comedy: the satire invites skeptics to congratulate themselves on their rationalistic superiority to the nutty holy rollers, only to have their faith in the voice of reason exposed for what it is— a faith no different in its essence from those who believe in the miraculous voice of conscience.

Franklin was intellectually at odds with Enlightenment rationalism and anticlerical ire (although he could really sock it to the clergy when the occasion called for it). He was a freethinking critic of Enlightenment freethinking. And he knew that such ire is based on the same moral intuitions and opinions as ground the experiences of the religious true believers. He thus bore no rationalistic illusions that religion could be eliminated from human life and was able, moreover, to imagine rationalist zealotry—and that is why he could be so cozy with the likes of George Whitefield and never stopped recommending the importance of rational religion for society.

Franklin was a stone-cold atheist in my view, but he came to his atheism not from dogmatic metaphysics (materialism) or from dogmatic psychological assertions (religion springs from ignorance and fear). He rather reasoned on the very same commonsensical turf shared by the believers. To Hobbes a believer could respond as did Philoclerus, and to the argument that religion springs from ignorance and fear the believer could respond as follows: "I'm not ignorant and I'm not afraid—if you've not experienced the miracle of the spirit moving within then it's too bad for you; and if the spirit does move you, you'll know it as surely as you know night from day."

But that same believer might not fare so well when cornered by the dialectical Franklin. All Franklin had to show was that, when his faithful neighbors were questioned as he had done to himself, their notions of virtue and vice and deserving blew up in their faces—and with this explosion perished too the meaning of particular providence. These explosions were not presupposed—he was able to and did really produce them during the time Franklin practiced his aggressive Socratic refutations as he describes in the *Autobiography*. That is why the good people of Boston ran him out of town as an abhorred infidel or atheist.

I disagree with the prevailing understanding of Franklin in another respect as well. Franklin could well have been in his youth the philosophical rascal he describes in the *Autobiography*. But in my book, I argue that the mature Franklin's skepticism did not make him a "nihilist" and so just a multitalented scoundrel. My book has two chapters (7 and 8) on Franklin's view of the good life, both private and political, and they include an account of Franklin's understanding of how moral indignation and anger are the roots of what we call vice and evil and of almost all the harms that people do to other people.

At the height of the revolution, Franklin published a hoax about a cargo of American scalps bound to the King from his Indian allies that subtly but clearly depicts both sides of the dispute as murderous moral fanatics.[16] And at the end of the war, he wrote to Joseph Banks not that justice had prevailed but rather that the whole affair was the wasteful result of stupidity on both sides.[17]

Franklin's moral and religious skepticism made him an egalitarian: he thought all men were equal not because they all have equal dignity but rather because no man could claim any moral dignity at all. And his related political pragmatism made him an opportunist as regards forms of government (the ends of liberty and modernity were all that really mattered, and there were many ways in his view to skin those two cats).

Franklin could look out for himself when his fundamental interests and circumstances really required, but he was not for that fact a mean or angry man. Other than to protect one's most fundamental interests, Franklin thought there is no good reason to harm anyone unless they intend to harm you; in any case, anger or indignation never make any sense. (How can they if someone who harms you is no different from a poisonous snake in the grass that cannot be held responsible for the bite that it inflicts?) So I disagree completely with Gordon Wood's argument that Franklin's political career was motivated by pride and anger as much as by Franklin's supposed view that the moral and religious obligation of public service trumps other interests he had and would otherwise have pursued. [18]

That is not to say that Franklin never got mad or felt proud—he was a human being after all. But whenever he did get mad or feel proud, at least in print, he always made it clear that on second thought his anger and pride made no sense. He was moved to politics, in my view, not by pride or anger and certainly not by a sense of moral obligation, but rather because he liked it as much as he liked chess, and as I say in my book, Franklin did what Franklin liked. That is certainly not to say that Franklin was a narrowly selfish or egotistical man. Far from it: he understood the attachments of the human heart and the pleasures of society and friendship too well to be a self-centered Scrooge or a tyrant (who, in Franklin's view, would both be men incapable of having fun).

But that said, he understood perfectly well the differences between the attachments of the heart and moral obligations as we understand them in our everyday common sense. And he understood how powerful the claims of that common sense are on just about every human being on the face of the Earth—even if on philosophical reflection they are totally incoherent.

I will close by addressing briefly the issues raised by Professor Pangle, in another chapter of this book, about Franklin's differences from Socrates. Saying anything about this requires some confidence that we know what Socrates was up to—and I have to admit that I lack that confidence, which is why I avoided such comparisons in my book. Franklin tells us that in his youth he adopted for a while the "Socratic" method of disputation, which for Franklin included aggressive dialectical refutations under the guise of humble doubt, and, later, a habit of expressing himself "in terms of modest diffidence." But what Franklin learned from these "Socratic" investigations we can learn from Franklin alone—he makes it possible for us to see what he learned and nowhere requires us to infer anything from Socrates himself.

I am just not sure what any comparison of Franklin to Socrates has to do with an assessment of Franklin's moral skepticism. But as regards Franklin, Professor Pangle seems to argue that his lifelong involvements in public service and Baconian natural science make no sense unless Franklin were at least some kind of moralist and bowed to an overarching duty to serve his fellow human beings.

As regards Baconian natural science, we must be careful not to confuse motive with effect. That true natural science—as opposed to Platonic metaphysics (which Bacon said was a pile of theological clap-trap)—does good to others has nothing to do with the fact that it enables us, as Bacon said, to see the world as it really is and not as we want it to be. And the latter could be the motive for natural science as easily as could the former. Baconian natural science solves the tension between theory and practice: discovering the truth about the world, which can be engaged in for purely selfish reasons, just happens to be in everybody's interest (well, at least under certain assumptions about God and the human good).

The same holds for public service. Again, Franklin did what Franklin liked, and we must be careful not to confuse motive and effect. That Franklin's public service resulted (mostly but not always) in good effects for others does not allow us to conclude that he liked politics and public service *because* it was good for others. And Franklin never stopped philosophizing—both as regards natural science and as reflection on the human condition. One floor of his house in London—while he was busy as a colonial agent and deeply involved in the mounting imperial crisis—was a laboratory he used for scientific experiments. And he wrote the *Autobiography*, his most philosophical work, over a period that stretched from 1771 to the end of his life. In the course of his life, and after he had become rich enough, Franklin had time for politics, natural science, and philosophy (and ladies and good food and wine and chess and more), and he saw no reason to have to choose among them.

True, Franklin says in the *Autobiography* that after his brush with selfish freethinking he came to see that God exists and governs the world by his providence and rewards virtue and punishes vice. And true, Franklin also says that he came to see that "the most acceptable service of God is doing good to man." But then there is the matter of the big fat lie at the root of the *Autobiography*'s moral saga—and the lessons Franklin learned on his own from getting run out of Boston, and from the Reverend Whitefield who failed to heed the warning that "the written word remains." Unless we can make this lie go away, we have to be very careful about judging why Franklin did whatever he had a mind to do.

NOTES

1. See Franklin to Joseph Banks, 1783, in Benjamin Franklin, *Benjamin Franklin: Writings,* ed. J. A. Leo Lemay (New York: Library of America, 1987), 1073–74. [Hereafter *Writings* (1987).]

2. Jerry Weinberger, *Benjamin Franklin Unmasked: On the Unity of His Moral, Religious, and Political Thought* (Lawrence: University Press of Kansas, 2005), ix.

3. Max Weber, *The Protestant Ethic and the Spirit of Capitalism*, trans. Talcott Parsons (New York: Charles Scribners, 1958), 48–56, 64–65, 71, 124, 189; see D. H. Lawrence, "Benjamin Franklin," in *Benjamin Franklin and the American Character*, ed. Charles L. Sanford (Boston: D. C. Heath, 1955), 57–64; John William Ward, "Who Was Benjamin Franklin?" *American Scholar* 32 (1963): 541–53.

4. Alfred Owen Aldridge, *Benjamin Franklin and Nature's God* (Durham, NC: Duke University Press, 1967); Walter Isaacson, *Benjamin Franklin: An American Life* (New York: Simon and Schuster, 2003), 84–85, 256; Edmund Morgan, *Benjamin Franklin* (New Haven, CT: Yale University Press, 2002), 17–25, 30; Gordon Wood, *The Americanization of Benjamin Franklin* (New York: Penguin, 2004), 13–15, 29–30, 66–70.

5. Franklin, *Writings* (1987), 1318–53.

6. Ibid., 1382.

7. Weinberger, *Benjamin Franklin Unmasked*, 49n16.

8. Ibid., chs. 5 and 6.

9. Franklin, *Writings* (1987), 155–57.

10. *Papers* 2:357; see Franklin, *Writings* (1987), 1172–73.

11. Franklin, *Writings* (1987), 180.

12. *Papers* 2:364.

13. Franklin, *Writings* (1987), 145–48.

14. Ibid., 148–51.

15. Thomas Hobbes, *Leviathan*, ed. Richard Tuck (Cambridge: Cambridge University Press, 1996), 76–77; cf. 273–79.

16. Franklin, *Writings* (1987), 956–60.

17. Ibid., 1073–74; see also Franklin to Priestley in *Writings* (1987), 1047–48.

18. Weinberger, *Benjamin Franklin Unmasked*, 222–23, especially n. 27.

Chapter Three

Early Modern Imperialism, Traditions of Liberalism, and Franklin's Ends of Empire

Carla Mulford

Franklin was born into a colony-based mercantilist political and social economy supporting Great Britain; he died as the new United States was starting an industrial era. He grew up believing himself to be a Briton, one who was geographically removed from England but nonetheless a subject within the British Empire and a part of the British nation. He died having lived through the colonists' rebellion against Great Britain and having seen the effects of colonial strife and civil war within his own family. He long believed it possible to accommodate the British nationalist imperialist agenda by consolidating colonial governments so as to create better colonial management inter-colonially and from Great Britain. Indeed, he worked so hard to accommodate both sides of the growing rift that American colonials worried he might be too pro-British, and Britons in England denounced him as a wily American. He ended by assisting Jefferson with the draft of the Declaration of Independence.

Through it all, and even through the difficult decade of the 1760s, when he had serious doubts as to whether the British ministry harbored any real concern for colonial Britons, Franklin attempted to find means, sometimes conciliatory and ameliorative, sometimes intentionally fractious, castigating, and divisive, to keep the colonies functioning within the British Empire and in support of a greater British Commonwealth. Some biographers and historians have accused Franklin of inconsistency in ideas, proposals, and policy, but the accusations are unfounded when taken in light of the inconsistent policies of the era and the differences among the colonies in the ways that policy was implemented. If Franklin seems to have been inconsistent, then it will be worthwhile to acknowledge the inconsistency of the times.

One consistent strand in Franklin's long life is the position Franklin held regarding the ends of empire. Phrased quite simply, the ends of the British Empire ought to be the creation, material support, and protection of the best possible living circumstances for the greatest number of people living within the borders of territories putatively held as British territory, whether on the mainland or in colonies geographically dispersed. His views are evidenced repeatedly, in what he printed in his newspapers and what he wrote in his published and circulated pamphlets and public and private letters—whether speaking to issues on the peopling of North America, Native Americans and imperial relations, immigrant non-Britons within British boundaries, colonial administration and changing colonial policies, or slavery and the conditions of living without owning one's own labor. Especially in the late 1750s and early 1760s, when he seems to have wanted to believe that colonial problems might still be resolved by better mutual understanding, Franklin seems to have taken every possible opportunity to make known his position about the mutual dependence and common bonds, the "interest of humanity," as he called it, of Britons on both sides of the Atlantic. For Franklin, the ends of empire *were* the interests of humanity.

FRANKLIN, MERCANTILISM, AND THE INTERESTS OF HUMANITY

Franklin's earliest readings in economics were in the mercantilist tracts of the late seventeenth century. Mercantilism, a term coined by Adam Smith to describe economic "interest" policies (thus creating what was called a "balance of trade,") was based in a philosophy of competition among nations for exclusive activity in the transport trades, in mercantile goods, and in the creation of specie at home. In general, mercantilists wished to regulate trade in such a way as to create a favorable trading circumstance for whatever goods or mineral wealth (especially silver and gold) they wished to benefit from. Their arguments held that trade regulation would benefit the nation, and if nations had to go to war in order to preserve favorable trade potential, then going to war functioned to serve a national agenda of wealth and well-being. Franklin was well-read in mercantilism as a young man. His interest in securing advantages in colonial trade to North America surely made him attentive to different policies regarding trade and bullion. But Franklin came to see the short-sightedness of trade regulation at about the time that he addressed economic and monetary problems in Pennsylvania with his tract, *The Nature and Necessity of a Paper-Currency* (1729). Within two decades, he would be creating full-blown arguments in support of what Adam Smith would later call "free trade" policies.

Evidence of Franklin's mid-life fascination with optimal trade circumstances and his shift from a closed economic system (represented by mercantilism) to an open one that would benefit all people appears in a letter Franklin wrote in the fall of 1760 to David Hume, after having received Hume's remarks on his own then-much-discussed "Canada Pamphlet."[1] In the pamphlet, Franklin argued in behalf of Britain's gaining French territories in Canada above those in Guadaloupe, in the protracted treaty negotiations ending the series of wars for empire over territory in North America.[2] Having read Hume's essays "Of Commerce" and "Of the Jealousy of Trade" (and evidently commingling them in his memory), Franklin used the opportunity of his letter to extend a long and urbane compliment to Hume for his presumed understanding of the economic situation of laboring peoples in colonial lands. Hume's letter to Franklin has not been found, but the import of Hume's remarks may be garnered from Franklin's response. Franklin wrote to Hume, "I am not a little pleas'd to hear of your Change of Sentiments in some particulars relating to America; because I think it of Importance to our general Welfare that the People of this Nation should have right Notions of us, and I know no one that has it more in his Power to rectify their Notions, than Mr. Hume."[3] Franklin's message both complimented and instructed Hume. Franklin made sure Hume understood the compliment by identifying, with great subtlety, what Hume's message *should* be. As the newly eminent historian of Britain whose examination of the British Empire and its history was then being published, Hume should inform Britons in Great Britain about the circumstances of Britons in colonial areas such as North America. Franklin played on the language of interest politics germane to the mercantilist system to make a point to Hume regarding the common interests, interests of humanity, of Britons in North America and those in Great Britain.

> I have lately read with great Pleasure, as I do every thing of yours, the excellent Essay on the *Jealousy of Commerce*: I think it cannot but have a good Effect in promoting a certain Interest too little thought of by selfish Man, and scarce ever mention'd, so that we hardly have a Name for it; I mean the *Interest of Humanity*, or common Good of Mankind: But I hope particularly from that Essay, an Abatement of the Jealousy that reigns here of the Commerce of the Colonies, at least so far as such Abatement may be reasonable.[4]

The rhetorical maneuver, typical of Franklin when addressing a learned audience, works to draw polite and witty attention to the selfishness of the game of the administration's interest politics being played at the expense of laboring people in colonial North America. The "interest of humanity," for Franklin, was the "good of mankind."

In making such an analysis, Franklin framed an elaborate and extended compliment of Hume's own views. Hume had pointed out in his essay, "Of Commerce," that war, by drawing people away from wealth-producing livelihoods, detracted from the ability of a nation to create wealth. If, rather than fighting with one another in an effort to gain exclusivity over the seas and in commercial matters, nations would aim to support freedom of commerce and trade by remaining in peace with one another, they could generate more products and thus greater profits to agricultural and manufacturing laborers and to the mercantile interests that benefited from agriculture and manufacture. Hume's critique of mercantilism was one that Franklin himself had been fond of making during these years, so Franklin did not miss the opportunity to lend a supportive ear to Hume's assertions.

Hume drove home his point about mercantilism in his essay, "Of the Jealousy of Trade," arguing, "It is obvious, that the domestic industry of a people cannot be hurt by the great prosperity of their neighbours; and as this branch of commerce is undoubtedly the most important in any extended kingdom, we are so far removed from all reason of jealousy. But I go farther, and observe, that where an open communication is preserved among nations, it is impossible but the domestic industry of every one must receive an increase from the improvements of others."[5] That is, a neighbor's wealth can increase a nation's wealth, because it creates a significant marketing opportunity for export of surplus manufactured goods, thus creating better livelihoods for those within the Commonwealth. Hume's particular case in point was the woolen manufacture, but his point leans toward the laissez-faire model already publicly favored by Franklin and adumbrated later on by Adam Smith.

In addition to confirming his agreement with Hume, Franklin's letter clarified the extent to which the British (considering the administration as the people's representative) did not, from the North American perspective, seem to care about the situation of Britons in North America, whether in peace or in war. Defense in North America, Franklin argued, was falling increasingly to the colonial North Americans alone, and they were prevented from appointing official military leaders from among themselves, as appointments were to occur at the prerogative of the Crown and ministry. Franklin reminded Hume that colonial troops were left defenseless in Canada in 1746, after the colonial administration in London had offered to support troops and send regimental leaders willing to make an expedition to Canada. Speaking specifically to the question of Canadian defense, Franklin wrote, "[T]ho' I am satisfy'd by what you say, that the Duke of Bedford was hearty in the Scheme of the Expedition, I am not so clear that others in the Administration were equally in earnest in that matter," Franklin wrote. Further, he offered:

It is certain that after the Duke of Newcastle's first Orders to raise Troops in the Colonies, and Promise to send over Commissions to the Officers, with Arms, Clothing, &c. for the Men, we never had another Syllable from him for 18 Months; during which time the Army lay idle at Albany for want of Orders and Necessaries; and it had begun to be thought at least that if an Expedition had ever been intended, the first Design and the Orders given, must, thro' the Multiplicity of Business here at home, have been quite forgotten.[6]

Franklin politely quibbled with what evidently had been Hume's representation of the British administration's concern about what happened to the North American colonies abutting Canada in the war there between Britain and France. Franklin's reply indicates that Hume had made a defense of the administration's concern about the colonies in North America.

The short version of Franklin's message to Hume was this: experience in Canada belied Hume's armchair representation of the administration. As did many of Franklin's letters to important people associated with elite group culture in England and Scotland, Franklin's letter to Hume works to instruct Hume about his implied obligation as an eminent historian and, thus, in effect, the spokesperson of British Empire, to instruct the administration on colonial policy matters. The letter clarifies to Hume that experience must always be taken into account when policy is devised, so that people are not left risking their lives and livelihoods attempting to save a British Empire that does not seem interested in saving them.

From a rhetorical standpoint, however, the most telling part of Franklin's long letter to Hume is his defense of having used the word *colonize* in the Canada pamphlet. Franklin, often fond of expressive neologisms, had used the word *colonize* as a reminder of an original intent regarding the lands of North America that present-day Britons, in their fears of drawing talent away from the mainland, had forgotten. He drew upon arguments he had been making against the old mercantilist theories beginning in the 1720s, arguments revealing a sophisticated theoretical understanding of the positive proportional ratio of land to population in areas not densely settled. "The objection I have often heard, that if we had Canada, we could not people it, without draining Britain of its inhabitants, is founded on ignorance of the nature of population in new countries. When we first began to colonize in America, it was necessary to send people, and to send seed-corn; but it is not now necessary that we should furnish, for a new colony, either one or the other."[7] Franklin's interesting rhetorical method was to create an intentional logic in behalf of peopling North America by calling up the former intentions of Britain for use in the present times. That is, the reminder behind Franklin's statement in the Canada pamphlet is that at one time it was policy to send people over the seas. Such venting occurred originally to secure better working conditions for a greater number of people in England. Venting also helped Britain gain a toe-hold upon which to build colonies and gain possible locations from whence it might engage in extractive measures to secure mineral wealth, the better to compete against Spain and France in the great contest for power over sea and land. In the Canada pamphlet, Franklin invoked that past initiative in an effort to remind readers that benefits would accrue to Great Britain with a greater number of people in North America, because they could take advantage of the productive *richesse* of the lands there.

In this portion of the Canada pamphlet, Franklin's point was like Hume's in the two essays Franklin cited in his letter. Franklin correlated land availability and cultivation to the support of the manufacturing interests of England, and he suggested that with free trade possibilities and free labor potential, Britain would flourish. "The annual increment alone of our present colonies, without diminishing their numbers, or requiring a man from hence, is sufficient in ten years to fill Canada with double the number of English that it now has of French inhabitants," Franklin wrote.[8] British North America could people itself, he indicated, without taking population or livelihood from people in Britain. He drove the point home when he published his 1760 Canada pamphlet by appending his treatise, originally written in 1751, *Observations concerning the Increase of Mankind.*[9]

Franklin's mercantilist leanings, while they comprehended the interest politics of Britain, nonetheless always led back to the greatest good for the greatest number of people. Herein he knew his view conflicted with the very interest politics he was confronting while attempting to deal with landholders and landholding policies of the Pennsylvania Proprietors during the 1750s and then with the colonial administration in London in the 1760s. And here we find Franklin's theories of empire beginning to develop into a view of a potential policy that he attempted again and again to foster among elite-group people and, especially, to the colonial administration. By using the phrase "the *Interest of Humanity* or common Good of Mankind," Franklin comprehended several factors but primarily that a free laborer ought to be able to earn a living wage sufficient to his and his family's needs and sufficient, too, that he would be free to sell his surplus goods from his own labor and free to begin setting aside an additional sum (whether in currency or in land) from his earnings for the proverbial rainy day. Franklin understood, by the 1760s, that this was not the view of the good of mankind supported by those in administration and even by many economists of the era. He had become painfully aware of the extent to which the discourse of "the nation" was trumping the opportunities of the nation's people, especially those living in colonial situations in North America, Ireland, and even in parts of Scotland not typically discussed by the legal, social, and political philosophers born there.

So Franklin employed the word *colonize* in his pamphlet. In so doing, Franklin spoke to a historical past that, he argued, accurately portrayed the situation of the first Britons in North America: they were colonizing the lands and peoples there in order better to serve the British Commonwealth. Yet David Hume, a Scot whose own country had its own burden of colonized history, found trouble with the word and the very notion of colonizing lands for England. Whereas Franklin wished to speak the facts as he saw them, Hume evidently paused at words that sounded too harsh, despite the truth of their representation in fact. One gathers this from what Franklin wrote in response to Hume's commentary: "I thank you for your friendly Admonition relating to some unusual Words in the Pamphlet. It will be of Service to me. The pejorate, and the *colonize*, since they are not in common use here, I give up as bad; for certainly in Writings intended for Persuasion and for general Information, one cannot be too clear, and every Expression in the least obscure is a Fault."[10] Franklin attempted to gloss over, as a difference of opinion regarding word usage merely, a difference of opinion regarding how to use facts as one sees them. That is, his response clarified that he agreed not to use the word, because it would fail to persuade; if he gave up anything, it was the word, but not the position, which he considered accurate. This interesting exchange between Franklin and Hume is a telling reminder of the extent to which Franklin came by his understanding of policy from having lived as the recipient of bad policy; Hume came by his policy by way of speaking about it and living from its benefits in the home economy rather than the colonial economy.

Unlike his friends in Great Britain and Europe, Franklin had witnessed great changes taking place in North America and understood the environmental and political promise of a consolidation of the colonies as productive parts of the British Empire. As he increasingly realized that his views would not be credited nor countenanced in England, he grew restive and began explicitly addressing the problems with the existing—and constantly changing—trade policies of Great Britain. His writings on economy and society are clear statements based on data he collected, readings he had done, and inquiries he had personally made among leading theorists. Recognizing the significant discrepancies between Britain's oppressive trade policies and its public, liberal face given to those policies, whether in Scotland, Ireland, North America, or India, Franklin engaged in a campaign to reveal the fractures in the façade. His many public letters to the British press, his letters both public and private to friends, his pamphlets from the 1750s through the early 1770s—all evince his attempts to write to the intersections of mercantilism and liberalism. If Franklin finally left England, sailing for North America again, this move was his last resort of last resorts, a recognition of his failure to persuade others to his views and a profound leave-taking that marked his final and complete understanding of the extent to which liberalism, a great China vase, was a pretty and fragile and empty promise of prosperity only for the few, not the many whom Franklin embraced as the most worthy—the laborers, the farmers, the manufacturers who simply, as he had done, wanted to live peaceful lives with hope for a better future for their children.

THE PROBLEM OF LIBERALISM

After many years of attempting to persuade people in Great Britain about the viability and utility of keeping the American colonies in the imperial system, Franklin finally gave up. Part of the problem Franklin faced in England was the fact that he was not born high, nor born in England, nor even born in Scotland, from whence England drew its great legal, social, and economic theorists by midcentury. Franklin was born in North America of parents who had emigrated there. Franklin was born a laborer into a family of laboring people, and he had had a trade. It was precisely his life condition that enabled Franklin to understand the problems in the imperial system.

And it was precisely Franklin's life condition that contributed to preventing those in power from being interested in what he had to say. This is, in part, the problem with Britain's vaunted liberalism, as Franklin viewed it from the colonial perspective. Franklin grew increasingly disgruntled with Britain as he wrote to the problems inherent in the intersections of mercantilism and liberalism. His views of early modern liberalism emerged against a rich historical context that is sometimes obscured by a too vague or general understanding of early modern liberalism, a vagueness or misunderstanding arising from viewing liberalism through the lens provided by several classical liberal writings of the nineteenth century. The few examples that follow will serve, I hope, to assist the beginning of the more deeply historicized inquiry that informs my scholarship. [11]

An interesting and telling example of the attitudes that cultured Britons held toward laborers, tradespeople, and all those in the marketing ends of commerce (as opposed to leaders in administration who were mercantilists bankrolling certain transport trades) appears in Samuel Johnson's 1755 *Dictionary of the English Language*, where Johnson reported: "Of the laborious and mercantile part of the people, the diction is in a great measure casual and mutable." [12] For Johnson, it was not lamentable that the words of laborers, tradespeople, and merchants would not appear in his dictionary. His clarifying remark indicates Johnson's condescension toward the work of most such people: their "fugitive cant, which is always in a state of increase or decay, cannot be regarded as any part of the durable materials of a language, and therefore must be suffered to perish with other things unworthy of preservation." Claiming that, for the purposes of his dictionary—the first such publication in the English language—he "could not visit caverns to learn the miner's language, nor take a voyage to perfect my skill in the dialect of navigation, nor visit the warehouses of merchants, and shops of artificers, to gain the names of wares, tools and operations," Johnson concluded, "it had been a hopeless labour to glean up words, by courting living information, and contesting with the sullenness of one, and the roughness of another." Laboring people, sullen and rough, would be dull-witted and certainly unskilled in language, Johnson assumed. His assumption taught the same values to all those who would read his dictionary in an effort to know better the English language. Surely Johnson was well aware that his presumed record of the language was both emancipating and disciplining of the middle classes who were increasingly becoming literate during the century.

Whereas Benjamin Franklin, who often visited wharves, ships, mills, and manufacturing plants, always had abundant curiosity about how things worked, what measures were used, how the laborers performed their work, and where they labored, Samuel Johnson would not stoop to do so, as the language of the laborer was, he sniffed, mere "fugitive cant." The uses of language—its diction, its speaking operations, its rhetorical power among initiates—differentiated people in Samuel Johnson's world. Franklin, well understanding this fact of life in his era, proposed that the primary skills students learn in his English school and his Academy (college), would be tied to the linguistic arts of reading, writing, and oratory. And for Franklin, himself once a laborer and merchant, Johnson's subtle obfuscation regarding which diction was "worth" recording and which was not would have been well understood—that is, understood, but disagreed with. Yet Franklin knew the audience he was seeking to persuade in England, and for that audience, Dr. Johnson served well as an index to its taste and self-cultivated sense of refinement. Franklin seems genuinely to have admired Johnson's learning, and he quoted Johnson in his Poor Richard almanacs.[13] The two met on May 1, 1760. One wonders how Dr. Johnson received this colonial man of laboring origins.[14]

Dr. Johnson's and Dr. Franklin's views on the word *liberal* are evident in the way each used it. The two primary meanings Johnson offered for the word, used as an adjective, imply class differentiation signaling elite-group assumptions about culture, precisely the elite-group assumptions that Franklin came to understand and quarrel with when attempting to negotiate for the colonies in England. Johnson's etymology for the word, used as an adjective, is based in Latin and French usages, and his definitions are these: "1. Not mean; not low in birth; not low in mind. 2. Becoming a gentleman." The third meaning that Johnson attached to the word speaks to displays of generosity: "3. Munificent; generous; bountiful; not parcimonious."

Examining Franklin's writings, one finds that Franklin used the term primarily to suggest two meanings, the first (and less-used) usage indicating "generosity," and the second as a descriptor for education, as in "liberal education." Franklin never used the term to suggest class functioning like the one Johnson enjoined in the first two meanings in his definition. Franklin conceived that the use of the term *liberal* ought to convey generosity, as, for instance, when he slightly revised and quoted the poem, "For Liberality," from *The Genuine Works* (1736) of George Granville, Baron Lansdowne (1667–1735) in *Poor Richard Improved* (1750):

> Tho' safe thou think'st thy Treasure lies,
> Hidden in Chests from Human Eyes,
> Thieves, Fire, may come, and it may be
> Convey'd, my Friend, as far from thee.
> Thy Vessel that yon Ocean sails,
> Tho' favour'd now with prosp'rous Gales,
> Her Cargo which has Thousands cost,
> All in a Tempest may be lost.
> Cheats, Whores and Quacks, a thankless Crew,
> Priests, Pickpockets, and Lawyers too,
> All help by several Ways to drain,
> Thanking themselves for what they gain;
> The *Liberal* are secure alone,
> For what they frankly give, for ever is their own. [15]

In his quotation, Franklin emphasized the word *Liberal* by taking the printer's liberty of italicizing it for his almanac readers. The poem provides a good index to Franklin's method when using the term, for it emphasizes that if one is a hoarder, one lives in fear of tempests and miscreants, whereas if one is generous, one has no fear of such things (instead, one has security), because one has already been generous in one's gifts and has sought to hoard nothing. Hoarding and insecurity about goods (and status) were qualities of the mercantilist era into which Franklin was born. Generosity of spirit and the security to be liberal—these were the qualities Franklin, by mid-life, had grown to value. Except when speaking of liberal education, Franklin always used the term *liberal* in this way, to convey generosity.

Franklin's educational models emphasized what he called a liberal education, but his educational plan was quite unlike those employed for gentlemen in England. The differences in his educational plans for Philadelphians, when compared to English educational models, are many: He sought to inculcate learning for middling-level people, including "handicrafts" (his word for tradesmen, artisans); he framed his educational plans to include the classical *trivium* and *quadrivium*, but such education was by design only for those entering into further academic life, such as ministers. For most other young men, he advocated training in practical arts and sciences; and he sought training in the English language and other contemporary, continental languages. [16]

For reading, Franklin suggested contemporary authors, or authors from the sixteenth and seventeenth centuries whose work influenced the great liberal traditions he had come to admire, from a youth. In his *Proposals*

Relating to the Education of Youth in Pensilvania (1749), Franklin argued that English ought to be central to the language training of young men, and it could best be learned by their reading exemplary writers: "The English Language might be taught by Grammar; in which some of our best Writers, as Tillotson, Addison, Pope, Algernon Sidney, Cato's Letters, &c. should be Classicks." Those writers he selected wrote into a tradition that critiqued church and state powers and emphasized the individual's power to grasp complicated conceptions such as liberty. He was recommending that all youth in Pennsylvania gain, in essence, formal training like the training he had given himself. Such authors as Algernon Sidney, John Locke, and John Trenchard and Thomas Gordon formed just a small part of Franklin's pantheon of liberal thinkers and writers.[17]

Just as he aimed to use his educational plan to model liberalism for the students, so Franklin used his almanacs to inform his readers about their cultural roots in liberal traditions and the potential for liberty in British North America. So, for instance, he called up the memory of Algernon Sidney for his readers in *Poor Richard Improved* for 1750. Under the entry for December, Franklin remarked:

> On the 7th of this Month, 1683, was the honourable Algernon Sidney, Esq; beheaded, charg'd with a pretended Plot, but whose chief Crime was the Writing an excellent Book, intituled, *Discourses on Government*. A Man of admirable Parts and great Integrity. Thompson calls him the British Cassius. The good Lord Russel and he were intimate Friends; and as they were Fellow Sufferers in their Death, the Poet joins them in his Verses,
>
> > Bring every sweetest Flower, and let me strow
> > The Grave where Russel lies; whose temper'd Blood
> > With calmest Chearfulness for thee resign'd,
> > Stain'd the sad Annals of a giddy Reign,
> > Aiming at lawless Power, tho' meanly sunk,
> > In loose inglorious Luxury. With him
> > His Friend, the British Cassius, fearless bled;
> > Of high, determin'd Spirit, roughly brave,
> > By ancient Learning to th' enlighten'd Love
> > Of ancient Freedom warm'd.[18]

Franklin quoted the poet, James Thomson, to consolidate the view—so that it is not Richard Saunders's view alone—that Algernon Sidney and Lord William Russell died unjustly, at the hands of a monarch who loved luxury, for a "plot" with which, it was said at the time, neither had anything to do. Sidney had been accused, with Russell, of plotting to take the life of Charles II and his brother, James II (heir to the throne), shortly after the Crown was restored to the Stuart line. A parliamentarian, Sidney had sought to use his pen and the press to express his views on representative government. Sidney's *Discourses concerning Government*, which circulated in manuscript during his lifetime, was published under several different titles beginning around 1698. By employing Thomson's poetry and his own memorial, Franklin reminded his readers that liberty of speech, liberty of person, and legislative freedoms are all contested values, and they ought not be taken for granted. By memorializing and thus celebrating Sidney's and Russell's martyrdoms for their presumed part in the Rye House Plot, Franklin used the opportunity to inform and remind his readers about the bravery involved in honoring "th' enlighten'd Love / Of ancient Freedom." This was an essential part of liberalism to Franklin: honoring ancient freedoms by challenging government when it attempted to usurp individual liberties.

Franklin's views of liberalism were based, in the earliest part of his life, in the writings and family memory arising from the era of the wars wracking Europe and England in the sixteenth and seventeenth centuries. The circumstances of the English Revolution and their impact upon Franklin's family were, I believe, more profound than most scholars have acknowledged.[19] Franklin attempted, across his lifetime, to come to terms with the problems of liberalism as it became implemented within the colonial systems constructing—or, attempting to construct—the British colonies, especially those in North America.

Franklin was generally working within traditions of republicanism and liberalism as these evolved from seventeenth-century politics, culture, philosophy, and religious history.[20] Several scholars have debated about the terms. Alan Bullock and Maurice Shock, for instance, remarked long ago that "English Liberalism . . . was born out of the seventeenth century struggle for freedom of conscience and the resistance of Parliament to the arbitrary authority of the King."[21] Stephen Holmes more recently has likewise argued that liberalism's earliest history "cannot be detached from the political history in the seventeenth and eighteenth centuries." Holmes has importantly expanded the locale of liberalism's inception to encompass England and Scotland, the Netherlands, France, and the then-new United States," an approach that more fully comprises several of the locales of Franklin's own activities.[22] Where Holmes features John Locke's career as "the best place to begin if we wish to cut to the core of liberalism,"[23] J. G. A. Pocock, whose emphasis is upon classical republicanism rather than liberalism per se, has emphasized the work of James Harrington as the paradigmatic case illustrating the importance of England in the 1650s to understanding the connection between the republicanism and liberalism of classical Rome and Florentine society in the Renaissance to ideals of republicanism appropriated during the eighteenth century by leaders of the American Revolution.[24] Annabel Patterson importantly revised the canon of liberal philosophers to include a wider range of writings political, philosophical, religious, and popular, even as she nonetheless emphasized that Milton stands in as her model of the early modern liberal.[25]

Among the revisionist stances taken in recent scholarship about republicanism and liberalism is Steven Pincus's most convincing analysis of a series of Commonwealth writers who shared many of the tropes common to classical republicanism, especially those reflecting an interest in "the common good" and a "hatred of tyranny," but who, rather than denouncing increasing commercialism as a corruption, instead celebrated the new commerce-driven "vocabulary of interests and rights in defense of the common good." Pincus has pointed out that in examining histories of liberalism, scholars must be attentive to the complete range of writings resulting from the Commonwealth tradition, whose work, rather than speaking with distress about the emerging commercial society of England, expressed "a new ideology applicable to a commercial society, an ideology that valued wealth but also the common good, an ideology, in short, that celebrated neither possessive individualism nor the anti-commercialism of republican Sparta."[26] Such an approach to studying liberalism—that as views evolved, they changed so as to embrace the new commercial society—enables us to see Franklin's interventions more clearly, as he wrote to the problems in the intersections of mercantilism and liberalism.

While Franklin might seem to have supported classical republican values, especially the traditional anti-luxury values associated with Milton's "Old Cause," Franklin's midlife theories about empire and, in later life, about statehood, reveal a central ideological position supporting laissez-faire trade and, in essence, a commitment to commercialism as constructive of equal opportunity within the social formation. The different framing of the problem of liberalism, one that removes us from classical republicanism as denoting "a description of political personality" (largely Pocock's position) into an area that allows for interest in commercial society, enables the exploration of a wider array of philosophical findings and geographically broader enunciation of the values of liberalism that found their way into later seventeenth-century and eighteenth-century writings. It also enables a more fruitful, because less class-driven, set of assumptions to emerge. Milton, Harrington, and many of their generation had celebrated the achievements of classical Sparta and Renaissance Venice, whereas, as Pincus rightly has observed, "many of the defenders of the Commonwealth came to prefer commercial Athens and Holland."[27] Franklin admired all of these writers—Sidney, Milton, Locke, Harrington, and many more—whose writings taken together represent a stream of liberalism founded in the English Revolution and held sacred by many in the so-called United States founding generation. Scholars today might quibble about whether the streams of argument were largely classical republican or liberal in their orientation; to someone like Franklin

who lived through the era, such rigid and categorical thinking could undermine the very usefulness of different positions at any particular time.

If some of the central tenets of Franklin's liberalism seem to have
changed across time, moving from interests primarily in free speech and
freedom of conscience to, ultimately, the freedom to own one's own labor,
there are several factors behind such a turn in his ideological positioning.
Perhaps the most important of these factors was Franklin's realization, finally, that by supporting Britain and the empire in North America, he was
supporting a corrupt system. The sources of the values Franklin believed in
might seem conflicting, in the historical scholarship, but in general, the values Franklin typically ascribed to and associated with early modern liberalism tend to have their root in the social contract theories of the seventeenth
century, theories that articulate the differences between what philosophers
called the state of nature, as compared to the state of civil society. In these
theories reside the political concept that all human beings are equal in the
state of nature and thus have equal rights by nature's laws, rights that become
constrained when they enter into civil society, creating compacts wherein
they abridge, by choice, certain of their natural rights in order to gain civil
advantages.

Franklin tended to admire John Locke and to distance himself from Machiavelli and Hobbes, all common theorists regarding the states of nature and
of civil society, yet Franklin was, by my estimation, often selective in his
arguments, depending on his current argument and audience. As his writings
attest, Franklin was a voracious and eclectic reader and a superb rhetorician.
He could at times reference Machiavelli, for instance, in denigrating terms,
whereas at other times, he gave Machiavelli a favorable reference and com-
mended him. In short, Franklin was a master rhetorician, and he was willing
to use whatever theoretical position would be most useful at any particular
time. He did not obsess about consistency the way historians of his life and
his work have done.

Franklin's writings reflect a remarkable flexibility of thinking, an inquirer's capability to embrace a position at one point but to reflect upon issues
continually in an effort to reach a better or more appropriate conclusion. As
the famous instance of his publishing and then retracting his "little metaphysical piece," as he called it in his autobiography, *A Dissertation on Liberty
and Necessity, Pleasure and Pain* (London, 1725) illustrates, Franklin would
work to get to know a position, test it out as he wished, use it if it proved
important to do so, and change his mind about it at some later point. His
theories on imperialism, liberalism, natural rights and obligations, the social
compact—all were open to continual interrogation, revision, reformulation.

FRANKLIN'S ENDS OF EMPIRE

Franklin's mature position on liberalism was not, to my thinking, formulated into self-conscious intellectual, social, and potential structural policy until perhaps the late 1760s, when he created sets of goals that might be used for retaining the British Empire intact, even as he understood that the liberalism he was advocating was in stark contrast to the special-privilege liberalist assumptions fostered by those in power in England upon a willing populace that feared British North Americans' economic independence and the political consolidation of the disparate peoples living within the boundaries of British-identified territories. Scholars have been confounded in their attempts to trace a seamless line of argument in Franklin's social, political, or economic philosophy. This confusion results from Franklin's own willingness to test hypotheses, formulate new plans, and develop strategies for fulfillment by taking positions that might seem, if considered in their totality and without attention to the particular political issue, era, or audience, inconsistent but which, taken across the time and territory Franklin covered, are understandable, given his particular political situation and the goals he was at a particular time seeking to implement.

Franklin's original goals for the colonies were that they remain within the British imperial system. Franklin held on to these goals for a long time, attempting to find workable solutions to the political and social impasses that he continually faced while attempting to negotiate, first for Pennsylvania alone and then for all of the colonies, when he was living in England. While in England, he began to realize, slowly but steadily, that he was being treated as a subaltern, that he was not taken quite as seriously as, he expected, a Briton from England who represented Britons in England might be taken. He also realized the extent to which the discourse of nationhood that was the foundation for England's imperial imaginings was, first, alienating of the disparate peoples living within the British Commonwealth system and second and more importantly, masking a political inequality Franklin perceived more and more to be acutely the condition of British American, Irish, and many Scottish people, not to mention the peoples in Asia and Africa that Britain was in the process of continuing to colonize. In these London years, Franklin's tone becomes more excoriating than conciliatory, more accusatory than accommodating.

Franklin was rankled that Britons in England did not consider British people all equal under the social compact that bound them all. He became deeply troubled that Britain's vaunted liberalism, a liberalism he had been raised to admire and cultivated as his own, was a sham. In some ways, Franklin's turn against England seems finally to be a turn into a political consciousness—indeed, political self-consciousness—that he had avoided recognizing for many years because he believed in the conception of love of country, a key aspect of the rhetoric of old Whig liberalism, that he often articulated in his writings.

Some of the core values of Franklin's mature liberalism lie in the insistence on individual dignity; the essential equality of all persons as social and political agents; the necessity for freedom of inquiry and freedom of expression; and the centrality of the freedom of labor (that one could own one's own labor) to the function of both local and global communities. Franklin formulated a theory of empire that was based in the primacy of labor and the importance of a living wage for all persons who ought to be considered equal politically in terms of their status in the citizenry and who could be interconnected with one another across land and water spaces. If we wish to trace a shift in Franklin's views, that shift can best be associated with Franklin's eventual critique of the discourse of nationalism and the racializing characteristics of the British nation, a view of nationalism that Franklin at one time embraced and then forcefully discarded when he realized the illiberal tendencies of the en-racing of any nation. Franklin finally argued, fully and consistently, in behalf of a necessary transparency of power that liberalism itself could often leave mystified or inarticulate. Franklin's greatest challenge and his greatest accomplishment was to identify and speak to the glaring inconsistencies in a system that yoked colonialism to liberalism and called it freedom.

NOTES

1. The formal title of this long pamphlet is *The Interest of Great Britain Considered, With Regard to her Colonies, And the Acquisitions of Canada and Guadaloupe. To which are added, Observations concerning the Increase of Mankind, Peopling of Countries, &c.* (London: T. Becket, 1760).

2. These wars are still commonly called the Seven Years' War, although many historians tend to agree that the wars lasted for about two decades.

3. Franklin to David Hume, 27 September 1760, in *Papers* 9:229.

4. Ibid.

5. David Hume, "Of the Jealousy of Trade," in *Essays and Treatises on Several Subjects: A New Edition* (London and Edinburgh: Millar, Kincaid and Donaldson, 1758), 187. This essay was printed separately, without being interleaved into the edition, as if it were a later addition to the compiled book, with directions as to its location in the already published edition. Both essays appeared in this volume. In writing to Hume, Franklin seems to have been working from memory. He commingled the two essays and called them Hume's "excellent Essay on the Jealousy of Commerce" (*Papers* 9:229).

6. Franklin to David Hume, 27 September 1760, in *Papers* 9:228–29.

7. Franklin, *Interest of Great Britain Considered*, in *Papers* 9:95.

8. Ibid.

9. *Papers* 4:227–34.

10. Ibid., 9:229.

11. The line of argument in this chapter is that of my book in progress, *Benjamin Franklin and the Ends of Empire*.

12. Samuel Johnson, preface to *Dictionary of the English Language* (London: William Strahan, 1755). The quotations that follow arise from the preface as well.

13. See, for instance, the *Poor Richard Improved* for 1750, where for the month of January Franklin quoted from Johnson's *Vanity of Human Wishes*, in *Papers* 3:442.

14. My thanks go to J. A. Leo Lemay who promptly answered my inquiry when I asked whether Franklin and Johnson had ever met (21 October 2007, e-mail correspondence). Lemay speaks of Franklin and Johnson in *Life of Benjamin Franklin, Volume 3, Soldier, Scientist, and Politician, 1748–1757* (Philadelphia: University of Pennsylvania Press, 2008). As Lemay has pointed out, information about their meeting appeared in Maurice J. Quinlan, "Dr. Franklin Meets Dr. Johnson," *Pennsylvania Magazine of History and Biography* 73 (1949): 34–44. Lemay also points out that Johnson commented on Franklin's *Observations Concerning the Increase of Mankind*, indicating he had read it sometime prior to 1775. It is likely that Johnson was a careful reader of Franklin's writings. For additional background, see Paul J. Korshin, "Benjamin Franklin and Samuel Johnson: A Literary Relationship," in *Benjamin Franklin: An American Genius*, ed. Gianfranca Balestra and Luigi Sampietro ([Rome]: Bulzoni Editore, 1993), 33–49; and Neill R. Joy, "Politics and Culture: The Dr. Franklin–Dr. Johnson Connection, with an Analogue," *Prospects* 23 (1998): 67–69.

15. [George Granville], *The Genuine Works in Verse and Prose of the Right Honourable George Granville, Baron Lansdowne* (London: J. and R. Tonson, 1736), 1:113–14. The changes made in the *Poor Richard* version interestingly draw light upon thieving, cheating, and quackery, when we consider Franklin's substitutions for words employed by Granville in the original: Franklin adds "Thieves" at line 3, emphasizes losses rather than the acquisitions of gold, and speaks to actual costs lost in a cargo. This is the original from Granville:

> Tho' safe thou think'st thy Treasure lies, Hidden in Chests from Human Eyes, A Fire may come and it may be Bury'd, my friend, as far from thee. Thy vessel that yon ocean stems, Loaded with golden Dust, and Gems. Purchas'd with so much Pain and Cost, Yet in a Tempest may be lost. Pimps, Whores, and Bawds, a thankless Crew, Priests, Pick-pockets, and Lawyers too. All help by several ways to drain, Thanking themselves for what they gain. The Liberal are secure alone, For what we frankly give, for ever is our own.

16. For background on Franklin's plans, see Carla Mulford, "Benjamin Franklin, Traditions of Liberalism, and Women's Learning in Eighteenth-Century Philadelphia," in *Educating the Youth of Pennsylvania: Worlds of Learning in the Age of Franklin*, ed. John Pollack (New Castle, DE, and Philadelphia: Oak Knoll Press and University of Pennsylvania Libraries, 2009).

17. See *Proposals Relating to the Education of Youth in Pensilvania* (Philadelphia: [B. Franklin], 1749), in *Papers* 3:405–7.

18. The quotation is from *Poor Richard improved: Being an Almanack and Ephemeris . . . for the Year of our Lord 1750. . . . By Richard Saunders, Philom.* (Philadelphia: B. Franklin, and D. Hall, 1750). Franklin quotes from "Summer" part of *The Seasons* (1730; revised 1744, 1746) by James Thomson (1700–48).

19. These matters are explored more fully in my book in progress.

20. The scholarship on liberalism, its early modern manifestation, and its relationship to the era of early nationalism in the United States and to modern democracy is vast. In addition to the scholars discussed here, readers might consult the several excellent essays in *Republicanism, Liberty, and Commercial Society*, ed. David Wootton (Stanford, CA: Stanford University Press, 1994); and in *Dimensions of Radical Democracy*, ed. Chantal Mouffe (London: Verso, 1992). But see also: Joyce Appleby, *Liberalism and Republicanism* (Cambridge, MA: Harvard University Press, 1992); Rowland Berthoff, "Peasants and Artisans, Puritans and Republicans: Personal Liberty and Communal Equality in American History," *Journal of American History* 69 (December 1982): 579–98; John Coffey, "Puritanism and Liberty Revisited: The Case for Toleration in the English Revolution," *The Historical Journal* 41 (1998): 961–85; Alan Houston, "Republicanism, The Politics of Necessity, and the Rule of Law," in *A Nation Transformed: England after the Restoration*, ed. Houston and Steven Pincus (Cambridge: Cambridge University Press, 1991), 241–71; James T. Kloppenberg, "Virtues of Liberalism: Christianity, Republicanism, and Ethics in Early American Political Discourse," *Journal of American Histo-*

ry 74 (June 1987): 9–33; Macpherson, *The Political Theory of Possessive Individualism: Hobbes to Locke* (Oxford: Clarendon Press, 1962); Daniel T. Rodgers, "Republicanism: The Career of a Concept," *Journal of American History* 79 (June 1992): 11–38. One of the earliest and most comprehensive studies of the Commonwealth tradition was a splendid book by Caroline Robbins, *Eighteenth-Century Commonwealthman: Studies in the Transmission, Development, and Circumstance of English Liberal Thought from the Restoration of Charles II until the War with the Thirteen Colonies* (1959; Indianapolis: Liberty Fund, 2004). Most who have worked over these materials and benefited from her work probably, as I do, disagree with her assessment that "the Commonwealthmen were only a fraction of politically conscious Britons in the Augustan Age, and formed a small minority among the many Whigs. No achievements in England of any consequence can be credited to them" (1).

21. Alan Bullock and Maurice Shock, *The Liberal Tradition: From Fox to Keynes* (London: A. and C. Black, 1956).

22. Stephen Holmes, *Passions and Constraint: On the Theory of Liberal Democracy* (Chicago: University of Chicago Press, 1995), 13.

23. Ibid., 15. While Holmes's is a useful analysis, I have found in a brilliant analysis by Jacqueline Stevens a most important revision of typical assumptions about Locke's idea of liberal individualism: Stevens, "Reasonableness of John Locke's Majority: Property Rights, Consent, and Resistance in the *Second Treatise*," *Political Theory* 24 (1996): 423–63.

24. J. G. A. Pocock, *The Machiavellian Moment: Florentine Political Thought and the Atlantic Republican Tradition* (Princeton, NJ: Princeton University Press, 1975) and *The Political Works of James Harrington*, ed. Pocock (Cambridge: Cambridge University Press, 1977).

25. Annabel Patterson, *Early Modern Liberalism* (Cambridge: Cambridge University Press, 1997).

26. Steven Pincus, "Neither Machiavellian Moment nor Possessive Individualism: Commercial Society and the Defenders of the English Commonwealth," *American Historical Review* 103 (1998): 708. Pincus's revisionism arises from his sense that the field of enquiry and the data sets used by Pocock and his followers frame an "argument [that] depends on a severely restricted sample of the ideological production of the defenders of the English Commonwealth" in the critical years of the 1650s (708). Another study by Pincus that has been useful for my conceptualizing of the problem of liberalism in Franklin studies is "From Holy Cause to Economic Interest: The Study of Population and the Invention of the State," in *A Nation Transformed: England after the Restoration*, ed. Alan Houston and Pincus (Cambridge: Cambridge University Press, 1991), 272–98. See also his "From Butterboxes to Wooden Shoes: The Shift in English Popular Sentiment from Anti-Dutch to Anti-French in the 1670s," *The Historical Journal* 38 (1995): 333–61; and "Popery, Trade and Universal Monarchy: The Ideological Context of the Outbreak of the Second Anglo-Dutch War," *The English Historical Review*, no. 422 (January 1992): 1–29. Pincus's book, *Protestantism and Patriotism: Ideologies and the Making of English Foreign Policy, 1650–1668* (Cambridge: Cambridge University Press, 1996) is a more complete analysis related to the study of Britain's changing ideological situation.

27. Pincus, "Neither Machiavellian Moment," 719.

Chapter Four

Benjamin Franklin, the Mysterious "Charles de Weissenstein," and Britain's Failure to Coax Revolutionary Americans Back into the Empire

Neil L. York

If America is finally, & irrevokeably determin'd to stake every thing on its independence—there is nothing left, but to play out this deep game—all good men on both sides will pathetically Lament that the Freedom of both Countries depends on so precarious a speculation. We trembling with apprehension, at the irresistable influence, & power of corruption, which must accede to the Crown, if we conquer—& you, to lose all the ties of personal Friendship, of family connections, & the heart felt prejudices of Education, similarity of Manners, & of Speech—to unite with strangers who heartily despise you already, & will despise those who have neither nobility, nor a profusion of Wealth—& to be obliged to submit to the supercilious haughtiness of those whose Language is different, whose principles of Law & Government are fundamentally & diametrically opposite to yours—& whose Religion hath ever been invariably, directly, & essentially, in practice and in Doctrine, the persecution, the compulsive Tyrant over that, which prevails amongst you. [1]

We can only imagine Benjamin Franklin's reaction as he read this paragraph, part of a much longer message delivered anonymously to his residence in Passy, outside Paris. It was late June 1778, and Franklin awaited news of the first fruits of the Franco-American alliance, an alliance that the author of this note condemned as a horrendous mistake. If Franklin had second thoughts about the pact—which, as the anonymous contact well knew, he had helped negotiate—he was not about to reveal them to this writer, who signed his cover letter "Charles de Weissenstein" but admitted it was an alias. Despite hiding his name he wanted Franklin to know that he was actually an Englishman, good and true, a friend seeking what was best for both Britain and America. John Adams, in France to work with Franklin, mocked the sender, his message, even his means of getting in contact, which had been to toss a packet of papers "through one of our grates." As Adams remembered it years later, he and Franklin thought so little of the proposal that they "never transmitted any account of it to Congress."[2]

Adams's dismissive views have more or less held sway ever since: an odd communication from someone with odd ideas, a curiosity of no consequence.[3] Understandable as that may be it is also unfortunate, for reasons that should become clear later if they are not evident now. Who was Charles de Weissenstein? We do not yet know; indeed, we may never know. The editors of Franklin's papers offered Philip Jennings Clerke as a possibility, an attribution based on a police report that identified Weissenstein as an Englishman named Jennings, a former captain in the king's guard regiment whose father had been a British diplomat.[4]

And how did the Paris police become involved? Weissenstein had enclosed detailed instructions so that Franklin could write a response and deliver it in person. Weissenstein would not be at the proposed rendezvous; instead, he told Franklin, he would send someone who knew nothing about the nature of their communication to meet him at Notre Dame de Paris. Franklin could hand his message to this third party. But Franklin had other plans. Determined to prove their loyalty to their new ally, Franklin and Adams agreed "to do nothing without previously informing the French Court."[5] They turned everything over to Charles Gravier, Comte de Vergennes, the foreign minister who orchestrated the Franco-American alliance. Vergennes in turn went to the Paris police, who sent agents to watch the cathedral on the designated day. They observed an individual behaving just as Weissenstein suggested would be done in his note to Franklin. Without being detected, they followed him back to the Hotel d'Hambourg. It turned out that the man they tailed was Weissenstein himself. The proprietor informed them of what little he knew about his lodger, which they relayed to Vergennes, but which Vergennes apparently did not pass along to the Americans. Weissenstein— that is to say Jennings—told the proprietor he had crossed over to Bordeaux on 20 June, thence to Paris, and was preparing to return to England the next day, 7 July, or soon thereafter. The police neither interviewed nor detained him; he presumably left as planned. They included this terse physical description: a somber fellow who appeared to be somewhere between thirty-six and forty, perhaps five foot five, thin face with a ruddy complexion, blonde hair in a tie. He had been well dressed, in a gray coat, white vest, and black pants; he wore a hat and sported a cane as well.[6]

No likeness of Jennings Clerke, if ever done, survives, so it is impossible to say if he matched the physical description. His father had been a diplomat and he had been an officer in the king's guard regiment—though he rose beyond captain to lieutenant colonel before resigning his commission in 1770.[7] As a boy he had attended Westminster School and then Oriel College, Oxford.[8] Upon his father's death he inherited Duddleston Hall, the family seat in Shropshire. He also owned a country house, Coxlease, in Hampshire, made his primary residence in London (Westminster, to be more exact), and sat in the House of Commons for the Devonshire borough of Totnes, from 1768 until his death twenty years later—a full decade after the Weissenstein business.

Jennings had added Clerke to his name by 1768 to honor his uncle, Sir Talbot Clerke, who made him his heir. He was elevated to baronet in 1774, despite his tendency to side with the Opposition.[9] If the baronetcy was an attempt to buy his political loyalty, it failed. Though not a leading voice in the Commons he had been critical of Lord North's policy toward the American colonies and the resulting conflict. Modeling himself on William Pitt, Earl of Chatham, "the greatest minister and the ablest statesman this country ever boasted," Jennings Clerke proclaimed during Commons debates in November 1777, that he condemned the war, "which has brought this country to the edge of its ruin, and which, if persevered in must end in destruction."[10] With the parliamentary session ending in June 1778 he could easily have traveled to France and back in order to deliver a message to Franklin. There are other hints of a connection and, collectively, there is at least enough to make the link to Weissenstein suggestive.[11]

Whoever Weissenstein was, Franklin did compose a response, although he gave it to Vergennes, not the mysterious caller. Judging by the tone, Franklin wrote it to reassure the foreign minister that Americans would not end the war, seek a separate peace, or settle for anything short of independence. By dismissing Weissenstein he reaffirmed to Vergennes the American commitment to France and their alliance.[12] Adams recalled Franklin telling him that there seemed to be internal proof of a connection to George III— that the proposal must have received royal approval. If Adams remembered correctly, Franklin's comment probably had more to do with the strained relations between the two diplomats than any belief on Franklin's part that the King had been privy to the plan. Adams, insecure and jealous of Franklin's stature, may just have gotten on the Pennsylvanian's nerves. In the opening days of 1778 Franklin had been seemingly inundated with English visitors looking to restore peace, and a couple did have royal connections. Franklin had no knowledge of the King's inner circle but, after his many years in London, he was far better connected than Adams, an international neophyte by comparison. Franklin may just have decided to have some fun at his testy colleague's expense.[13]

Adams belittled Weissenstein's proposal as "very weak and absurd," demonstrating "a gross ignorance of the American People."[14] He exaggerated. The proposal was undeniably unrealistic but it was not, pointedly, any more absurd than other proposals that had come before or that would follow, some of which I discuss below. Adams fixated on Weissenstein's American "house of peers," which was but a small part of his overall plan. Most important, Weissenstein called for a "continental congress"—effectively a validation of what Revolutionary Americans had already created for themselves—to unite the colonies and act as an intermediary between London and the individual provinces, which he also referred to as "states." The Crown would call it into session at least once every seven years, Parliament's own septennial act serving as the model. The American congress could not vote money to the crown unless Parliament concurred. Parliament would determine military needs; the American congress would meet those needs by the same requisition system it used to take care of internal affairs. Funds requisitioned from the individual states would be based on proportionate shares, to be determined by population. Individual colonies could keep whatever governmental structure they preferred and determine for themselves how executive officials would be selected—which could have been read to mean that governors would no longer be appointed by the crown. "Nor shall the King, nor the British Parliament, assume the authority, ever to make Laws for or to tax America other than according to this Compact"—and that Compact made no such provision. All laws then binding the colonies to Britain were to be vacated; the empire was to be formed anew.[15]

"A Supreme Continental Court" with jurisdiction over all the individual colonial courts would be created to resolve disputes, with appeals going to the House of Lords in London. The crown would name the members, who would never exceed two hundred. They would be appointed for life, with inheritable titles—what Adams ridiculed as the American "house of peers." Weissenstein called for "great officers of state" as well, but kept that part vague—presumably a detail to be worked out in the actual negotiations. He also left open the possibility of someone with "royal blood" presiding as a resident "viceroy." In a notable revision of the troublesome navigation system, "American ships shall sail at their own Choice to any & every Port of the World, provided" they obtained proper clearances and paid the required duties.

All of this was to be created through "A Great & Solemn Compact" which would "be Perpetual & unrevokeable but by the free, & mutual Consent of both Countries." The existing American Congress would appoint commissioners who would come over to London, there to treat with counterparts appointed by Whitehall and Westminster. If in those negotiations details were altered, then so be it, provided both parties agreed to the changes. Once the terms had been agreed to and ratified by crown and parliament on one side, and congress on the other, rebel soldiers were to go home and British forces were to occupy leading American ports, all in anticipation of reconstituting the empire according to this thoroughly federalized plan.[16] The

King would determine what should be done about the Franco-American alliance. "If these Preliminaries are not agreed upon before the 1st of January 1779 next ensuing, they shall be taken to be null & void, as if they never had existence."[17]

No apologist for Britain's imperial policy, Weissenstein conceded "that every provocation capable of piquing national, or private resentment has been exercised on America—Insolence—Contempt—wanton injustice—tyrannick violence—& all those mischiefs, which stupid narrow minded Despotism command."[18] He was careful not to accuse the King himself of that "despotism;" rather, he attributed the foolish actions leading to war as "conjured up by the Spells of Scottish witchcraft"—not a Shakespearean reference, but a thinly-veiled allusion to the Earl of Bute and his supposed behind-the-scenes influence on the King. It was a common rhetorical device, which Franklin knew well, to distinguish between the King and his ministers. Imperial reform could put an end to the need for such fictions. And, Weissenstein emphasized, Americans had much more to fear from their ostensible ally. France had long been a thorn in Britain's side, playing it false again and again. Americans should not assume that France would be any more trustworthy in its dealings with them. Better to be shielded from French treachery by Britain's navy than to face France alone—which, in time, they would have to do, once the French showed their true colors. And besides, why should Americans think that they could win, even with French aid? "It is one thing to elude" defeat; it is quite "another to vanquish your Adversary."[19] Americans had gone to war to better secure their rights in the empire, a worthy goal to which they should return, urged Weissenstein. Continuing to seek independence would only expose them to greater dangers and put their freedoms more at risk.

That Weissenstein played an anti-French, anti-Catholic card made perfect sense, given the traditional enmity between France and British America. That he also emphasized the common political cause and cultural ties of Britain and America—and that they both would suffer by separation—also made sense. Weissenstein did not hide his doubts about Americans being able to realize greatness on their own. He wanted Franklin and his fellow Revolutionaries to distinguish between problems caused by bad policies and the possibility of a better empire to come. Working together, Britons and Americans could help the empire fulfill its destiny.

Even though he did not say anything too disparaging about American aspirations, it seems doubtful that his proposal would have been welcomed in either London or Philadelphia, had it been made public. Franklin was emphatic in his response that Weissenstein's proposal would be unappealing to Americans. Franklin had not always read his countrymen correctly, but in this instance he probably did. For his part, George III would not have appreciated being linked to "stupid narrow minded Despotism," even if only as a type of guilt by association.

Whatever the merits of Weissenstein's ideas, George III and Parliament had already endorsed another peace proposal, entrusted to the Carlisle commission, which was playing itself out on the far side of the Atlantic even as Weissenstein made his overtures to Franklin.[20] It had been preceded by others made informally to the Americans in Paris during the first days of 1778 to stave off a Franco-American alliance. All had been preceded by efforts dating before 1776 to keep Americans from declaring independence.

It would be easy enough to sweep all of these failures into the dustbin of history—unappealing offers by free agents like Weissenstein or emissaries sent by the King and his ministers. Not surprisingly, British attempts during the war to reconcile with the Americans end up as mere footnotes to the larger story, all of them more or less fitting into the same category where Adams dumped Weissenstein's proposal. Francis Wharton, editor of the diplomatic correspondence generated by members of the Continental Congress, sought to change this perspective, contending that if Whitehall and Westminster had granted in 1775 what they only grudgingly offered later in the war, "independence would not have been declared in 1776."[21] Echoing Wharton, the distinguished historian John Richard Alden would later contend that the war had been avoidable and the early political damage from it reparable, but "George III and his political friends," too proud to bend, too blind to see, "bungled" it.[22]

As with all counterfactual historical speculation, there is no way to either prove or disprove Wharton's or Alden's point. But we can put the failed peace proposals back into the American Revolutionary narrative. That the British would end up trying to negotiate with the Americans even as they fought them was not strange in the least, since war and diplomacy are inextricably connected. Before criticizing British leaders for refusing to accept the "reality" of American independence once Revolutionaries claimed it in 1776, we should recall that it took sixteen months of fighting for those Revolutionaries to reach that point. Wharton and Alden were right to emphasize the malleability of American ideas in this setting. Odd as Revolutionary Americans settling for something short of independence may now seem—our frame of reference being the nationalistic assertion of 1776, with everything else before it mere prologue—we forget the state of mind then. Britain's secretary of state for American affairs, interestingly enough, thought that the Declaration might in fact hasten reconciliation by alienating British leaders who had been sympathetic to American protests before the shooting started and Americans themselves who were willing to fight for rights within the empire but had no desire to leave it.[23] Even in July 1776 there were those in the Continental Congress—avowed patriots, not loyalists, not neutralists— who did not relish parting ways with Britain. Thomas Jefferson's original draft of the Declaration of Independence included a lamentation about separation, an expression of sadness that Britain and America could no longer share the same future.[24] It was excised, probably because most of Jefferson's congressional colleagues decided that such an expression could be misread as doubt about the course they had chosen, a complication they did not need as they attempted to build a nation in the midst of war and assure potential allies that they would not falter.

True enough, Congress had moved beyond the sentiments it expressed in the Olive Branch petition the year before, in what historian Stephen Conway considered the first "peace initiative" offered by either side.[25] It was first only in the sense that it was the first after Lexington and Concord; it had been preceded, informally, by others. British leaders remembered that colonial protesters before the fighting at Lexington and Concord had denied that they sought independence. Some called, instead, for a return to policies in place before 1763. Americans, by their own words, were reluctant revolutionaries. Therefore it should be no surprise that British proposals stumbled about, the more modest seeking a return to conditions as they were—or at least as they were idealized—before the unpopular policies of the 1760s, the more ambitious looking to some sort of imperial restructuring to prevent future clashes. Just as Americans had been slow to become Revolutionaries, Britons were slow to respond to a changing reality. But slow is not the same as unmoving. Few if any at either Whitehall or Westminster would have disagreed with a pamphleteer who concluded: "we must either give up the colonies, or strike out some method of reconciling British superiority with American 'liberty.'"[26] Advice like this had been offered on both sides of the Atlantic, well before the shooting started.

The most public of the prewar proposals to avoid war by restructuring the empire was made in Thomas Pownall's new 1774 edition of a treatise that Pownall had first published anonymously a decade before.[27] He revised his argument several times over the years and, with each subsequent revision, his argument became more involved—a critic might say more convoluted. If so, it was because of the deep-seated nature of the problem at hand, not the author's ineptness. In effect, Pownall tried to square the circle, an impossible task given the attitudes of the moment, *not* the inherent difficulties of the structural problem. He accepted the underlying logic of unitary sovereignty, which assumed that there must be one supreme power in any state, one court of last resort, one ultimate authority. Britain was necessarily supreme; the colonies were necessarily subordinate. As Pownall saw it, colonists were never outside the King's dominions even if they had left the realm. Colonies only existed because of crown charters to those who funded and settled them. Parliament did not have the authority to tax the colonists directly. It did, however, have the right to regulate their commerce, and they, in turn, had the responsibility to help cover the costs of empire. Therefore the navigation system had to be maintained, for the good of the larger empire.[28]

Pownall hoped that the issue of supremacy versus subordination would not arise once a mutually beneficial, mutually acceptable relationship had been worked out. At the time he wrote he had good reason to believe that protesting Americans would not reject his ideas out of hand. They professed to love the empire, to be loyal subjects of the King, and to be willing to accept—or as the more insistent would see it, permit—some parliamentary role in controlling their trade.[29] What he offered as his solution to the heretofore intractable problem, but not in so many words, was a power-sharing, federal arrangement. To have any chance of success, it obliged colonists to ignore their subordinate status while concentrating on the notion of reciprocity, a belief in all parts of the empire sacrificing for the greater good of the whole, with all ultimately benefiting because of it.

Pownall—like Weissenstein four years later—blamed both Britons and Americans for the political impasse that had developed. Imperial administrators had been too insensitive to colonial rights; colonists had been too strident in defending them. When, echoing Machiavelli, he called for a return to "first principles,"[30] he wanted rival interests to be subordinated to shared identity. "I wish the government of this country to define its own rights and standing on that sure ground, to acknowledge those of others," Pownall wrote, in words directed at Whitehall and Westminster. "I wish the people of America, as they love liberty, so to honour true government, which is the only basis on which *real liberty* can stand," he admonished aggrieved colonists.[31] "No other line of pacification remains, than either the Colonies be admitted into the Parliament of Great Britain by a general *British Union*," he concluded, "or that they have a *Parliament of their own under an American Union*."[32]

Neither option presented by Pownall—seating Americans at Westminster or allowing Americans their own intercolonial congress—appealed to the masters of empire. In their protests against imperial policy few Americans expressed any interest in having seats at Westminster and did not seem all that enamored of an intercolonial congress. Their political rhetoric trailed behind their political behavior. They acted as if they were independent long before they claimed independence; indeed, they repeatedly denied that independence was their goal. And yet they had challenged London's suzerainty by stepping outside the lines of legitimate authority, many of them supporting provincial conventions to supersede assemblies before the end of 1774. Those conventions were effectively shadow governments, calling on the people to pay taxes to them, not royal authorities, and to reorganize their militias and support the Continental Congress, which became a proto-national government long before there was a conscious choice to found a new nation.[33] In that sense the real revolution occurred on a subconscious level first, the conscious choice based on it coming months, even years, later—which should give us a better sense of what British peace negotiators were up against.

Given the pre-1776 professions of loyalty that almost invariably accompanied American grievances, Crown and Parliament are to be forgiven in thinking that the rebellious colonies should not be considered lost. Formally recognizing or even negotiating with provincial conventions or the Continental Congress meant accepting a future that they wanted to avoid, a future that protesting Americans themselves claimed not to want. London's response in early 1775 to conciliatory moves begun by dissident colonists the summer before would be in the form recommended by Lord North, after first rejecting a proposal made by William Pitt, now Earl of Chatham. North characterized his approach as conciliatory. Compared with Chatham's, it was not conciliatory in the least. Seeking to sidestep constitutional issues raised by disagreements over the range of authority and distribution of power within the imperial structure, North offered Americans the opportunity to tax themselves under a requisition system, without renouncing Parliament's authority to tax directly if it saw fit. He refused to deal with the Continental Congress or provincial conventions; rather, he addressed only those governments existing under royal charters.

Chatham, by contrast, was willing to accept the de facto as de jure, and proposed significant structural change. He did reaffirm basics: Britain must be sovereign and Parliament supreme. Nevertheless that supremacy, he contended, did not mean unlimited authority. Americans were right to argue that they should not be taxed where they were not represented. Parliament could regulate colonial trade; the King had the prerogative to station troops in the colonies. Those troops were not to impose order if that meant depriving the colonists of their rights as Englishmen, and Parliament was not to use its right to regulate trade as an excuse to unconstitutionally raise revenue from it. Imperial needs could be met through a requisition system, not through individual colonies paying their share—North's way—but by recognizing the Continental Congress as a legitimate legislative body and letting it set the rates that colonists would contribute to meet imperial needs. Congress would recognize Parliament's supremacy and Parliament, for its part, would repeal the Coercive Acts and no longer subject the colonists to abuses of power. In short, Chatham stressed, if both sides gave a little, each would gain a lot. [34]

Chatham, admittedly, was long past his prime, riding on his fame and unable to form and lead a solid Opposition in either the Lords or the Commons. Remembered more for his oratory in these later years than his attention to practical policy, it is too easy to dismiss him as out of touch because unpersuasive. Chatham's stock as a "friend" to America has fallen posthumously as Edmund Burke's has risen, Chatham's January 1775 speech in the Lords setting the stage for his February resolutions suffering by comparison with Burke's speech on reconciliation in the Commons the following month. But then, Burke's moving March speech had no more effect on policy than Chatham's, and Chatham was far ahead of Burke in what he was willing to concede in order to save the empire. Chatham had never endorsed the Declaratory Act pushed through by the Rockingham ministry in 1766. Burke did and would not give up on it until 1778, when creation of the Carlisle commission effectively made it dead letter law.

Congress offered conciliatory gestures from the beginning but never sent peace commissioners to London. Its status at its first meeting in the fall of 1774 was so nebulous that half of the colonial agents in London chose not to be associated with its petition to the Crown. When reconvened in the spring of 1775, Congress had a firmer footing, but it was still not a national government—nor did it profess to aspire to be—and chose again not to send anyone to London to speak for it, on the presumption that whoever was sent would not be granted an audience anyway.[35] Congress's hands were tied because Whitehall and Westminster would not deal with it as a legitimate government. By contrast, there were peace commissioners sent by London to the war-torn colonies from 1776 through the end of the war in 1783—seven years of attempted reconciliation, with no success.

George III had been reluctant to appoint any commissioners at all. Accusing rebellious Americans of seeking "an independent Empire" when he opened a new session of Parliament in October 1775, he did not authorize the first peace commission until near the year's end.[36] Even then he was skeptical that it could accomplish anything. The Earl of Dartmouth, his secretary of state for American affairs at the beginning of the fighting, had been hopeful that reconciliation could be reached by working with the Continental Congress, at least informally, perhaps only behind the scenes.[37] George Germain, his successor, was much closer to the King in his sentiments. Before Germain took office North had queried him about going to the colonies as a peace commissioner if the King approved. Germain declined, convinced that dealing with Congress in any form would legitimize it and undercut imperial authority.[38]

George III appointed his first peace commissioners, the brothers Howe—Admiral Richard and General William—with that fear in mind. They were not to deal with Congress or with any individual colony where duly constituted, royally recognized authority had been displaced. Although colonial leaders had behaved "traitorously," having "usurped" power, the Howes could meet with, even pardon, whomsoever they chose—essentially do anything "as may tend to the Advantage and Stability" of the colonies "and to a lasting Union of each of them respectively with Great Britain upon the true Principles of the Constitution."[39] The King empowered the Howes to recognize rightful civil authority and assist those willing to swear allegiance to him when forming new governments. North's conciliatory proposal of February 1775, bolstered by the prohibition of trade with New England since then,[40] could be the basis for discussions. The rebels were not to impose any conditions of their own.

The Duke of Grafton complained that this amounted to a demand for "unlimited submission" and predicted that it would produce no positive results. It was not the assumption that "all Our Colonies should be maintained in a due subordination to the Authority of the Parent State" that bothered him; rather, it was that too few incentives had been presented to induce a return to the fold. Events would prove him correct, even though the vast majority of his colleagues in the House of Lords thought him wrong.[41]

The misery that the Howes experienced as they tried to drive rebels to the bargaining table has become an all too familiar tale.[42] They issued a series of proclamations before the end of 1776, each one an attempt to persuade and cajole simultaneously. Officially, of course, they could not negotiate with Congress; unofficially, Lord Richard—his brother William was busy leading the troops driving Washington's army out of New York—met in September on Staten Island with a three-man congressional delegation that included Benjamin Franklin. The Americans matched British maneuvering with their own: independence, they emphasized, had been declared and there was nothing to discuss—unless, that is, the Howes received authorization from London to deal with them as representatives of a sovereign nation. Then they could talk. Frustrated, embarrassed, the Howes reported that "the Infatuation and Perseverance of the People and their Leaders have hitherto afforded no opportunity for the effectual operation of the Civil Commission with which His Majesty hath been pleased to charge us."[43] Cutting through the ponderous language: they confessed to having failed. Nonetheless, they could not bring themselves to concede that all efforts at reconciliation and restoration were doomed, that there was nothing to be done, which is why they also searched desperately for signs of change, for any evidence that the revolutionary tide could be turned. Hence their report at the end of 1776 that pacification seemed to be working here and there. Political gains had followed in the wake of their successful military campaign, with nearly five thousand colonists swearing oaths of loyalty to the Crown, over half of those in New Jersey alone.[44]

Even if they had enjoyed greater success, how would London have responded? The Howes promised that Parliament would repeal legislation that the colonists had found offensive; the House of Commons in fact refused to even consider repeal, an indication of how little George III and his ministers were willing to give, despite the Howes' charge as peace commissioners.[45] Opposition leaders became so frustrated at their seeming intransigence that they contemplated a walkout at Westminster but then decided against it, since it was all too obvious that their leaving would have no effect on policy—except to make it easier to pass legislation sustaining the war.[46] As

George Savile, a longtime parliamentary ally of Rockingham, lamented, the more that Americans insisted on independence, the easier it was for war enthusiasts to characterize them as foreigners and the conflict as a fight for national survival.[47] Nevertheless he and Rockingham and others wanted to do something, especially when they learned that Congress had sent Franklin to France to find succor there. The French had been aiding the rebels surreptitiously from the beginning and any sort of formal alliance could prove utterly disastrous—not just militarily, but to any political plans for reconciliation.

The year 1776 closed with the Marquess of Rockingham complaining that no one with the King's ear had the courage to tell him that his policies "towards America," though fully sanctioned by Parliament, "are erroneous" and that "the adherence to them is destruction."[48] Understandably there would be those who believed that the future could have been dramatically different if someone other than North had headed the ministry. So, at least, claimed the Duke of Grafton many years later in his autobiography;[49] so too others at the time, who thought that if some envoy from London could get to Franklin before he began talks with the French, peace could be restored.[50] They grasped at straws, perhaps, but then their hope that the Franklin of 1776 could be turned back toward the Franklin of 1775 can hardly be dismissed as groundless. His Articles of Confederation, drafted in July of that year, had held out the possibility of reconciliation and provided for an intercolonial union that could be temporary or permanent, depending on London's response to their grievances.[51] Congress, still of a divided mind, let Franklin's proposed articles sit. Even after Congress moved ahead with proclaiming independence, Edmund Burke thought it might have empowered Franklin to cross over to London to negotiate some sort of peace based on a return to the empire, should he be spurned at Versailles.[52] Franklin, though ambivalent about leaving the empire in the early days of the war, appears to have passed the point of no return well before he arrived in France: independence had become the irreversible goal.[53]

Before dismissing Burke's supposition as naively out of touch, we should remember that course reversals are not uncommon in diplomacy and that the purportedly nonnegotiable often ends up being negotiable after all. American Revolutionaries were not ignorant of the world of realpolitik and would not have even contemplated rising against Britain if they had not thought they could turn Europe's balance of power competition to their advantage. They were hardly innocents, venturing into the unknown; they already knew that politics could make strange bedfellows.[54]

The King and his ministers eventually recognized that the old empire could not be reassembled and that something different would have to take its place. Military stalemate at the end of 1776 and again at the close of 1777 nudged them there, with New England surrendered to the rebels, the southern colonies above Florida all but abandoned, the outcome in the area between the Susquehanna and Hudson Rivers still uncertain, and France apparently on the verge of entering the war. With North showing early signs of discouragement, Opposition leaders tried again in the spring of 1777 to sway the King toward offering a more generous peace. They drafted a "humble address" that emphasized how blood continued to be shed needlessly; meanwhile, Britain's trade was disrupted, its debt continued to rise, and the possibility of foreign intervention increased daily. Consequently, urged these dissident parliamentarians, the Howes had to be empowered to offer more generous terms and the King needed to be prepared to stand behind them; otherwise, "the Colonies may be lost" and rival nations could ally with them and "reap those advantages" which Britain, by its own failed policies, had opened.[55] Some became so worried France was about to enter the contest that they urged Whitehall and Westminster to recognize American independence, then, as allies, Britain and the United States could go to war against France—voila, problem solved.[56] Although the proposal went nowhere, it reflected the growing desperation in some minds.[57]

Those like the Duke of Richmond who were willing to let the colonies go in order to end the war and seek reconciliation outside the imperial framework were a tiny minority and would remain so for some years to come.[58] Convinced that Britain teetered on the edge of disaster, with Americans unbeaten—possibly even unbeatable—and France edging closer to intervention, Chatham roused himself once again and in mid-1777 returned to his failed prewar proposal: "If an end is not put to this war, there is an end to this country," he thundered in the House of Lords.[59] He could not get the ministry to change policy, but in the months to come he still did not change his mind. "Be the victory to which ever Host it pleases the Almighty to give it, poor England will have fallen upon her own Sword," he prophesied.[60] His last speech, delivered in April 1778, during which he collapsed and was carried from the Lords' chambers, never to return, was on that very same subject: end the war, but—*but*—reconcile with the Americans rather than let them go.[61]

By then the King had finally decided to pursue reconciliation in earnest, even if still at too great a distance from the throne. Early in 1778 he appointed the Carlisle commission to join in what the Howes had begun. He had in fact opened the new parliamentary session that began in November 1777 with a speech hinting he was headed that way. He promised that he would be "ever watchful for any opportunity of putting a stop to the effusion of the blood of my subjects and the calamities that are inseparable from a state of war" because he still hoped "that the deluded and unhappy multitude will return to their allegiance."[62] Both Houses supported the King's message, with large majorities. A couple of weeks later Thomas Pownall, firmly aligned with the Opposition, contended that the "sovereignty of this country over America is abolished and gone for ever." Nonetheless, what to him was a self-evident truth was not evident to most members of the Commons.[63] For them, American independence remained unthinkable.

There would be a flurry of behind-the-scenes diplomatic activity between the King's message in November 1777 and the appointment of the Carlisle commission the following spring. It occurred with the King's knowledge and, in a couple of cases, possibly even his complicity. The presumed impact of the Saratoga campaign on all of this is actually a matter of some debate. The British position was already shifting before London learned of Burgoyne's surrender; the American position had long been staked out; the French were more or less committed to entering the war by the coming spring anyway. Only utter disaster on all fronts would have changed French thinking. The primary issue was how the threat of formal French or Spanish intervention could be used by either the British or Americans to give themselves a negotiating edge.[64] Thus Whitehall's informal turn toward Franklin.

Franklin was not alone in Passy. Silas Deane, who had landed in France many months before him, and Arthur Lee, were also there. (John Adams would not arrive as Deane's replacement until the following April.) They stood very much in Franklin's shadow, even though Deane, in theory, was senior of the three. By the time that visitors from London turned up on their doorstep, Congress had decreed that it would not settle for anything less than independence from Britain—a statement aimed at France as much as at Britain, which Franklin and his colleagues did not receive until most of the visitors had come and gone.[65] Those essentially self-appointed negotiators who crossed the channel were determined to change Revolutionary American minds. So too the King who stood back to see what their efforts might bring, though even he—like North—was beginning to realize how slim their chances had become.[66]

None in London knew, though many suspected, that before the end of December 1777 Vergennes had promised the Americans an alliance. Anticipation of that offer is what had prompted the train of visitors as well as a more flexible approach by the King's men.[67] Cloaked in the mystery of his own making, Charles de Weissenstein would not arrive until many months later, after others had tried and failed to affect Franklin's thinking. Among those descending on Franklin (and to a lesser extent, Deane) was Paul Wentworth, who in effect acted at the behest of William Eden—someday a member of the Carlisle commission, but for the moment the head of a rudimentary spy ring for the North ministry. Eden was convinced that the war had devolved into stalemate. He realized that getting Americans to accept that "fact" would be as difficult as changing the minds of colleagues in the Commons who wanted to press on with the war. He urged Wentworth to help Franklin see that Americans, while claiming to be independent, were not really free at all. They were caught up in a bloody, expensive struggle with no end in sight, contemplating alliance with a former enemy who cared nothing for them. What did Britain need to do to win them back: Ease the navigation system? Guarantee the sanctity of colonial charters? Desist from taxation? If Franklin the realist rather than Franklin the ideologue came to the fore, there was a chance for reconciliation, or so Eden preferred to believe. Wentworth's report dashed those hopes. Franklin could not be moved from insisting on independence and would not really engage Wentworth in any meaningful dialogue. Wentworth, frustrated, canceled a second meeting, deciding it would be a waste of time. [68]

Franklin's meetings with James Hutton and William Pulteney were, by contrast, much friendlier but still accomplished nothing tangible. Franklin and Hutton, a London bookseller, had been friends for some twenty years. Hutton knew the King; the King apparently encouraged him to go to Passy, even though he did not share Hutton's sympathy for the American cause or his admiration of Franklin. [69] Hutton went convinced that he could persuade Franklin to settle for something short of independence. Like so many others, he did not really hear Franklin's response—that it was too late, that even though Britain could not be trusted to be a loving parent, it could still prove itself to be a friend, *if* it would accept the new nation as an equal. "A Peace you may undoubtedly obtain, by dropping all your Pretensions to govern us," Franklin told him, at once an assurance and a warning. It appears that Hutton returned to a royal audience, but his news brought no joy when it was shared with the King's closest advisers and even members of the Opposition. In a tantalizing glimpse of what went on behind the scenes, Horace Walpole reported that "both the Court and Chatham were so mad" that whatever compromise was in the works came apart and Chatham decided not to attend the House of Lords, where he would presumably have made some sort of motion for peace that the King's men would then have endorsed—stipulating what, exactly, we cannot say. [70]

Pulteney, a member of the Commons, did not have Hutton's long connection with Franklin. He had been trying to act as a go-between for some time, though kept at arm's length by the Pennsylvanian and initially rejected as an intermediary by the ministry. He went to Passy basically on his own, determined that he could find the middle ground that would preserve the empire by first persuading Franklin to tell him what it would take for America to agree to "lay down its arms." [71] He could not. By the time of his visit to Passy in March 1778 the Franco-American alliance had already been signed (which he did not know) and the Carlisle commission was being put together (which he did know). So desperate was he to reach an agreement that he implied misleadingly in a subsequent pamphlet that Franklin had given him the impression that independence was still negotiable. [72]

Pulteney did not insist that the colonies remain in the empire forever. On the contrary; he and most of his contemporaries understood that Americans would be independent someday—that most colonists eventually chafe at their subordination, that no empire lasts forever. He conceded American charges that Crown and Parliament had exceeded their constitutional authority and that the colonial protests against being taxed had been appropriate. But, he intoned, the time was not right for Americans to leave the empire, especially if they left allied to a duplicitous France. Pulteney contended that North's requisition system, as proposed back in February 1775, could be the first step toward a restoration of harmony. His pamphlet enjoyed a wide circulation, going through five printings within a single year, which gives some indication of how much interest there was among Britons in finding a peaceful resolution to the crisis.[73]

Perhaps the most intriguing of the British contacts with Franklin was by post rather than in person: letters from David Hartley, longtime friend, a member of Parliament, an independent who usually lined up with the Opposition, especially on American matters. Hartley had protested against the use of force before it was even applied, condemned the war once it began, and went from calling for American legislative autonomy, with a nominal tie through the King, to embracing Americans as independent and equal, and entering into an alliance with them against France. With Franklin emphatic that independence was irreversible because of what Britain had done, and could no longer be depended upon to undo, initially Hartley had scrambled to find a solution that would not alienate Britons opposed to American independence and Americans who would not settle for anything less. When addressing his Hull constituents publicly, he emphasized American independence as a last resort, with a tie through the King the preferred solution and a "foederal alliance" joining Britons and Americans as the solution to the problem. With Franklin in private he conceded the need for full independence, with the "foederal alliance" a partnership between equals.[74] He was inconsistent without being disingenuous, believing that the first object was to end the war and break the Franco-American tie. Everything else was secondary, with details to be worked out after the essentials had been achieved.[75]

It made more sense to Hartley—as it had to Pulteney—that negotiations be conducted between Franklin and his companions in Passy and British diplomats crisscrossing the channel rather than through commissioners in far-off America. Nothing had been accomplished by the Howes; he saw no reason to expect more success with three new commissioners, who would join the brothers, not replace them. Berating the ministry for not wooing Americans back into the fold, Hartley urged that the commissioners be empowered to proclaim a cease-fire and promise Americans the full rights of Englishmen, including the power to tax themselves, in something vaguely anticipating the future commonwealth.[76] Concluding that, without such guarantees, the commissioners would again fail, Hartley finally gave up on his approach. The secondary had to become primary, he concluded: American independence must be the starting point of any discussion, as Franklin had labored so long to persuade him.[77]

The king, his ministers, and a majority in Parliament disagreed. Despite three years of fighting they still hoped that the majority of Revolutionary Americans could be reconciled to the empire. North, for his part, stood by his February 1775 propositions as the basis of discussions. He simply did not believe that *"All America"* wanted independence.[78] George III, not wanting North to resign even though he was losing heart, urged him to offer more and he did. John Wilkes pushed too hard when he tried to get the Declaratory Act repealed; his motion in the Commons went down to a crushing defeat.[79] Although not willing to see the Declaratory Act repealed or let the Opposition shape the direction of any conciliatory effort, North was willing to suspend that legislation and to repeal other acts that Americans had protested in the years leading up to the war. Taking a page from Rockinghamites who had opposed Grenville in the 1760s on the Stamp Act, North planned to give up taxing without formally renouncing the right, on the assumption that constitutional issues would fade as political and economic disputes subsided.[80] He did so as part of an endeavor to get the Continental Congress to negotiate "as if it were a legal body"—the "as if" a crucial indicator of Whitehall's intentions.[81]

By early 1778 the king and his men were finally willing to deal with Congress directly. They would not, however, explicitly recognize its legitimacy because they expected it to disappear in the wake of successful talks, after which the colonies—each acting individually—would once again accept a place in the empire.[82] That those colonies had proclaimed themselves states in a new nation could be ignored; the claim of independence itself could be forgotten, as if it had never happened, or so went Whitehall's exercise in political optimism.[83] Wilkes came around in support, even as he chided, "may we regain by treaty what we have lost by tyranny of arms."[84] North's proposal subsequently passed easily in the Commons; it did likewise in the Lords, the objections of an unbending Earl of Abingdon notwithstanding. The Earl accused North of being disingenuous, of conceding only as much as he felt obliged to, thereby giving the appearance rather than the substance of compromise. Abingdon had almost no discernible effect on other peers; Carlisle and his colleagues went forth to do North's bidding.[85]

If Congress should prove unwilling to negotiate, then the new commissioners, like their predecessors, could talk with other groups or individuals who would be willing to form new governments swearing fealty to the king. In effect, Whitehall and Westminster were trying to take a chapter from the rebels' political notebook, using extralegal methods to undercut what the new American regime deemed legal. They would start their own shadow governments to challenge those who purported to be "state" officials, just as dissidents had done against imperial authority in 1774. Popular opinion and popular support would be the ultimate determinants of who would prevail and what would stand as legitimate. With luck the commissioners could turn the tables on those who had usurped power, using revolutionary methods to reverse revolutionary results.

North did not expect to win over all the disaffected. A revitalized peace commission, coupled with the repeal legislation as a show of good faith, might enable him to divide and conquer, reconverting some rebellious Americans, even if not others, in the Continental Congress, in the government of individual provinces, even in the general population.[86] "The object of the Commission is not simply to restore Peace between Great Britain & the Colonies, but to form such a Plan of Government as shall tend to remove all jealousies and bind the Colonies more firmly to the Mother Country."[87] Carlisle and his two new fellow commissioners, William Eden and George Johnstone, like the Howes two years before, had a fair amount of leeway granted them and a certain amount of ambiguity in their charge. North hoped that in those gray areas a new loyalist constituency could be formed that would reclaim political power and with it the governmental authority London had lost.[88] The commissioners could promise fewer restrictions on trade, an American say in setting requisition amounts, even discuss American seats at Westminster—provided those seats were not so numerous as to affect the balance of power there, which shows how far London remained from any true federal sense of power sharing within the empire.

Not having any word from France in months and hearing rumors that the new commissioners were en route from Britain, there were those in Congress who yearned for an end to war and reconciliation with Britain in the aftermath. Not sure of where they stood with the French, John Jay, for one, stated, "If Britain would acknowledge our independence, and enter into a liberal alliance with us, I should prefer a connection with her to a league with any power on earth."[89] Others in Congress, less outspoken, apparently felt the same.[90] Just as Congress began to consider a resolution expressing a wish for reconciliation—but without dropping its assertion of the previous November that independence was nonnegotiable, it received word of the French alliance being sent for its ratification. It then shifted emphasis, calling for the American people to stand firm, to press on until they had won victory. "It hath now become morally certain, that, if we have courage to persevere, we shall establish our liberties and independence," Congress proclaimed. That meant driving the enemy "away from this land of promise."[91] Members of Congress who may have been wavering, who may have leaned toward meeting with the peace commissioners without any guarantees going in, had their spines stiffened.

According to the traditional view the timing could not have been worse for the Carlisle commissioners, because they stepped ashore in a Philadelphia about to be evacuated by the British army. But we should not let hindsight skew our perspective. As Whitehall saw it, this was not a permanent abandonment of the region or the beginning of the end for the larger conflict. North's divide–and–conquer approach had a military as well as a diplomatic component. Although Henry Clinton was replacing William Howe as army commander, Clinton was to pick up where Howe left off. Howe had never been relieved of his duties as a peace commissioner and, as army commander, his primary task had been to try and force the rebels to negotiate.[92] Frustrated as both of the Howes had become (the Admiral too wanted to be relieved), they kept giving London the impression that victory was close, perhaps just a new campaign away.[93] Germain's orders to Clinton for the 1778 campaign season were similar to what the Howes had been instructed to do in 1776. He was to think of diplomatic efforts and military operations as opposite sides of the same coin. Like the civilian commissioners, he had been given a fair amount of leeway. He was to take the war to the South and attempt a pacification program there that had thus far failed in the North. But evacuating Philadelphia—or not—was his call. If he wanted to use the city as a base from which he could send out naval raiding parties to points near and far, that was his choice. In any event, he was not to think of London's reallocation of resources to meet the French threat as a winding down of the war or acceptance of irreversible defeat anywhere on the mainland of North America.[94]

As Clinton prepared to withdraw across New Jersey and set up headquarters in New York City before beginning his southern campaign, the Earl of Carlisle—in theory Clinton's colleague on the peace commission—tried to interest Congress in peace talks. "We are vested with powers equal to the Purpose and such as are even Unprecedented in the Annals of our History," he proudly informed Henry Laurens, president of the Congress.[95] Laurens' response was polite but firm, repeating what he had already stated to General Clinton and Admiral Howe: the United States would happily discuss terms with Great Britain, but only when Britain recognized its independence and not before. Carlisle did what he could to get Congress to reconsider its position, to contemplate accepting a place in the empire "on the Basis of equal Freedom and Mutual Safety"—a deliberately vague promise, meant to sidestep the issue of sovereignty and subordination. Congress remained unmoved.[96] The noted American diplomatic historian Samuel Flagg Bemis did not criticize Congress for being inflexible, but he did lament that with that refusal passed the last chance for a grand "Pax Britannica" that could have changed the destiny of the world.[97]

Bemis, to be sure, had engaged in a bit of wishful thinking—as had the Howes, the members of the Carlisle commission, the king who sent them, and Weissenstein when he approached Franklin. Carlisle and his companions remained in New York many months before finally returning home. Their departure did not bring an end to peace commissioners in the colonies, how-

ever. Clinton stayed on; Admiral Arbuthnot took up Lord Howe's charge and
joined him. Clinton would be succeeded by General Guy Carleton after
Yorktown, Arbuthnot by Admiral Richard Digby. Carleton made it clear that
he did not want to preside over a surrender. He still did not believe that most
Americans wanted independence and chafed at not having more authority to
use a veiled military threat to compel the Revolutionaries into reconsidering
their position.[98] His peace-seeking duties, irritating as they were, did not end
until the spring of 1783, shortly after a cease-fire had been declared and a full
year after clandestine negotiations had begun in France.[99]

We should not express wonder at such apparent thickheadedness—this
refusal to accept what many now deem to have been the unchangeable reality. Instead, we should combine what we already know about the larger war
with Britain's peace-seeking efforts, a connection too seldom made. For
example, it is common knowledge that not every American embraced the
Revolutionary cause and the peace commissioners did not have to contrive
evidence of loyalism. Thus the tone of a letter that Carlisle wrote to Germain
in October 1778, when he was in New York City. Despite having witnessed
the evacuation of Philadelphia and the contracted range of British authority,
he sounded optimistic. "The Crisis is certainly favourable for the rise of
measures tending to break the whole Rebellion," he assured the American
secretary, "and to make a Great Proportion of the Inhabitants of this continent to restore themselves to the Intercourse and Affection of their fellow
subjects."[100] Notice that he wrote "a Great Proportion," not "all"—an acceptance on his part that imperial authority could not necessarily be restored
everywhere. Even so, New York City stood securely under British control;
the loyalists dominated locally, and patriots still in the city had to keep quiet.
Events over the next couple of years during Clinton's southern campaign
would show that Carlisle's optimism had not been harebrained. Savannah
fell, Charleston surrendered, and a pacification program led to the restoration
of imperial authority in some areas of the deep South.

Cornwallis's disaster at Yorktown notwithstanding, Piers Mackesy, one
of the foremost historians of the conflict, contended that "if the British had
persevered a little longer, they could have won the war."[101] He emphasized
that even though they had military options they had not exercised, they
succumbed to war weariness. Mackesy, like another notable historian, Don
Higginbotham, depicted the British as caving in after Yorktown. Lord
North's supposed "O God! It is all over!" comment upon hearing of Cornwallis's surrender probably had too much of an impact on their thinking.[102]
In actuality, Yorktown did not change many minds in London very quickly.
George III wanted to continue the war, Yorktown regardless; George Germain likewise. Even as late as February 1782, Henry Conway's motion to
end military campaigns in North America barely passed the House of Commons and had no chance of passing in the House of Lords. It said nothing

about granting Americans their independence. Rather, it did just the opposite, sounding very Chatham-like in declaring that continued fighting would only make reconciliation that much more difficult.[103] Yet, limited as that resolution was, it helped drive George III to contemplate abdication.[104] He feared that if he let one part of the empire go the rest would follow, until Britain was reduced to inconsequence, a great power no more.[105]

First Germain, then North, stepped down from their posts, a new ministry formed under Rockingham, and George III reconciled himself to losing thirteen of the American colonies as peace negotiations began in the spring of 1782.[106] The Earl of Shelburne, who had supported Chatham's attempts to achieve reconciliation and swore he would ever-resist granting Americans independence, ended up, ironically, heading the ministry that succeeded the deceased Rockingham, accepting, as Rockingham had, American independence as the price of ending the war.[107] Even then Shelburne hoped for some sort of Anglo-American federation, an informal partnership as the next-best-thing to restoring formal ties. Before reaching that point, Whitehall and Westminster had rejected recommendation after recommendation that they pursue a different approach to the American war, even if that meant letting some of the colonies go in order to keep others. Ultimately, that is precisely what they ended up doing anyway. To return to Mackesy's point: the British might have held onto other areas that they eventually signed away in Paris, had they conducted the war differently—if, for example, they had given up New England as lost from the beginning and concentrated their efforts elsewhere, or if they had pursued pacification earlier and more consistently in the deep South.[108]

There is no need to pile up the what-ifs to underscore the point that British attempts to persuade American Revolutionaries to rejoin the empire cannot be dismissed as delusive. The Charles de Weissensteins of the Revolutionary Era are a reminder that many people knew then, as scholars emphasize now, that identities and boundaries were fluid in the British Atlantic world, that most Americans who turned to revolution did so reluctantly, and that many did not embrace it at all. The Revolutionaries themselves found that they could not export their ideas wherever they chose and that they had to shorten their reach as they radicalized their aims. Although some Anglo-Irish leaders expressed sympathy for rebellious Americans, they shared no real empathy with them.[109] The West Indies showed little interest in following the American lead, despite complaints made there against the navigation system.[110] Most Canadians, for their part, had shown little interest in joining the rebellion as it expanded to become a revolution. Nova Scotia, anglicized for generations, had that identity intensified with the arrival of Loyalist émigrés. The Floridas, returned to Spain after just twenty years, had hardly been anglicized at all. Vermont, part of the new republic, had dissidents who contemplated returning to the empire.[111] Whitehall and Westminster, understandably, had wanted to reclaim everything they had lost. Even though they failed, the reasons for that failure were much more involved than a simple inability to deal with change.

No doubt they put too much stock in what imperial administrators told them before the fighting erupted and they repeated the error when accepting too uncritically what loyalists during the war said about American sympathies.[112] Perhaps, too, more policy makers should have listened to critics like Josiah Tucker, who had advised, even before Lexington and Concord, that Americans should be cut loose—that it would be easier to dominate their trade outside of the formal imperial arrangement rather than attempt to control their behavior within it and bear the financial burden and suffer the political costs that came with the navigation system.[113] Whitehall and Westminster thought they knew better. Events often proved them wrong, but using hindsight to critique what we deem their lack of foresight breeds its own kind of hubris.

At the very least, to dismiss the Carlisle commission as a "farce" and to conclude that London failed at reconciliation because it was incapable of embracing a federal notion of empire oversimplifies.[114] The Carlisle commission may indeed have been empowered to offer too little too late, but it did reflect a signal shift in imperial thinking—a willingness to restructure the empire to meet new conditions which, again, most in Whitehall and Westminster knew would have to be done eventually anyway. Reluctant as they had been to change at that moment, they accepted the logic behind the platitude that change is the one constant.[115] They were not ready to remake Parliament in order to include colonists as part of what would someday become known as "responsible government"—nor would their successors, for that matter. And they remained averse to any sort of intercolonial American congress. But their willingness to allow individual colonial legislatures to operate under a requisition system and to have a voice in setting the amounts required represented a sea change in imperial thinking—yes, imposed by war, but potentially irreversible once begun, which North and George III probably realized. Repeal of the Declaratory Act rather than mere suspension may well have followed, hastening the sort of relationship between mother country and colonies only finally achieved under the Statute of Westminster in 1931.[116]

The king and his men recognized American independence most reluctantly, obliged by what they came to see as geopolitical necessity. Early on that reluctance had been fed by American denials that independence was the goal. That George III should send the Howes as peace commissioners looking to restore peace and order within the empire was logical enough: they were appointed six months before the Declaration of Independence and arrived at a time when patriot political ambitions were greatly in flux. American defeats in 1776 and again in 1777 fed the British tendency to believe that the rebels could not sustain independence, despite their having claimed it.[117] Even though the Continental Congress formed itself as a national government and thirteen provinces proclaimed themselves states in a new nation, there were those in London who believed that the political clock could be turned back— that if the revolutionaries failed to make good on their political claims through military success, restoration of the empire would follow as a matter of course. George III's endorsement of behind-the-scenes diplomatic maneuvers with Franklin should be viewed in that light; likewise Charles de Weissenstein's impetuous trip to France.

Even with the French alliance only New England had clearly established itself as a region outside of imperial purview. The American cause appeared to be in such desperate straits as late as the summer of 1781 that some in Congress were sympathetic when they heard rumors that Britain would welcome mediation by Austria or Russia, even though that would have meant a much smaller country.[118] Whether, before Yorktown, the United States— whatever the projected national boundaries at that point would have been— could have insisted on independence as a condition to ending the war remains a moot point.

In any event, British aversion to American independence was not a sign of an inept king or dysfunctional Parliament. George III, Lord North, the Earl of Shelburne, and others at Whitehall and Westminster did not want to surrender any of their American colonies and yet they eventually separated personal preference from national need and approved a treaty that they did not like—a realistic, pragmatic response. As much as they resented the new reality, they accepted it once they saw that further resistance would be foolish.[119] In seeking to salvage victory from defeat they could have done much worse than they did.[120]

NOTES

1. As taken from Benjamin Franklin Stevens, *Facsimiles of Manuscripts in European Archives Relating to America, 1773–1783* (London: Charles Whittingham and Co., 1898), vol. 8, no. 835, dated 16 June 1778, Brussels, which acts as a cover letter for a proposal to end the war (no. 836) and restructure government in North America to prevent future conflict (no. 837). It appears that Brussels was a ruse; possibly the date too. Stevens made photostatic copies from originals in the Archives Du Ministère Des Affaires Étrangères in Paris. Microfilm copies of the originals can be found in the Manuscripts Division of the Library of Congress.

2. John Adams to Elbridge Gerry, 9 July 1778, with notes appended later to explain what he only alluded to in that letter. Printed in *Diary and Autobiography of John Adams*, ed. Lyman Butterfield (Cambridge, MA: Harvard University Press, 1961), 4:150, 153.

3. Carl Van Doren reviewed this episode in *Benjamin Franklin* (New York: Viking Press, 1938), 603–5, and returned to it in *The Secret History of the American Revolution* (New York: Viking Press, 1941), 80–83. Cecil Currey also touched on it in *Code Number 72* (Englewood Cliffs, NJ: Prentice Hall, 1972), 221–23, and the Weissenstein business figured in an exchange involving Currey and historians Alan Brown and Forrest McDonald in "Letters to the Editor," in *William and Mary Quarterly*, 3rd ser., 32 (1975): 179–82. Thomas J. Schaeper, *Edward*

Bancroft: Scientist, Author, Spy (New Haven, CT: Yale University Press, 2011), 198–206, does not allude to Weissenstein, but puts no stock in virtually any of Currey's arguments. Weissenstein turns up, ever so briefly, in Stacy Schiff's *A Great Improvisation* (New York: Henry Holt and Company, 2006), 158–59; and William Doyle, *Aristocracy and Its Enemies in the Age of Revolution* (New York: Oxford University Press, 2009), 93–94. Weldon A. Brown, *Empire or Independence?* (Baton Rouge: Louisiana State University Press, 1941), the most detailed examination of British attempts at peacemaking during the war, gave (an unnamed) Weissenstein short shrift, at 281–82: "Someone threw a proposal over his [Johns Adams's] gate in Paris recommending an American peerage of two hundred colonists, such as Franklin, Washington, Samuel Adams, and John Hancock. It was a peculiar offer, and one can easily imagine the laughter it aroused in Samuel Adams and John Hancock." But Adams and Hancock may never have known about it at all. Weissenstein did not make it into standard accounts such as Samuel Flagg Bemis, *The Diplomacy of the American Revolution* (New York: D. Appleton-Century, 1935); Jonathan R. Dull, *A Diplomatic History of the American Revolution* (New Haven, CT: Yale University Press, 1985); H. M. Scott, *British Foreign Policy in the Age of the American Revolution* (Oxford: Clarendon Press, 1990); and Steven Conway, *The British Isles and the War of American Independence* (Oxford: Oxford University Press, 2000).

   4. See the editorial note in *Papers* 26:637. *The Complete Works of Benjamin Franklin*, ed. Jacob Bigelow (New York: G. P. Putnam's Sons, 1887–96), 6:187–96 included Franklin's (unsent?) letter to Weissenstein of 1 July 1778 and discussed Weissenstein's "curious and remarkable" proposals, which he had apparently seen in a Parisian archive. Jonathan R. Dull, *Franklin the Diplomat: The French Mission* (Philadelphia: American Philosophical Society, 1982) does not discuss Weissenstein's plan. Perhaps it should be fit into the "grandiose proposals" category (p. 12) that Dull emphasized Franklin avoided in order not to jeopardize Franco-American relations.

   5. John Adams, *Diary and Autobiography of John Adams*, ed. Lyman Butterfield (Cambridge, MA: Harvard University Press, 1961), 4:151.

   6. A copy of the police report, in French and dated Tuesday, 7 July 1778, the day after Weissenstein was tailed back to his hotel from Notre Dame, ended up (curiously) in the Arthur Lee Papers, Houghton Library, Harvard University. My colleague Chris Hodson only needed a few minutes to translate the report which, with my pidgin French, would have taken me hours.

   7. There are two brief biographical essays on Jennings Clerke, the first in Lewis Namier and John Brooke, *The House of Commons* (New York: Oxford University Press, 1964), 2:680–81; and the second in Martyn Powell's 2008 online addition to the print version of H. C. G. Matthew and Brian Harrison, eds., *Oxford Dictionary of National Biography* (Oxford: Oxford University Press, 2004), www.oxforddnb.com/view/article/93442?docPos=1. Most of the details of Jennings Clerke's life have been lost, and there is not perfect agreement on the accuracy of those that survive. His will is in the National Archives/Public Record Office [hereafter PRO], Prerogative Court of Canterbury, 11/1162 (also available online), dated 3 November 1784, with a codicil added on 9 July 1787 and proved 9 February 1788. There are brief obituary notices in the *Gentleman's Magazine* 58, part 1 (January 1788): 85, and *The Annual Register... For the Year 1788* (London: J. Dodsley, 1790): 230.

   8. G. F. Russell Barker and Alan H. Stenning, *The Record of Old Westminsters*, 2 vols. (London: Chiswick Press, 1928), 1:194; Joseph Foster, ed., *Alumni Oxonienses*, 4 vols. (London: Parker & Co., 1888), 2:751.

   9. He appears as Jennings Clerke in William Cobbett, ed., *The Parliamentary History of England*, 36 vols. (London: T. C. Hansard, 1806–20), 16:432, for the parliamentary session that began in May 1768, his first. The note for his promotion to a baronetcy in October 1774 appeared in *The Annual Register... For the Year 1774*, 2nd ed., (London: J. Dodsley, 1778), 188.

   10. Jennings Clerke in the Commons, speech of 18 November 1777, in Cobbett, *Parliamentary History*, 19:428. In his reminiscence Nathaniel Wraxall made a backhanded compliment, writing that Jennings Clerke was "a man of unquestionable integrity, but not endowed with superior parts." Henry B. Wheatley, ed., *The Historical and the Posthumous Memoirs of Sir Nathaniel William Wraxall, 1772–1784* (London: Bickers and Sons, 1884), 2:99–100. Wraxall referred to Jennings Clerke in the context of the baronet's proposal that the Commons ban

government contractors from sitting there. His bill made it through a third reading before going down to defeat in May 1778—"which we threw out with great difficulty," Lord North admitted to the King. In Sir John Fortescue, ed., *The Correspondence of King George III, from 1760 to 1783* (London: Macmillan and Co., 1927–28), 4:131. Jennings Clerke had supported Chatham's 1 February 1775 proposal that Crown and Parliament accept the legitimacy of the Continental Congress, at that moment a de facto intercolonial government. That gives credence to the claim that Jennings Clerke was Weissenstein. He mocked North's supposedly "conciliatory" resolution passed later that month. See Cobbett, *Parliamentary History*, 18:350.

11. For example, could the *Charles* in Weissenstein have come from his oldest son's name, Charles Philip? And, as Richard Reeves, a historian with the New Forest Visitors Centre, wondered (in an e-mail response to a query from the author), could *Weissenstein* have been an allusion to the white paint used on the stucco facade of the Georgian mansion at Coxlease (now Foxlease)? Perhaps; perhaps not. In any event, Charles died just a few months after his father and the baronetcy expired with him. There is a beautiful shrine to his memory in St. Michael and All Angels Church in Lyndhurst, not far from Foxlease (which is in the heart of the New Forest), erected by his sister Frances, the sole surviving child. To add yet another wrinkle, Jennings Clerke's younger son, John Edward, was in 1778 a cornet in the Twenty-First Light Dragoons. His unit was posted in Yorkshire to patrol for smugglers. Had he taken an unofficial leave and dashed off to France? Not likely. And there is the age factor again: he was twenty-one, not close to forty. He died the next year; there is a plaque honoring him in the nave of Exeter Cathedral. Then there is the Colonel Jennings who was involved in a dust-up between George III and his brother, the Duke of Gloucester, during the Duke's tour of the continent in the fall of 1777. Horace Walpole recorded it with his usual glee at royal peccadilloes in *The Last Journals of Horace Walpole during the Reign of George III, from 1771–1783*, (New York: J. Lane, 1910), 2:47–69. This was definitely not Phillip Jennings Clerke and doubtful if he was the Jennings in Paris the following June who contacted Franklin.

12. Franklin's response of 1 July 1778 is in *Papers* 27:4–10.

13. Again, see Adams's reminiscence in Adams, *Adams Diary and Autobiography*, 4:150. Adams's memory was sketchy; he thought Weissenstein's real name "was Colonel [Mc] Fitz—something[;] an Irish name I have forgotten, the Place he came from and the time he sett off to return." (Ibid., 4:152.)

14. Ibid., 4:152.

15. Rather than dismiss Weissenstein's proposal as "absurd"—John Adams's characterization—would it be going too far in the other direction to call it visionary? Had, for example, Weissenstein read Pufendorf and become intrigued by Pufendorf's "system of states," which moved beyond traditional unitary notions of sovereignty? For Pufendorf and others who dabbled in such things see Alison LaCroix, "Drawing and Redrawing the Line: The Pre-Revolutionary Origins of Federal Ideas of Sovereignty" in *Transformations in American Legal History*, ed. Daniel W. Hamilton and Alfred L. Brophy (Cambridge, MA: Harvard Law School, 2009), 58–84, which acted as a précis for LaCroix's *The Ideological Origins of American Federalism* (Cambridge, MA: Harvard University Press, 2010).

16. Stevens, *Facsimiles*, vol. 8, no. 837. In his details on how the treaty was to be negotiated, in ibid., vol. 8, no. 836, Weissenstein stipulated that if the king did create an American peerage, then George Washington, breveted to lieutenant general in the British Army, ought to head the list. Franklin too was on that list. Weissenstein knew enough about how the Continental Congress had arranged for veterans to be granted western lands after the service that he carried a like arrangement into his proposal.

17. "The Crown shall take upon itself to adjust the treaty between America & France, which shall be laid before his Majesty in entire, for his full information with respect thereto, a mode of notifying it to the Court of France shall be settled." Ibid., vol. 8, no. 836.

18. From Weissenstein's cover letter, no. 835 in ibid., vol. 8. The extracts that follow are from the same source.

19. Ibid.

20. Jennings Clerke had endorsed North's conciliatory motion in February 1778 (see Cobbett, *Parliamentary History*, 19:770–71) that paved the way for the Carlisle commission, but only after criticizing North for bringing on war in the first place. Even so, that does not rule him

out as Weissenstein. He may have become impatient waiting for results, or he could have decided that Carlisle had not been authorized to offer Americans enough to placate them.

21. Francis Wharton, ed., *The Revolutionary Diplomatic Correspondence of the United States*, 6 vols. (Washington, DC: Government Printing Office, 1889), 1:295.

22. John Richard Alden, "Again, the American Revolution—Inevitable?" *Phi Kappa Phi Journal* 55 (1975): 3. Also see Brown, *Empire or Independence?* 296.

23. George Germain to Richard, Lord Howe, 18 October 1776, in the George Sackville Germain Papers, vol. 5, William L. Clements Library, University of Michigan [hereafter Germain Papers]; printed, with minor changes, in the Historical Manuscripts Commission [hereafter HMC], *Report on the Manuscripts of Mrs. Stopford-Sackville* (London: His Majesty's Stationery Office, 1904–1910), 2:22.

24. See the facsimile printed in Julian Boyd, *The Declaration of Independence* (Washington, DC: Library of Congress, 1999), Document V.

25. Stephen Conway, *The War of American Independence, 1775–1783* (London: Edward Arnold, 1995), 215.

26. [John Lind], *Remarks on the Principal Acts of the Thirteenth Parliament of Great Britain* (London: T. Payne, 1775), 499. Lind is better remembered for *An Answer to the Declaration of the American Congress* (London: T. Cadell, 1776). Lind was a barrister affiliated with Lincoln's Inn.

27. That first version appeared as [Thomas Pownall] *The Administration of the Colonies* (London: J. Wilkie, 1764). G. H. Guttridge discussed this and the later versions in "Thomas Pownall's *The Administration of the Colonies*: the Six Editions," *William and Mary Quarterly*, 3rd ser., 26 (1969): 31–46. Daniel Baugh and Alison Gilbert Olson wrote an introduction for a reissue of the 1768 edition, published by Scholars' Facsimiles & Reprints in 1993. John A. Schutz, *Thomas Pownall, British Defender of American Liberty* (Glendale: A. H. Clark, 1951) remains the basic study. Pownall turns up here and there elsewhere, such as in Jerome R. Reich, *British Friends of the American Revolution* (Armonk, NY: M. E. Sharpe, 1998); and in Brendan McConville's *The King's Three Faces* (Chapel Hill: University of North Carolina Press, 2006).

28. Thus *A Letter from Governor Pownall to Adam Smith* (London: J. Almon, 1776), where Pownall defended the rationale behind the navigation acts and critiqued Smith's free trade notions. Although Pownall condemned the "roundabout trade"—in effect, the smuggling—that resulted from misapplications of the navigation system, he hoped that a more permissive "circuitous trade" within an improved system would replace it.

29. See the careful wording of the fourth of their ten resolutions, discussed in Neil L. York, "The First Continental Congress and the Problem of American Rights," *Pennsylvania Magazine of History and Biography* 122 (1998): 353–83.

30. Thomas Pownall, *Administration of the British Colonies, Part the Second* (London: J. Wilkie, 1774), 14.

31. Ibid., x–xi.

32. Ibid., 82.

33. For the "real" revolution preceding the declaration of it, see Jackson Turner Main, *The Sovereign States, 1775–1783* (New York: New Viewpoints, 1973), 99–142; for Congress's gradual emergence as a national government, see Jennifer Greene Marston, *King and Congress* (Princeton, NJ: Princeton University Press, 1987).

34. See Chatham's speech in the House of Lords of 20 January 1775, in R. C. Simmons and P. D. G. Thomas, eds., *Proceedings and Debates of the British Parliaments Respecting North America, 1754–1783* (Millwood, NY: Kraus International, 1982–87), 5:268–71, 275–82; and Pitt's formal proposal of 1 February, in the Pitt Papers, PRO 30/8/97, part II, fos. 111–26, which was also printed in William Stanhope Taylor and John Henry Pringle, eds., *Correspondence of William Pitt, Earl of Chatham* (London: John Murray, 1838–40), 4:533–36. For North's "conciliatory" motion of 20 February, see Simmons and Thomas, *Proceedings*, 5:432–51, 466–81.

35. See John Dickinson's notes for a speech that he made in May 1775, calling for Congress to send peace commissioners to London. Printed in Paul Smith et al., eds., *Letters of Delegates to Congress, 1774–1789* (Washington, DC: Library of Congress, 1974–2000),

1:371–91. In a letter of 24 February 1776, David Hartley urged Franklin to press Congress to be specific about what Americans wanted, which would help those in Parliament sympathetic to their cause to press for reconciliation. In *Papers* 22:363–66. But Congress was not that clear in its thinking yet and, even if it had been, George III was not willing to deal with it as a legitimate government.

36. Speech in Simmons and Thomas, *Proceedings*, 6:69–70. The authorization, dated 9 December 1775, is in the PRO/Colonial Office [hereafter CO] 5/159, fol. 138. Also see George Germain to Attorney General Thurlow and Solicitor General Wedderburn, instructing them to draft that authorization, in PRO/CO 5/350, fols. 299–300. For George III's hardening toward Americans as they escalated from protest to rebellion, see Andrew Jackson O'Shaughnessy, "If Others Will Not Be Active, I Must Drive," *Early American Studies* 2 (2004): 1–46.

37. See Dartmouth to William Knox, 6 August 1775, in the William Knox Papers, Box 2, Correspondence, 1773–1776. William L. Clements Library, University of Michigan [hereafter Knox Papers]. For Knox as imperial reformer, see Leland Bellot, *William Knox* (Austin: University of Texas Press, 1977).

38. For developments in London during the closing months of 1774 and early 1775, see Charles R. Ritcheson, *British Politics and the American Revolution* (Norman: University of Oklahoma Press, 1954); Peter D. G. Thomas, *From Tea Party to Independence* (Oxford: Clarendon Press, 1991); and, for Germain, Gerald Saxon Brown, *The American Secretary* (Ann Arbor: University of Michigan Press, 1963).

39. From the copy of the commission found in Auckland Papers, Add. Ms. 34413, fol. 32, British Library. Other copies of the commission and instructions can also be found in the PRO/CO 5/177 and the Knox Papers, Box 9, Miscellaneous Manuscripts.

40. For the statutory sequence whereby the rebellious colonies that went on to declare independence, beginning with New England, were cut off from trade in the empire between 1775 and 1776, see *The Statutes at Large*, ed. Danby Pickering (Cambridge: Joseph Bentham, 1762–1807), 31:4-11 (25 George III c. 10); 31:37–43 (25 George III c. 18); and 31:135–54 (26 George III c. 5).

41. During debates in the House of Lords, 14 March 1776, as printed in Cobbett, *Parliamentary History*, 18:1249.

42. A story well told in Ira D. Gruber, *The Howe Brothers and the American Revolution* (Chapel Hill: University of North Carolina Press, 1972). Eric Robson, *The American Revolution* (London: The Batchworth Press, 1956), 93–152, puts their problems into a much broader context.

43. Howe to Germain, 20 September 1776, in PRO/CO 5/ 177, fol. 69; Franklin to Congress, 13 September 1776, in Wharton, *Revolutionary Diplomatic Correspondence*, 2:140.

44. See the Howes' report to Germain of 22 December 1776 in the PRO/CO 5/177, fol. 135.

45. The Commons, on learning the content of the Howes' proclamation of 19 September 1776, refused overwhelmingly (109–47) on 6 November to convene as a committee of the whole to consider repeal of any recent legislation concerning the colonies. Cobbett, *Parliamentary History*, 18:1432–48.

46. See Charles James Fox to the Marquess of Rockingham, 13 October 1776, in Earl of Albemarle, *Memoirs of the Marquis of Rockingham and His Contemporaries* (London: Richard Bentley, 1852), 2:297. Some continued to see secession as necessary, even into the next year. See Richmond to Rockingham, 2 November 1777, Wentworth Woodhouse Muniments [hereafter WWM], R1/1739, Sheffield Archives, UK.

47. Savile to Rockingham, 15 January 1777, in WWM, R1/1705.

48. Rockingham to ?, sometime in December 1776, in Albemarle, *Memoirs*, 2:303.

49. Sir William R. Anson, ed., *Autobiography and Political Correspondence of Augustus Henry, Third Duke of Grafton* (London: John Murray, 1898), 284, 303.

50. See, for example, the Duke of Manchester to Rockingham, 18 December 1776, WWM R1/1696. For one of the more interesting, after-the-fact, "what if" arguments, see Fitzmaurice, *Life of Shelburne* (London: Macmillan and Co., 1875), 2:19–20, who contends that if Pitt had been healthier and lived longer, and if he had headed a new ministry, the outcome could have been better for Britons, even better for the Americans, who might have returned to the empire. Even if Fitzmaurice's argument about what might have happened is not especially persuasive,

it is nonetheless a good reminder that, with just a few small changes, there could have been a dramatically different outcome to the American war—but that also entails accepting that Britain could have done worse as well as better.

51.   Franklin's July 1775 articles, too often ignored by historians in the rush to get John Dickinson's articles, drafted *after* independence was declared, are in Worthington C. Ford, ed., *Journals of the Continental Congress* (Washington, DC: Government Printing Office, 1904–1937), 2:195–99. In Franklin's articles, all of Canada—St. Johns and Nova Scotia as well as Quebec—are invited to join in a union, as are the Floridas, Bermuda, and the West Indies. This version ought to be compared with the handwritten draft in the Papers of the Continental Congress, 1774–1789 [hereafter PCC] (Washington, DC: Government Printing Office, 1959; 204 reels microfilm), Item 9 (reel 22), which includes Ireland. Also see the copy and editorial notes in *Papers* 22:120–25; the discussions in Edmund Cody Burnett, *The Continental Congress* (New York: Macmillan, 1941), 90–93; and Marston, *King and Congress*, 189–92.

52.   Burke to Rockingham, 6 January 1777, in Thomas W. Copeland, ed., *The Correspondence of Edmund Burke* (Chicago: University of Chicago Press, 1958–78), 3:310.

53.   See Jack P. Greene's "The Alienation of Benjamin Franklin, British American" in Greene's *Understanding the American Revolution* (Charlottesville: University of Virginia Press, 1995), 247–84, for Franklin as a "trimmer"—which gives a more nuanced view than the opportunistic, even duplicitous Franklin painted in Currey's *Code Number 72* (though even a caustic Currey admitted, on p. 10, that "Getting at the truth about Benjamin Franklin is no easy matter.") Upon arriving in France, Franklin played "the courted virgin," as Jonathan Dull put it in *Franklin the Diplomat*, 11. He knew that the British and the French needed to believe that he and his nation would consider reconciliation if he were to have any leverage. Some in both Paris and London may have inferred that he treated independence as negotiable—something he never stated explicitly, but what he misleadingly left implicit is another matter. That is why it is called the "art" of diplomacy.

54.   For a brief but insightful discussion of an American approach to diplomacy before there was an independent American nation or any aspiration to create it, see James H. Hutson, *John Adams and the Diplomacy of the American Revolution* (Lexington: University of Kentucky Press, 1980), 1–32; Richard W. Van Alstyne, *Empire and Independence* (New York: John Wiley & Sons, 1965); and Felix Gilbert, *To the Farewell Address* (Princeton, NJ: Princeton University Press, 1961).

55.   Grafton wrote the address, which he sent to Rockingham for his perusal on 28 April 1777. In WWM R1/1721b.

56.   See, for example, John Cartwright to the Earl of Dartmouth, 10 April 1777, in the Dartmouth Papers, D (W) 1778/II/1750, Staffordshire Record Office. On the eve of war Cartwright had written *American Independence: The Interest and Glory of Great Britain: A New Edition* (London: H. S. Woodfall, 1775), but then he had advocated legislative independence only, with the colonies still joined to the empire through the crown. For context, see Robert Toohey, *Liberty and Empire* (Lexington: University of Kentucky Press, 1978); and more broadly still, Colin Bonwick, *English Radicals and the American Revolution* (Chapel Hill: University of North Carolina Press, 1977); and G. H. Guttridge, *English Whiggism and the American Revolution* (Berkeley: University of California Press, 1966).

57.   For a later instance, see Richmond to Rockingham, 15 March 1778, WWM R1/1770. Richmond followed that private missive with a public proposal the next month in the House of Lords that Britain recognize American independence (as part of his call for an address on the state of the nation from the Lords to the king). It was voted down, 33–50, with both Shelburne and Pitt as well as supporters of the ministry arrayed against him. Cobbett, *Parliamentary History*, 19:1012–59 passim.

58.   See Richmond to Rockingham, 19 August 1777, WWM, R1/1731.

59.   From his speech in the House of Lords, 30 May 1777, printed in Taylor and Pringle, *Correspondence of Pitt*, 4:432n–436n; quotation from 433n. As the year drew to a close, Shelburne stood by Chatham in believing that Americans could be offered something short of independence, but he recognized that Rockingham and others in opposition were beginning to waver and were considering letting the Americans go. Shelburne to Chatham, 23 December 1777, in ibid., 4:480–84, and Rockingham to Chatham, 26 January 1778, ibid., at 4:489–91.

Also see Chatham's speech of 20 November 1777 in ibid., 4:450n–459n (and Cobbett, *Parliamentary History*, 19:360n–370n).

60. Chatham to Earl Temple, 24 September 1777, Grenville Papers, Add. Ms., fols. 187–88, British Library.

61. For various versions of this relatively short (given his weakened condition) speech, see Taylor and Pringle, *Pitt Correspondence*, 4:518n–522n; and Cobbett, *Parliamentary History*, 19:1022–31. Also see Walpole, *Last Journals*, 2:74.

62. Speech from the throne on 18 November 1777, as taken from Cobbett, *Parliamentary History*, 19:355. The Lords' supportive response passed, 97–28; the Commons' like response passed, 174–47.

63. From Pownall's speech in the Commons on 2 December 1777, in Cobbett, *Parliamentary History*, 19:527. That same day Charles James Fox's motion that there be an inquiry into the state of the nation went down to defeat, 89–178.

64. Which is reviewed nicely in Chris Tudda, "'A Messiah That Will Never Come': A New Look at Saratoga, Independence, and Revolutionary War Diplomacy," *Diplomatic History* 32 (2008): 779–810.

65. This resolution, passed 22 November 1777, is printed in Ford, *Journals of Congress*, 9:951–52.

66. North advised the king that a Franco-American alliance loomed—see his letter of 30 December 1777, in Fortescue, *Corres. George III*, 3:530; the king recognized that the Americans in Paris would most likely not treat independence as negotiable. See his letter to North of 13 January 1778, ibid., 4:14–15.

67. See the note from Franklin, Deane, and Lee to Congress of 18 December 1777, in Wharton, *Revolutionary Diplomatic Correspondence*, 2:454–56; also in *Papers* 25:305–9. See too Arthur Lee to Samuel Adams, 19 December 1777, in Richard Henry Lee, *Life of Arthur Lee, LL.D.* (Boston: Wells and Lilly, 1829), 1:116. For a growing sense of urgency among British leaders, see the Earl of Hardwicke to Dartmouth, February [?] 1778, in D (W) 1778/II/ 1839.

68. See Eden to Wentworth, 5 December 1777, and Wentworth to Eden, 7 January 1778, in Stevens, *Facsimiles*, vol. 5, nos. 483 and 489, resp., the latter of which is printed, in part, in *Papers* 25:435–40. For context, see Samuel Flagg Bemis, "British Secret Service and the French-American Alliance," *American Historical Review* 29 (1924): 474–95. Eden was an undersecretary of state for the northern department, under the Earl of Suffolk, which enabled him to dabble in espionage. He ended up on the Carlisle commission in large part because he and Carlisle had been friends, going back to their days at Oxford. There is no modern full biography of him. There is even less about Wentworth, who was somehow connected to the powerful Wentworth family of New Hampshire.

69. George III complained to North in a letter of 26 March 1778, in Fortescue, *Corres. George III*, 4:80, that Franklin had proved again and again that he hated Britain and that he would not support any sort of reconciliation. The king's resentment toward Franklin probably reinforced his belief that reconciliation could only come through other channels—a reason to send Carlisle to America rather than try to work with Franklin in France. George III took all of this very personally and it is well to remember that even though the days of the divine right of kings had long since passed in Britain, the king was still encouraged to think of himself as the embodiment of the national will. Therefore, when George III expressed reluctance to end a war that the nation had embarked upon, he had a difficult time distinguishing between himself and the people or separating his disappointments from theirs. As James E. Bradley, *Popular Politics and the American Revolution in England* (Macon, GA.: Mercer University Press, 1986) noted, there had been widespread popular support for the Americans early on, but whether it ever penetrated the king's thinking—in the way that it undoubtedly affected many around him—is difficult to say. For the personal element in Franklin's behavior, see n. 74 below.

70. See Walpole, *Last Journals*, 2:74 and 4:154. Walpole, of course, must always be used advisedly. Also see Hutton to Franklin, 27 January 1778, and Franklin to Hutton on 1 and 12 February, in *Papers* 25:529–30, 562–63, 653–54, and the editors' note on 401–2; plus Hutton to George Germain, 25 and 26 January, in the Germain Papers, vol. 7. The episode is discussed

briefly in John W. Jordan, "Some Account of James Hutton's Visit to Franklin in December 1777," *Pennsylvania Magazine of History and Biography* 32 (1908): 223–32.

71. Pulteney to Germain, 6 December 1777, Germain Papers, vol. 6, only part of which is printed in HMC, *Stopford-Sackville*, 2:82–84. As is clear in his letter to Germain of 5 March 1777, in Germain Papers, vol. 5, Pulteney had been wanting to work on Franklin for some time. His name was actually on the list of twenty-one potential members of the Carlisle commission submitted to the king by Alexander Wedderburn in February 1778—see Stevens, *Facsimiles*, vol. 4, no. 356—even though he felt that sending a commission to the colonies made no sense when Franklin was so close by in France. Pulteney's brother George Johnstone would serve as a commission member. Frustrated by his failure, Pulteney suggested that Franklin, still smarting from his treatment by Wedderburn in the cockpit over four years before, was actually an impediment to peace. See his letter to John Temple, 1 May 1778, in James Bowdoin's "Bowdoin and Temple Papers," *Massachusetts Historical Society Collections*, 6th ser., 9 (1897): 416–17.

72. For the pamphlet, see n. 73 below. George Johnstone, Pulteney's brother, gave the commissioners notes that they took with them, which may have misled them about Franklin's position—and therefore that of Congress too. They are in Stevens, *Facsimiles*, vol. 1, no. 68. In fairness to Pulteney, perhaps he misled unintentionally, because Franklin had used evasive language that he fastened onto, to hear what he wanted to hear. Still, it does not seem likely that Franklin would have told Pulteney something different from what he said to the others, all of whom he apparently informed that American independence was nonnegotiable.

73. William Pulteney, Esq., *Thoughts on the Present State of Affairs with America* (London: J. Dodsley and T. Cadell, 1778). For an overview, see Frederick B. Tolles, "Franklin and the Pulteney Mission: An Episode in the Secret History of the American Revolution," *Huntington Library Quarterly* 17 (1954): 37–58.

74. As quoted from his *Letters on the American War* (London: J. Almon, 1778), 120, which was a bit vague and reminiscent of what John Cartwright had first proposed in 1774, then revised, in *American Independence*. Also see Franklin to Hartley, 14 October 1777, in *Papers* 25:65; also printed in Wharton, *Revolutionary Diplomatic Correspondence*, 2:409; Hartley's reluctance to take independence as a given, in his letter to Franklin of 25 December 1777, in *Papers* 25:349–52; and Franklin's frustrations with him in a letter of 12 February 1778, in *Papers* 25:650–53. For yet another Franklin friend in London who still thought reconciliation possible, see William Strahan to Franklin, 13 March 1778, in *Papers* 26:108–10.

75. The "foederal alliance" that he proposed to Franklin in a letter of 15 May 1778, was with a fully independent United States. *Papers* 26:465–66.

76. Hartley in the Commons, 9 April 1778, in Cobbett, *Parliamentary History*, 19:1072, 1088.

77. See Hartley to John Temple, 16 May 1778, in the "Bowdoin and Temple Papers," 418. For Hartley in general, see George Herbert Guttridge, *David Hartley, M. P.* (Berkeley: University of California Press, 1926); Reich, *British Friends*, 127–38, leans heavily on Guttridge. Neither Hartley nor his successor, Richard Oswald, would attempt to move Franklin from that position when they acted as negotiators in 1782. But both would believe that Franklin was amenable to some sort of "federal union" after Britain recognized American independence. Thus Oswald's letter to Shelburne on 10 July 1782, in the Shelburne Papers, 70:43–44.

78. As Walpole, *Last Journals*, 2:137, has him contending during debates in the Commons, 17 March 1778.

79. The vote, on 10 December 1777, was 10–160. Cobbett, *Parliamentary History*, 19:589.

80. North to the King, 29 January 1778, in Fortescue, *Corres. George III*, 4:27–28.

81. North during debates in the Commons, 17 February 1778, Cobbett, *Parliamentary History*, 19:764.

82. See Pickering, *Statutes at Large*, 18 George III c. 11 (repealing the 1774 Massachusetts Government Act and restoring charter protections); c. 12 (repealing provisions on tea dating from 1767, with a promise not to pass acts like it again); and c. 13 (empowering the peace commissioners to suspend the Declaratory Act and exercise executive authority in other areas, subject to the approval of Parliament). For the debates over North's peace proposals, see Cobbett, *Parliamentary History*, 19:762–815 (in the Commons) and 19:834–70 (for the Lords).

83. Without straining the analogy, think here of the later Lincoln view of an indestructible American union, where states that claimed to have seceded could be treated as if they never had because secession was a constitutional impossibility. Rather, as Lincoln saw it, wrongheaded leaders had temporarily—and wrongly—removed the people in their states from their proper relationship to the nation.

84. Wilkes on 2 March 1778, in Cobbett, *Parliamentary History*, 19:815.

85. Abingdon's protest is in ibid., 19:867–70. His pamphlet is *Thoughts on the Letter of Edmund Burke, Esq.; To the Sheriffs of Bristol, On the Affairs of America* (Oxford: W. Jackson, 1777). Walpole, *Last Journals*, 2:43 thought his argument against the Declaratory Act and the thinking behind it "shrewd and clear, and destructive of Burke's sophistry." *Proposals for a Plan Towards a Reconciliation And Re-Union With the Thirteen Provinces of America* (London: G. Kearsly, 1778), called for a new council of state to make American policy and to set the requisition rate that the assemblies in each of the colonies would be responsible for meeting.

86. See North to the king, 29 January 1778, in Fortescue, *Corres. George III*, 4:27–28.

87. D (W) 1778/II/1825.

88. Germain, the American secretary, claimed to have been kept out of the loop in most of the planning—presumably because of his hardline preferences. See his letter to John Irwin of 13 February 1778, in the Germain Papers, vol. 7, also printed in HMC, *Stopford-Sackville*, 1:139. Also see the skepticism expressed in Walpole, *Last Journals*, 2:110–12. Walpole wondered if the new commission might be all for show—that the king and his men had not really changed their attitudes about how power ought to be distributed in the empire. For the instructions to Carlisle and the others, see Auckland Papers, vol. 14, Add. Ms. 34415, British Library, and HMC, *The Manuscripts of the Earl of Carlisle* (London: Eyre and Spottiswoode, 1897), 322–35. Thurlow and Wedderburn's message to Germain of 27 March 1778 on replacing the commission issued to the Howes in May 1776 with this new one, is in PRO/CO 5/160. The commission itself, dated 12 April 1778, is in PRO/CO 5/180; and Stevens, *Facsimiles*, no. 1075.

89. Jay to Robert Morris, 29 April 1778, in Wharton, *Revolutionary Diplomatic Correspondence*, 2:566.

90. Without citing a particular individual, Edmund Body Burnett, ed., *Letters of Members of the Continental Congress* (Washington, DC: Carnegie Institution of Washington, 1921), 3:xv–xvi, contended that some members of Congress were shaky on the matter of independence—that even two years past the Declaration they might have considered reversing course. He includes (at p. 208) a proposed resolution of 30 April for negotiating peace with Britain, with independence as nonnegotiable, but another on 1 May 1778 (at p. 213) where the wording is not so clear—"that it is the true Interest of America to be an Independant power, she will be inclined to relinquish her Independency, only from the most absolute necessity to do so." Apparently neither motion came to a formal vote. See Burnett's comments on both, in the accompanying footnotes.

91. The "Address" of 8 May 1778 is printed in Ford, *Journals of Congress*, 11:474–81; quotations from 477 and 479, respectively.

92. See Germain's orders to Howe of 18 February 1778, in PRO/CO 5/95, fol. 30.

93. "From concurrent intelligence which we have obtained the people in these parts appear to be very generally desirous of seeing an end to the war and to be satisfied that a reconciliation with the mother country ought to take place upon grounds" laid out by North in the bills that he had pushed through Parliament, the Howes reported to Germain on 7 May 1778. In PRO/CO 5/177, fol. 103.

94. Germain's orders to Clinton of 8 March 1778 are in PRO/CO 5/95, fols. 35–37; and Stevens, *Facsimiles*, vol. 4, no. 1062; also printed in HMC, *Stopford-Sackville*, 2:94–99. Germain explained the strategy to Clinton with the proviso that it be pursued only if peace talks had failed. Clinton's options and choices are ably discussed in Ira D. Gruber, "Britain's Southern Strategy," in *The Revolutionary War in the South*, ed. W. Robert Higgins (Durham: Duke University Press, 1979), 205–38.

95. The Carlisle commission to Congress, 9 June 1778, in PRO/CO 5/180; also in Stevens, *Facsimiles*, vol. 11, no. 1104. See Laurens to Clinton and Lord Howe, 6 June 1778, PCC, Item 13, pp. 355–56 (reel 23); also in PRO/CO 5/180, fol. 97; Laurens to George Johnstone, one of

the new commissioners, on 14 June 1778, in Smith, *Letters of Delegates*, 10:91; and to the commissioners in general, on 17 June 1778, in Stevens, *Facsimiles*, vol. 11, no. 1110.

96. The commission to Congress, 11 July 1778, PRO/CO 5/180. Carlisle had already written a note to Germain four days before, admitting that he had failed with Congress and there was "no room for hope . . . except through the exertions of His Majesty's arms or by an appeal to the people at large by negotiation with separate bodies of men and individuals." In ibid. Even so, Carlisle did not think reconciliation utterly hopeless. He might not be able to woo back all of the rebels, but he would continue to believe for many months that some could be persuaded to return to their old loyalties—and not just in the southern colonies, where Clinton had carried the war in earnest, but in the New York area where the commissioners had gone with the evacuation of Philadelphia.

97. Samuel Flagg Bemis, *The Hussey-Cumberland Mission and American Independence* (Princeton, NJ: Princeton University Press, 1931), 3. Bemis was not a specialist in British imperial history. His contemporary, Charles McLean Andrews, who was, shared his internationalism. Brown, *Empire or Independence*, 244–92, offers a different characterization of and postmortem on the Carlisle commission, concluding that it had all been an exercise in futility, a sad case of too little, too late. In *The Peacemakers* (New York: Harper & Row, 1965), 149, Richard B. Morris would call it a "tragic fiasco signalizing the end of the first British empire." I am not sure that it was the former or indicated the latter.

98. Carleton's frustrations, the awkwardness of his position, and the never-say-die attitude of some American loyalists in the New York area are reviewed nicely in Paul David Nelson, *General Sir Guy Carleton, Lord Dorchester* (Madison, NJ: Fairleigh Dickinson University Press, 2000), 137–56.

99. For Clinton alone, see Alexander Wedderburn (attorney general) and James Wallace (solicitor general) to Germain, 28 June 1779, in PRO CO 5/177; for Clinton and Arbuthnot, see Germain's charge to them of 3 August 1780, in PRO/CO 5/178, fols. 99–110. For orders to Carleton and Digby in March 1782, see PRO/CO 5/8, fols. 255–65. Carleton had not wanted to succeed Clinton if his only task was to make arrangements to withdraw from New York. As late as November 1782 he forwarded a letter to Shelburne from Joshua Upham, urging another attempt at reconciliation since, the author claimed, three-quarters of the "*common* people of America wish for Peace & Reconciliation with Great Britain." Upham called for an imperial reconfiguration reminiscent of what Arthur Young had outlined in 1759. In the Shelburne Papers, vol. 69, pp. 101–8. Carleton and Digby had already dutifully informed George Washington that the king accepted independence as a nonnegotiable given, in a letter of 2 August 1782 (that they made public), in PRO/CO 5/175, fol. 349. Carleton knew that Shelburne would not think him impertinent in sending along Upham's letter anyway, despite the peace negotiations begun under his ministry. Shelburne wanted reconciliation within the empire as well, although he was obliged to keep that his preference rather than make it his policy. John Norris discusses Shelburne's desire to avoid American independence in *Shelburne and Reform* (London: Macmillan & Co., 1963), 164–70, 240–70.

100. Carlisle to Germain, 15 October 1778, PRO CO5/181, fols. 36–37.

101. Piers Mackesy, *Could the British Have Won the War of Independence?* (Worcester, MA: Clark University Press, 1976), 28. Also see William B. Willcox, "Why Did the British Lose the American Revolution," *Michigan Alumnus Quarterly Review* 62 (1956): 317–24; and the closing comments in Jeremy Black, *War for America* (New York: St. Martin's Press, 1991), 245–49.

102. North's comment was recorded in Wheatley, *Wraxall*, 2:138. As told to Wraxall by George Germain. "This was the universal feeling" stated Piers Mackesy, *The War for America, 1775–1783* (London: Longmans, 1964), 435. "Realistic Englishmen recognized that the former colonies were lost forever," echoed Don Higginbotham, *The War of American Independence* (New York: Macmillan, 1971), 383. Both quoted Wraxall.

103. Conway's motion passed on 27 February 1782, 234–215. It is recorded in Cobbett, *Parliamentary History*, 22:1071; the vote is at p. 1085. The results of the vote were sent to Clinton by Welbore Ellis, Germain's successor, soon after. In PRO/CO 5/264, fols. 39–40. See Ian Christie's comments in *The End of North's Ministry* (London: Macmillan, 1958), 319–40;

and Neil L. York, "Ending the War and Winning the Peace: The British in America and the Americans in Vietnam," *Soundings* 90 (1987): 444–74.

104. North talked him out of it. The draft of his March letter is in Fortescue, *Corres. George III*, 5:425. See his reaction to what the Commons had determined ought to be done, along with a second resolution, on 4 March in Cobbett, *Parliamentary History*, 22:1086.

105. A fear he expressed to North in a letter of 11 June 1779, in Fortescue, *Corres. George III*, 4:351.

106. According to William Knox, upon hearing of Rockingham's death, North hoped that negotiations would lead to the Americans accepting something short of independence. See his letter to Germain of 6 July 1782 in HMC, *Stopford-Sackville*, 1:79.

107. For a cabinet meeting of 18 May 1782, where British acceptance of American independence as the basis of peace talks was reaffirmed, see "Secret Instructions and Official Papers, Autograph Letters & State Documents relating to the Negotiations for the Independence of America, 1782–83," in Thomas Townshend, 1st Viscount Sydney Papers, vol. 1, William L. Clements Library, University of Michigan; and Fortescue, *Corres. George III*, 6:32–34. It is notable that George III did not use the news of Rodney's victory over de Grasse at the Saintes, received later that same day, as an excuse to reverse himself and insist on something short of American independence.

108. For some of the more notable examples, see William Knox's critique of British strategy, in which Knox urged London to leave recalcitrant New Englanders to themselves while concentrating on securing or winning back friendlier areas, in an undated essay, ca. 1777, in the Knox Papers, Box 9, fol. 21; Major Charles Cochrane's December 1780 recommendation to let the colonies north of Delaware go, while strengthening efforts to the south, in the Germain Papers, vol. 21, pp. 5–19; and James Anderson, *The Interest of Great-Britain with Regard to Her American Colonies Considered* (London: T. Cadell, 1782), which made a similar recommendation. George Chalmers, a Scotsman who had emigrated to Maryland before the war, then returned, embittered, to Britain in 1775, wrote a long letter to the Earl of Mansfield on 18 September 1780—now in the John Carter Brown Library—suggesting how the colonies and mother country could be reconciled. That Chalmers, who distrusted Revolutionary Americans and considered them chronically contentious, could believe reconciliation possible shows just how pervasive that feeling could be.

109. Neil L. York, "American Revolutionaries and the Illusion of Irish Empathy," *Eire-Ireland* 21 (1986): 13–30.

110. Explained adroitly in Andrew Jackson O'Shaughnessy, *An Empire Divided* (Philadelphia: University of Pennsylvania Press, 2000).

111. Peter S. Onuf, *The Origins of the Federal Republic* (Philadelphia: University of Pennsylvania Press, 1983), shows how disputes over authority that plagued the empire could be carried into the new nation, with Vermont as a case study of the phenomenon.

112. A point made, variously, in Paul H. Smith, *Loyalists and Redcoats* (Chapel Hill: University of North Carolina Press, 1964); Wallace Brown, *The Good Americans* (New York: William Morrow, 1969); and Alan S. Brown, "The Impossible Dream: The North Ministry, The Structure of Politics, and Conciliation," in *The American Revolution and "A Candid World,"* ed. Lawrence S. Kaplan, (Kent, OH: Kent State University Press, 1977), 17–39. Maurice Morgann, who had been Shelburne's personal secretary, traveled to New York (to work with Carleton) and informed Shelburne in a letter of 12 June 1782 that "*nineteen* out of *twenty* throughout the Provinces are our well wishers, at least and perfectly disposed to a Reunion." His source for that information? Local loyalists. That Morgann himself could not get an audience with anyone of notable authority on the patriot side was, in Morgann's view, beside the point. In the Shelburne Papers, 69:373–87; quotation from pp. 373–74.

113. Josiah Tucker, *Four Tracts, together with Two Sermons on Political and Commercial Subjects* (Glocester: R. Raikes, 1774) and *Tract V* (Glocester: R. Raikes, 1775).

114. See Robson, *American Revolution*, 205, for the commission as farce; and two essays by J. G. A. Pocock: "Contingency, Identity, Sovereignty," in *The Making of British History*, ed. Alexander Grant and Keith B. Stringer (London: Routledge, 1995), 292–302, and "Empire, State and Confederation: The War of American Independence as a Crisis in Multiple Monarchy" in *A Union for Empire*, ed. John Robertson (Cambridge: Cambridge University Press,

1995), 318–48, for British inability to embrace federalism as the great stumbling block. See also the nuanced discussion in Eliga H. Gould, *The Persistence of Empire* (Chapel Hill: University of North Carolina Press, 1999), 208–14; and, broader still, the longing for an *imperium britannicum* discussed in Anthony Pagden, *Lords of all the World* (New Haven, CT: Yale University Press, 1995) that would someday have its American analogue.

115. Although as A. F. M. Madden noted in "1066, 1776 and All That: The Relevance of English Medieval Experience of 'Empire' to Later Imperial Constitutional Issues," in *Perspectives of Empire,* ed. John E. Flint and Glyndr Williams (London: Longmans, 1973), 9–26, the builders of empire did not always remember, or understand the implications of, their own imperial history.

116. Which is not to say that, with this new law, all of the questions about sovereignty and supremacy dogging the empire had at last been answered, as K. C. Wheare pointed out in *The Statute of Westminster and Dominion Status* (Oxford: Oxford University Press, 1953; orig. ed., 1938), particularly in his discussion of the "constitutional conventions" that continued to be employed to smooth over misunderstandings between Britain and its dominions.

117. For such thinking among British field officers, see Matthew H. Spring, *With Zeal and with Bayonets Only* (Norman: University of Oklahoma Press, 2008).

118. Discussed in Burnett, *Continental Congress,* 518–21; and Morris, *The Peacemakers,* 147–217, passim, the issue of American independence, as Morris put it, being the "Gordian knot" (p. 151) that so many in Europe during the war tried—and failed—to untie. As William M. Fowler Jr., *American Crisis* (New York: Walker & Company, 2011) argued recently, the American cause suffered some of its most desperate moments *after* Yorktown.

119. Vincent Harlow, *The Founding of the Second British Empire, 1763–1793* (London: Longmans, Green, 1952, 1964); treated Shelburne as a visionary who tried to keep Chatham's dream of the empire alive. Harlow conceded that Shelburne's ideas about a "federal union" between Britain and an independent United States, ca. 1782–83, are hard to pin down. Shelburne's directions to Carleton and Digby as peace commissioners on 5 June 1782, PRO CO 5/178, fols., 437–61, illustrate Harlow's point nicely. Interestingly enough, the much more hard-headed John Simcoe, former officer in the Queen's Rangers, as a civilian official in postwar Canada became interested in somehow bringing Americans back into the imperial fold. But like his king, and like Shelburne too, he was able to separate personal longing from practical politics. See Alan Taylor, *The Civil War of 1812* (New York: Alfred A. Knopf, 2010), 45–56, 72.

120. See John Cannon's "The Loss of America" in H. T. Dickinson, *Britain and the American Revolution,* 233–57 (London: Longman, 1998): for an interesting view on the outcome of the war and Britain's hopeful prospects despite it.

Chapter Five

Benjamin Franklin, Student of the Holy Roman Empire

*His Summer Journey to Germany in 1766 and His
Interest in the Empire's Federal Constitution*

Jürgen Overhoff

I found a very fine country—Benjamin Franklin on his trip to Germany in a
letter to Daniel Wister, 27 September 1766. [1]

When the British House of Commons met in February 1766 as a Committee
of the Whole to consider problems resulting from colonial opposition to the
Stamp Act of 22 March 1765, that assemblage devoted most of the sessions
of February 11–13 to the examination of twenty-six witnesses speaking to
the causes of the American discontents. [2] These informants, who attended at
the bar of the House, included English merchants, colonials, and others conversant with the attitude of the Americans. All of them were asked to explain
why the Stamp Act—originally proposed by prime minister George Grenville as a plan for taxing the American colonies in a rather modest way,
thereby reminding the Americans of their share of the burden of the commonly fought victory against France in the Seven Years' War—had sparked
a firestorm of protest that swept up and down the American continent. [3] The
principal witness was America's greatest celebrity, the deputy postmaster
general of North America and agent of the Pennsylvania Assembly Dr. Benjamin Franklin, inventor of the lightning rod. Because of his generally recognized familiarity with the American colonies at large and his personal standing and reputation as an ingenuous scientist, his testimony was regarded as
especially important. [4]

When his questioning was opened on Thursday, 13 February, Franklin insisted that the Stamp Act should be totally and absolutely repealed as an erroneous policy of the British government. Asked to specify his reservations about the new British fiscal policy, he replied that demanding a new and heavy tax by stamps without the consent of the Americans "was not just, nor agreeable to the nature of an English constitution."[5] For, as Franklin continued:

> The stamp-act says, we [Americans] shall have no commerce, make no exchange or property with each other, neither purchase nor grant, nor recover debts; we shall neither marry, nor make our wills, unless we pay such and such sums, and thus it is intended to extort our money from us, or ruin us by the consequences of refusing to pay it. (139)

Like all faithful subjects of his Majesty the King, he argued, the American colonists were "intitled to all the privileges and liberties of Englishmen" as "declared by Magna Charta, and the petition of right," which meant that they were "not to be taxed but by their common consent" (156).

Although the colonies in North America considered themselves "as a part of the British Empire" (150), they were "not supposed to be within the realm" (153) of Great Britain, as Franklin went on to explain. They had "assemblies of their own," which were "their parliaments," and they were "in that respect in the same situation with Ireland" (153) or "the West-Indies" (145). Like the Americans, the Irish and West Indians "considered themselves as a part of the whole" (155), loyal subjects of the King, yet on equal terms with all Englishmen living in the mother country. Clearly, Franklin believed the global British Empire to be composed of several political entities whose inhabitants saw themselves compelled to elect their own assemblies, as no very extensive empire could exercise parliamentary sovereignty over people very remote from the seat of government. According to Franklin, the separate British dominions around the globe were indeed forced by the vast scale of the empire to manage a great deal of their political affairs in an entirely autonomous manner.

Grenville himself now queried whether the American colonists would voluntarily "pay [a] part of the expense" (133) for their protection, "[i]f the stamp-act should be repealed, and the Crown should make a requisition to the Colonies for a [particular] sum of money?" (154). "I believe they would" (154), said Franklin. Another member of Parliament then probed the stamina of the American opposition. Would the colonists not eventually yield to the demands of the British government if they were forced by arms? "No power, how great soever," Franklin calmly replied, "can force men to change their opinions" (158).

Franklin's proud and inspired defense of the American opposition to the Stamp Act had the desired effect. By the testimony of the London printer William Strahan, the Marquis of Rockingham, first lord of the Treasury, told a friend of his "a few days after, That he never knew Truth make so great a Progress in so very short a Time."[6] From the day of Franklin's appearance in the Commons, the repeal "was generally and absolutely determined, all that passed afterwards being only mere Form, which even in Business the most urgent must always be regarded."[7] "Happy Man!" Strahan exlaimed, "In truth, I almost envy him the inward Pleasure as well as the outward Fame, he must derive from having it in his Power to do his Country such eminent and seasonable Service."[8] And indeed: On 18 March 1766, almost a year to the day after the act had received royal approval, both Houses of Parliament agreed on the repeal of the Stamp Act.

When word reached America of the repeal, the colonists rejoiced. From Philadelphia Franklin's friend Joseph Galloway wrote him on 23 May: "I have now the inexpressible Pleasure of informing you that we have [now] the great News of the Royal Assent to the Repeal of the Stamp Act."[9] Like most Pennsylvanians, Galloway was especially pleased about the fact that their agent in London had contributed a great deal to the happy ending of the Stamp Act Crisis, "which has been the Occasion of great Distress and Anxiety to the Colonies for Several Months past."[10] For "[t]he Numerous Accounts we have of my Dear Friends's Integrity and Address in procuring the Repeal," as Galloway emphasized, "give us all the greatest pleasure."[11]

FRANKLIN PLANS AN EXTENDED TRIP TO GERMANY

By the time he received Galloway's letter, Franklin's popularity had risen to new heights, though very much to his chagrin. In a letter to his wife, Deborah, he complained about an almost endless flow of visitors to his house in Craven Street:

> I am excessively hurried, being every Hour that I am awake either abroad to speak with Members of Parliament or taken up with People coming to me at home, concerning our American Affairs, so that I am much behind-hand in answering my Friends Letters.[12]

And in a letter to his cousin Jonathan Williams he also sighed that his time in London was "extreamly taken up, as you may imagine in these general Affairs of America."[13] Still in June he felt so beleaguered by well-wishers and inquisitive people that he decided to beg for leave from his London duties: On 10 June the sixty-year-old Franklin informed the Pennsylvania Committee of Correspondence about his intention to set out for "a Summer Journey, to which I have been so many Years accustomed, and which I omitted last year, necessary to my Health, of late sensibly impair'd" by a restless commitment to "the Affairs of America."[14] "At my Return," he promised, "I shall apply myself diligently to what concerns the Interest of our Province."[15]

The country Franklin wanted to visit during his summer vacation and where he sought relaxation was Germany, the mainland of the Holy Roman Empire, also known as the Roman-German Empire or simply the German Empire. On 13 June he notified his wife of the state of his travel preparations: "To-morrow I set out with my friend Dr. Pringle (now Sir John)[16] on a Journey to Pyrmont," a spa in the north central part of Germany, "where he goes to drink the Waters; but I hope more from the Air and Exercise."[17] "[T]ho[ugh] I was not quite to say sick," as Franklin went on:

> I was often ailing last Winter and thro[ough] this Spring. We must be back at farthest in Eight Weeks, as my Fellow Traveller is the Queen's Physician, and has Leave for no longer as she will then be near her Time.[18] I purpose to leave him at Pyrmont, and visit some of the principal Cities nearest to it, and call for him again when the Time of our Return draws nigh.[19]

On 15 June, one day later than originally intended, Franklin and Pringle left London, and after a week's journey by road, channel packet, and again road, they arrived at Pyrmont in the principality of Waldeck, near the southern border of the electorate of Hanover.

Now, up to this day, Franklin's trip to Germany has not been of great interest to historians, and, accordingly, not much has been written about it. In America only Carl Van Doren and H. W. Brands briefly mentioned the summer journey of 1766 in their voluminous biographies of Franklin, and in Germany Paul Ssymank, Hans Walz, and Rudolf Vierhaus discussed the great American's trip to Pyrmont in extremely brief sketches.[20] While Van Doren guessed that Franklin primarily wanted to visit Germany because of the exceptional quality of the waters at Pyrmont, being "famous for their iron,"[21] Brands assumed that he rather wanted to "s[ee] the source of all those Germans who had emigrated to Pennsylvania over the years."[22] Approximately 60,000 of Pennsylvania's 160,000 white inhabitants were Germans, as Franklin himself had stated when being examined by the Commons on 13 February 1766.[23] Vierhaus believed that Franklin's decision for a summer vacation in Germany was a quite arbitrary one, and he supposed that the trip to Pyrmont scarcely made a lasting impression on Franklin's mind. At least, evidence for such an impact was not detectable anywhere in his writings, as Vierhaus argued, and the German scholar also believed—rather too dismissively—that a lasting impression would have been a highly unlikely result of a trip to Pyrmont anyway.[24]

But was Franklin's summer journey to Germany really so uninteresting as Vierhaus wants to make us believe or as uneventful as Van Doren or Brands suggest? First of all, there is ample proof in a variety of very interesting eighteenth-century sources, that the trip was by no means a spontaneous journey, but a carefully planned tour not only to Pyrmont, but also to Hanover, Göttingen, Cassel, Marburg, Frankfurt, Mainz, Trier, and Cologne. As a letter from the Hanoverian minister Burchard Christian von Behr to Franklin indicates, the summer journey to Germany was planned months ahead.[25] Although Franklin certainly sought to recover in Pyrmont from his exhausting duties as colonial agent in London, the main reason for his trip to Germany was nevertheless his wish to see the principal cities of the Holy Roman Empire and to pay a visit to the University of Göttingen, one of the leading academies of the time. Above all, as Franklin pointed out in a letter to a German friend, Rudolph Erich Raspe, he wanted to talk to certain "professors at Göttingen."[26]

FRANKLIN'S CONVERSATION WITH JOHANN STEPHAN PÜTTER ON GERMAN FEDERALISM

Only a few days after his arrival in the principality of Waldeck, Franklin left Pyrmont for Hanover, where the Hanoverian prime minister Baron Gerlach Adolph von Münchhausen provided him with a letter of recommendation for two professors in particular: in his letter Münchhausen strongly recommended Franklin as a distinguished doctor of law to Gottfried Achenwall, professor of the history of the Roman-German Empire, and Johann Stephan Pütter, professor of German constitutional law.[27] Both scholars were held in the highest esteem in the whole of Germany for their unparalleled knowledge of the constitutional history of the Holy Roman Empire.[28] When Franklin eventually arrived at Göttingen, where he stayed for almost two weeks until 26 July, he immediately made the long-awaited acquaintance with Pütter and Achenwall. During his stay at Göttingen he met both men repeatedly and for hour-long conversations at the house of Pütter, who was the person he talked to the most. Since Franklin could not converse in German, the three men must have talked in English. The use of this language is confirmed by Achenwall's repeated introduction of English technical terms into the report he later wrote of their meeting. The report was published in 1767 as a small treatise bearing the title *Einige Anmerkungen über Nord-Amerika und über dasige Grosbrittanische Colonien. Aus mündlichen Nachrichten des Herrn D. Franklins* (Some observations on North America and her British Colonies. From Oral Information by Dr. Franklin).[29]

In the preface to his detailed report Achenwall told his readers that the famous American had primarily sought to learn from Pütter as much as possible about the political structure and organization of the German Empire. According to Achenwall, Franklin himself had freely admitted how "begierig" [greedy] he actually was for that kind of knowledge.[30] But why was Franklin so inquisitive about the political constitution of the Holy Roman Empire, and what could Pütter have told him about the peculiar features and operations of this old European body politic? Most probably it was Pütter's understanding of the Roman-German Empire as a state with a distinctly federal constitution that attracted Franklin's great interest.[31] For, on the one hand, Pütter's interpretation of the Holy Roman Empire as a real federation, designed to protect all its members against the menacing predominance of Austria and Prussia, was a rather new and unwonted theory, unmatched by any other contemporary description of Germany's political constitution. On the other hand, it almost seemed to be a blueprint for the markedly federative empire that the British Empire was meant to be—at least according to Franklin's elaborate explanations in the House of Commons. Finally, Pütter's theory also served in many respects as an interesting model for the type of confederacy that Franklin sought to establish among the American colonies since 1754 when he had composed his Albany Plan of Union.[32]

So what could Franklin have learned from his long and intense conversation with Pütter? Since Achenwall's report of their meeting does not give us a clear picture of the exact contents of their discussions, we need to turn to Pütter's most important writings of the late 1750s and early 1760s if we seek an answer to that question. In particular, we need to consult his *Historisch-politisches Handbuch von den besonderen Teutschen Staaten* (Historical and Political Handbook of the Several German States) of 1758 and his *Kurzer Begriff des Teutschen Staatsrechts* (Concise Account of the German Constitutional Law) of 1764.[33]

In these books Pütter defined the German Empire as a "Staat, dessen einzelne Glieder wieder förmliche Staaten sind," thus as a state composed of states.[34] He emphasized that the several political units of the Holy Roman Empire—Austria, Bavaria, Baden, Würtemberg, the Palatinate, Hesse, Saxony, Anhalt, Hanover, Brandenburg (not Prussia, as the mainland of the Kingdom of Prussia was situated outside the empire), Mecklenburg, Holstein, and Hamburg—were not to be called provinces, but "förmlich" (formally) and really "Staaten" (states), as their rank could be perfectly compared with the status of the smaller European realms or republics.[35] As a truly compound body politic, as a state composed of states, Pütter believed, the German Empire was unique, "[der] einzige [Staatskörper] seiner Art" (the only body politic of its kind).[36] Not even the thirteen cantons of Switzerland or the seven provinces of the United Netherlands, he argued, were apt to be compared with the German States, for only the German States had a common sovereign or overlord, namely the Roman-German emperor, whose decisions were at times binding for all member states of the empire. Especially in cases of military conflict with neighboring states, the emperor was entitled to ask all member states of the German empire to deploy troops and to support the imperial army, necessary for the defense of all.[37]

Usually, however, the several German states enjoyed a great measure of freedom and independence. As Pütter pointed out, all member states had "seine besonderen" (their own) parliaments, so called "Landtage," where they conducted the negotiations about their political concerns or problems in a highly autonomous manner.[38] The German state parliaments, Pütter explained, had the authority to negotiate commercial treatises with other German as well as European states. They had to be consulted when another German or European state made territorial claims in the empire. They had the duty to protect the individual rights of their subjects when these subjects were travelling through another German state. And they could determine the amount of taxes that their subjects were liable to pay for the upkeep of the imperial administration. Only in the case of a prolonged dispute between the different German states did the *Reichstag* (Imperial Diet) at Regensburg or the German Empire's *Reichskammergericht* (supreme court) at Wetzlar have to overrule the decisions of the state parliaments in the interest of the whole of the German Empire. How some of the most pressing conflicts between German states had thus been solved in the past was analyzed and described by Pütter in painstaking detail, especially in his *Historisch-politisches Handbuch von den besonderen Teutschen Staaten*.[39] Accordingly, his writings contained a host of exemplary studies about the different ways and means of solving conflicts within the political boundaries of a federation.

Of course, Franklin was not blind to the deficiencies of the German Empire's federal system, since neither the state parliaments nor the Imperial Diet could be compared with the Parliament at Westminster or with the North-American assemblies: Whereas the various British parliaments and assemblies around the world were—at least in part—elected by the freemen of Great Britain and the diverse British dominions, the German parliaments were parliaments of estates, summoned without an election (with the single exception of the assembly of the city-state of Hamburg, the *Bürgerschaft*). This is why Franklin had once called the German Empire a state whose subjects were not used to liberty.[40] And yet, even a federation with an essentially monarchical structure, lacking the democratic element of the British constitution, could teach some very important lessons about the functioning of a "state composed of states"—which is why Franklin decided to take Pütter's books back to London.[41]

"HOLY ROMAN MOMENT" IN THE HISTORY OF THE UNITED STATES

So let us ask again: Did Franklin's journey to Germany have a lasting impact on his political thinking? If we carefully study the letters he wrote in autumn 1766, shortly after his return to London, it becomes clear that he considered his sojourn in Göttingen and his conversation with Pütter and Achenwall to have been a very special and important experience: to Raspe he wrote on 9 September 1766:

> Be so kind as to present my respectful Compliments to the good Baron Munchhausen, and assure him that I have the most grateful Remembrance of the Civilities I receiv'd from his Excellency at Hanover, and thro' his Recommendation at Göttingen [. . .] I never think of the Time I spent so agreeably at Hanover, without wishing it could have been longer. Remember me also affectionately to the Professors at Göttingen, whose Learning and Politeness impress'd me with the highest Esteem for them: I wish every kind of Prosperity to them and their University.[42]

Whether Pütter's political theory of the German Empire was of any relevance for Franklin's political thought of the late 1760s or the mid-1770s, when he composed his *Articles of Federation and perpetual Union of The United Colonies of North America*, is an intriguing question that can only be answered if more research about the development of his federalist theories is carried out.[43] Research of that kind seems all the more promising since it must not be forgotten that still in the 1780s the Holy Roman Empire figured largely in the debates of the American Federalists. The Federalist Papers, for example, whose importance for American constitutional thought can hardly be overestimated, mention the Holy Roman Empire in seven out of eighty-five essays,[44] and in a letter to Thomas Jefferson of 24 October 1787 James Madison explicitly regarded the federal organization of the United States as a variant of the federal constitution of the Roman-German Empire.[45] To conclude: Franklin's interest in the federal constitution of the Holy Roman Empire was at least as serious as his interest in the Iroquois confederacy which he famously uttered in a letter of 1751 to James Parker.[46]

Thus the German Federation might have influenced his plan of colonial union just as much as the Iroquois example. Since the Iroquois influence thesis has now grown into a cottage industry, resulting in numerous books and articles for scholarly and popular audiences,[47] it might be just about time to opt for a fresh look at the genesis of colonial union in America and to discover the "Holy Roman moment"[48] in the early history of the United States.[49]

NOTES

1. *Papers* 13:429. This article was first published in *German Studies Review* 34, no. 2 (2011): 277–86. © 2011 The German Studies Association. Reprinted with permission of The Johns Hopkins University Press.

2. A good and accessible account of these sittings of the Committee of the Whole, which are not recorded in detail in the Journal of the House of Commons, has been offered by Lawrence H. Gipson, "The Great Debate in the Committee of the Whole House of Commons on the Stamp Act, 1766, as reported by Nathaniel Ryder," *Pennsylvania Magazine of History and Biography* 86 (1962): 10–41.

3. The best account of the Stamp Act crisis has been written by Edmund S. Morgan and Helen M. Morgan, *The Stamp Act Crisis: Prologue to Revolution* (Chapel Hill: University of North Carolina Press, 1953).

4. The last decade has seen an unprecedented advance of interesting new research on the life of Benjamin Franklin. Cf. Walter Isaacson, *Benjamin Franklin: An American Life* (New York: Simon & Schuster, 2003), Alan Houston, *Benjamin Franklin and the Politics of Improvement* (New Haven, CT: Yale University Press, 2008), Edmund S. Morgan, *Benjamin Franklin* (New Haven, CT: Yale University Press, 2002), H. W. Brands, *The First American: The Life and Times of Benjamin Franklin* (New York: Doubleday, 2000), Jürgen Overhoff, *Benjamin Franklin: Erfinder, Freigeist, Staatenlenker* (Stuttgart: Klett-Cotta, 2006), Gordon S. Wood, *The Americanization of Benjamin Franklin* (New York: Penguin, 2004).

5. Benjamin Franklin, "The Examination of Doctor Benjamin Franklin, before an August Assembly, relating to the Repeal of the Stamp Act, &c." *Papers* 13:138.

6. *Papers* 13:125.

7. Ibid.

8. Ibid.

9. Ibid., 13:284.

10. Ibid., 13:290.

11. Ibid., 13:285.

12. Ibid., 13:165.

13. Ibid., 13:253.

14. Ibid., 13:299, 296.

15. Ibid.

16. Pringle was made a baronet on 3 June 1766.

17. *Papers* 13:315.

18. The Queen gave birth to a daughter, Charlotte Augusta Matilda (1766–1828), on 29 September. In 1794 the princess married Prince Friedrich Wilhelm Karl of Württemberg, who was made King of Württemberg by Napoleon in 1806.

19. *Papers* 13:315.

20. Cf. Carl Van Doren, *Benjamin Franklin* (New York: Viking Press, 1938), 356–57, and Brands, *First American*, 393–94. Cf. Paul Ssymank, "Benjamin Franklin und die erste Berührung deutscher und nordamerikanischer Wissenschaft," *Mitteilungen des Universitätsbundes Göttingen* 15, no. 2 (1934): 1–16, Hans Walz, "Benjamin Franklin in Hannover 1766," *Hannoversche Geschichtsblätter: Neue Folge* 21 (1967): 61–65, Rudolf Vierhaus, "Benjamin Franklin. Rede anläßlich der Enthüllung einer Gedenktafel am 24 September 1981, Prinzenstraße 21 (Michaelishaus)" *Göttinger Jahrbuch* 30 (1982): 206–8.

21. Doren, *Benjamin Franklin*, 356.

22. Brands, *The First American*, 393.

23. Franklin, *Examination*, 132.

24. Vierhaus, *Benjamin Franklin*, 208.

25. This is indicated by the contents of a letter of Baron Behr to Benjamin Franklin, 10 June 1766 (cf. *Papers* 13:300).

26. *Papers* 13:409.

27. Münchhausen referred to "Francklin, der Doctor juris"; cf. Ssymank, *Benjamin Franklin*, 5.

28. A full-scale study of Achenwall's life and work is still sorely missed, but two excellent books on Pütter have been published: Ulrich Schlie, *Johann Stephan Pütters Reichsbegriff* (Göttingen: Verlag Otto Schwartz & Co, 1961), and Wilhelm Ebel, *Der Göttinger Professor Johann Stephan Pütter aus Iserlohn* (Göttingen: Verlag Otto Schwartz & Co, 1975).

29. Gottfried Achenwall, *Einige Anmerkungen über Nord-Amerika und über dasige Grosbrittannische Colonien: Aus mündlichen Nachrichten des Herrn D. Franklins* (Helmstedt: Johann Heinrich Kühnlin, 1777).

30. Achenwall, *Anmerkungen*, 4

31. On Pütter's political theory see Schlie, *Johann Stephan Pütters Reichsbegriff.*

32. On Franklin and his Albany Plan of Union see Timothy J. Shannon, *Indians and Colonists at the Crossroads of Empire: The Albany Congress of 1754* (Ithaca, NY: Cornell University Press, 2000).

33. Johann Stephan Pütter, *Historisch-politisches Handbuch von den besonderen Teutschen Staaten* (Göttingen: Vandenhoeck, 1758); Johann Stephan Pütter, *Kurzer Begriff des Teutschen Staatsrechts* (Göttingen: Vandenhoeck, 1764).

34. Pütter, *Historisch-politisches Handbuch*, S. IV.

35. Ibid.

36. Ibid.

37. On Pütter's comparison between Switzerland, the Netherlands, and the German Empire cf. Schlie, *Johann Stephan Pütters Reichsbegriff*, 48.

38. Pütter, *Historisch-politisches Handbuch*, 193.

39. Pütter's commentaries on the rights and privileges of the *Landtage* are to be found in *Historisch-politisches Handbuch*, 332–35, 466–68, 470.

40. See Benjamin Franklin to Peter Collinson, 9 May 1753, in *Papers* 4:484.

41. See Benjamin Franklin to Rudolph Erich Raspe, 9 September 1766, in *Papers* 13:407. In this letter Franklin talks about his "books brought from Göttingen." In his autobiography Pütter mentions the fact that he presented Franklin with some of his books. See Johann Stephan Pütter, *Selbstbiographie* (Göttingen: Vandenhoeck, 1798), 490.

42. *Papers* 13:408–9.

43. A comprehensive research project on the development of Franklin's federalist theories and his interest in the German Empire's federal constitution is now being carried out at the University of Regensburg by Volker Depkat (University of Regensburg), Johannes Burkhardt (University of Augsburg, Institut für Europäische Kulturgeschichte) and Jürgen Overhoff (University of Hamburg/University of Regensburg). This research project "Das frühneuzeitliche deutsche Reich als politisches Referenzsystem der amerikanischen Föderalisten im Entstehungsprozeß der USA (1754–1788)," is currently financed by the Deutsche Forschungsgemeinschaft.

44. See Alexander Hamilton/John Jay/James Madison, *The Federalist*, ed. Jacob E. Cooke (Middletown, CT: Wesleyan University Press, 1961), no. 12, p. 74; no. 14, p. 86; no. 19, p. 117–22; no. 21, p. 132; no. 42, p. 284; no. 43, p. 292; no. 80, p. 536–37.

45. Thomas Jefferson, *The Papers of Thomas Jefferson*, vol. 12, ed. Julian P. Boyd (Princeton, NJ: Princeton University Press, 1955), 274.

46. See Benjamin Franklin to James Parker, 20 March 1751, in *Papers* 4:118–19: "It would be a very strange Thing, if six Nations of ignorant Savages should be capable of forming a Scheme for such an Union, and be able to execute it in such a Manner, as that it has subsisted Ages, and appears indissoluble; and yet a like Union should be impracticable for ten or a Dozen English Colonies, to whom it is more necessary, and must be more advantageous; and who cannot be supposed to want an equal Understanding of their Interests."

47. See Bruce E. Johansen, "Native American Societies and the Evolution of Democracy in America 1600–1800" *Ethnohistory* 37 (1990): 279–97; Donald A. Grinde Jr. and Bruce E. Johansen, *Exemplar of Liberty: Native America and the Evolution of Democracy* (Los Angeles: American Indian Studies Center, 1991).

48. This is, of course, an allusion to J. G. A. Pocock's highly influential *Machiavellian Moment*, a book first published in 1975: J. G. A. Pocock, *The Machiavellian Moment: Florentine Political Thought and the Atlantic Republicanism* (Princeton, NJ: Princeton University

Press, 1975). The title of Pocock's book has been picked up and cited by an increasing number of scholars of the ideological origins of the American Revolution.

49. The only scholarly articles on the very important question of whether the German Federation might have influenced Franklin's (or indeed Jefferson's and Adams's) conception of a North American federation are Helmut Neuhaus, "The Federal Principle and the Holy Roman Empire," in *German and American Constitutional Thought: Contexts, Interaction, and Historical Realities*, ed. Hermann Wellenreuther (New York: Berg, 1990), 27–49; and Hartmut Lehmann, "Another Look at Federalism in the Holy Roman Empire," in ibid., 80–85.

Chapter Six

Benjamin Franklin and the Leather-Apron Men

The Politics of Class in Eighteenth-Century Philadelphia

Simon P. Newman

Benjamin Franklin is both the best-known and yet paradoxically the most enigmatic member of America's founding generation. A true master of spin, Franklin enjoyed an enviable ability to construct and popularize certain public faces and images for himself while yet contriving to obscure others. As his autobiography makes abundantly clear, Franklin was enormously sensitive to the ways in which his contemporaries and posterity might regard him. He constantly attempted to fashion and refashion his own image and admitted as much almost as a point of honor, recording that "In order to secure my Credit and Character . . . I took care not only to be in *Reality* Industrious and frugal, but to avoid all *Appearances* of the Contrary."[1] The result of such self-conscious and adept self-fashioning is that for two centuries historians have made what they will of the archetypal self-made American and author of what is quite possibly the world's most widely read autobiography, pursuing in his life, his writings, and his actions whatever aspect of eighteenth-century British North American life and culture most interests them.

The excellent recent studies by Edmund S. Morgan, Gordon S. Wood, and David Waldstreicher illustrate the point.[2] To Morgan, Franklin was a man who "could never stop thinking" and who privileged public service.[3] Wood recounts the inadvertent Americanization of a provincial Pennsylvanian who was drawn like a moth to the burning lights of the imperial metropolis of London. Wood's Franklin longed for acceptance into the imperial inner sanctums of Whitehall, but was burned by the rejection he experienced in the later 1760s and early 1770s and thus was driven into radical politics and the Patriot cause. A very different man emerges from Waldstreicher's study of the runaway servant who became wealthy and successful through his exploitation and usurpation of the labor of others, including African-American slaves. All of these studies reveal elements of his life that Franklin sought to celebrate, and others that the authors contend he kept hidden.

Perhaps, however, these very processes of self-revelation and of self-concealment are what draw us to Benjamin Franklin. For all that he was one of the oldest members of the founding generation, his life, his interests, and his self-promotion make him the most identifiably modern, universally accessible, and popular American of his age. Franklin was a self-made man in far more than a literal sense: how he constructed and presented himself, and the ways in which such performances succeeded and failed, reveal a great deal about life and society in eighteenth-century British North America.

And yet for all of the many studies of different aspects of Benjamin Franklin's life and character, his enduring working-class identity has been largely forgotten. This is somewhat surprising, given that it was a readily identifiable facet of Franklin's self-image and popular representation during his lifetime and was very familiar to contemporaries in Philadelphia and beyond. Of all the Founding generation, none were so readily identified with the leather apron and the life, the work, and the identity of the craftsman as was Benjamin Franklin. From Boston apprentice to runaway, from journeyman to master craftsman, his was the story of success that America appeared to promise, in which hard work could secure independence. In eighteenth-century British America the few men who actually rose from the obscurity of manual labor to genteel status usually distanced themselves from their laboring pasts and refashioned their identities in terms of their hard-earned elite rank and privilege. In stark contrast, Franklin never tired of celebrating both his own and others' labor and craftsmanship. He reveled in the life that commercial success and financial independence afforded him, writing, conducting scientific experiments and exchanging ideas with some of the greatest minds of his generation, and he told all who would listen that he had succeeded. Yet throughout his life Franklin never looked down upon honest and capable workers, identifying with them and affording them a remarkable status and level of respect. If, as Wood suggests, Franklin would eventually become the heroic prototypical American "for hundreds of thousands of middling Americans," during his own lifetime Franklin appeared as a champion of the leather-apron men, among whom were included both working-men and those whose success had made them into semi-independent or independent master craftsmen.[4]

Franklin's articulation of his pride in his identity as a craftsman, long after he had become a gentleman who no longer needed to work for a living, endeared him to mechanics and craftsmen in Revolutionary and early national America. On Independence Day in 1795, for example, the members of

New York City's General Society of Mechanics and Tradesmen raised their glasses to the sentiment:

> The memory of our late brother mechanic, Benjamin Franklin, may his bright example convince mankind, that in this land of freedom and equality talents joined to freedom and frugality, may justly aspire to the first offices of government.[5]

In their toast these workingmen remembered neither a gentleman nor a philosopher and scientist, but rather a workingman, a skilled craftsman who embodied the democratic spirit of the new republic. It was an image that Franklin had helped fashion throughout his life, and which endured even after his death in the pages of his autobiography.

Franklin grew up relatively poor in Boston, a provincial town in which widening class differences would play a significant role in the coming of the revolution. A half century later Franklin visited his ancestral home in Ecton, Northamptonshire, and in the register of St. Mary Magdalene parish church he learned "that I was the youngest Son of the youngest Son for 5 Generations back."[6] This reminiscence, early in his autobiography, recorded not only Franklin's pride in his own ability to rise out of inherited poverty, but also the dignity and self-respect of a man who is not ashamed of his or of his family's working-class origins.

At the tender age of ten Franklin began assisting his father, Josiah, who worked as a tallow chandler and soap boiler, but the boy strongly "dislik'd the Trade and had a strong Inclination for the Sea." Fearing that their youngest son would follow his brother Josiah Jr. and run away to sea, never to return, Franklin's father

> sometimes took me to walk with him, and see Joiners, Bricklayers, Turners, Braziers, &c. at their Work, that he might observe my Inclination, and endeavour to fix it on some Trade or other on Land. It has ever since been a Pleasure to me to see good Workmen handle their Tools; and it has been useful to me, having learnt so much by it, as to be able to do little Jobs my self in my House, where a Workman could not readily be got; and to construct little Machines for my Experiments.[7]

There is an almost lyrical quality to Franklin's descriptions of the work of leather-apron men, and throughout his life his pleasure in "an excellent Craftsman" or an "ingenious" mechanic was almost tangible.[8] Labor and craft were, for Franklin, far more than the means of survival and prosperity.[9]

While his autobiography records the limited options available to the sons of poorer craftsmen and laborers in early eighteenth-century Boston, Franklin nonetheless reminisces about and identifies with the joy and pride of skilled craftsmanship. He was the prototypical self-made man who escaped the legal indenture and the social realities that trapped most of the younger sons of poorer artisans and workers in the same or even lesser professions than their fathers, reducing some of them to unskilled wage labor. Franklin combined celebration of his success with respect for the skill and the honest labor of ordinary workingmen. Almost three-quarters of Franklin's autobiography chronicled his working life as an apprentice, a runaway, a journeyman and a master craftsman, a remarkably unusual self-presentation by a wealthy and successful businessman and gentleman. He did not think less of an apprentice or journeyman who had not yet achieved independence, and even at the end of his life he remembered with deep resentment the unfair beatings he had received from his brother and master James, recalling that "I fancy his harsh and tyrannical Treatment of me, might be a means of impressing me with that Aversion to arbitrary Power that has stuck to me thro' my whole Life."[10]

In one of his earliest publications Franklin noted that "the Generality of People" were unwilling to judge what they read until they knew "who or what the Author of it is, whether he be *poor* or *rich*, *old* or *young*, a *Schollar* or a *Leather-Apron Man*." When Franklin did identify himself it was most often in terms of his early-life status and craft, as a printer or a tradesman. This continued long after commercial success meant that he did not need to work for a living. In an age when class and status were profoundly significant in the ways in which people judged one another, Franklin continued to think of himself with pride as a skilled craftsman. Even after he had become a gentleman he repeatedly identified himself as "Benjamin Franklin, Printer," or more anonymously as "a Tradesman."[11] Franklin's almanacs had been filled with Poor Richard's celebrations of honest labor, and the collection of proverbs and aphorisms that Franklin pulled together and that eventually became known as *The Way to Wealth* can easily be read as a manual for controlling the terms of one's own labor, albeit as a humorous one.[12] Self-presentation, popular image, hard work, and frugality are presented by Franklin as the ways in which an honest worker may both succeed and command respect.

Franklin's social and political education came as a working child in Boston. The options facing Franklin's father were severely limited by economic circumstances, which in turn restricted the career options of his youngest son. Franklin experienced these domestic circumstances in the context of a decline in the enforced unity of the Puritan town, which had been replaced by increasing social and political tensions. Mechanics who resented the control of the town's only liberal church by wealthy gentlemen had combined in 1714 to found their own New North Street Church.[13] Many, including Franklin's older brother and master, James, were supporters of the Old Charter and opponents of colonial governors' attempts to rule by prerogative. In James's printing office the young Franklin was surrounded by the political discussions of workingmen and their friends, and he was hardly in his teens when he first started contributing to them. [14]

But perhaps the most enduring lesson was less in the mechanics of printing and the principles of politics than in the potential of the man who worked. When Franklin formed the Junto in Philadelphia in 1727, originally named the "Leather Apron Club," its members included other print workers like himself, a scrivener, a surveyor, a shoemaker, a clerk, and "a most exquisite Mechanic and a Solid and Sensible Man."[15] The nascent American Philosophical Society may have been a self-help group for Franklin and his co-founders, but its very creation rested on the assumption that leather-apron men could and should be respected for their "exquisite" skills and their intellectual abilities. The Junto was in the tradition of artisanal mutual aid societies, designed not just to protect members and help advance their careers, but also to celebrate their lives as skilled craftsmen. [16]

Such beliefs informed much of what Franklin thought and did. In an impressive argument in favor of paper currency, the twenty-three-year-old journeyman printer expounded the labor theory of value in such clear terms as to later merit the approval of Karl Marx, who applauded Franklin's formulations. [17] "Labouring and Handicrafts Men . . . are the chief Strength and Support of a People," wrote Franklin, and he proposed that "Men have invented Money, properly called a Medium of Exchange, because through or by its Means Labour is exchanged for Labour, or one Commodity for another."[18]

He held these beliefs with conviction throughout his life. In some ways, Franklin harkened back to medieval and early-modern artisanal concepts of work as far more than utilitarian physical labor but rather as highly skilled productive activity with as much moral and social as economic value. This larger social role for skilled craftsmanship in the community encouraged artisans to regard themselves as equal to all other men, and Franklin inherited this proud belief. [19] But with his clear articulation of the labor theory of value, Franklin bridged the gulf between the medieval and modern worlds. In his autobiography he recalled that these ideas, contained in a defence of an expanded paper currency, were "well receiv'd by the common People in general; but the Rich Men dislik'd it."[20]

The proud memoirs of his own skilled labor by America's most famous gentleman, his clearly stated belief in the labor theory of value, and Franklin's lifelong respect for those who worked with their hands earned him a kind of respect from workingmen that was unparalleled among the Founding Fathers. During his lifetime wealth inequality rose in American towns and cities, and the economic security of craftsmen and unskilled laborers diminished. By the late eighteenth century the traditional route to competency and independence that many workingmen had dreamed of and that Franklin and some others had traveled, had become increasingly difficult. It had been undermined by the import of mass-produced manufactured goods; by increasing immigration, which flooded urban labor markets; and by the growing employment of semiskilled or unskilled workers in the manufacture of goods. This trend helped fuel the artisanal radicalism that surfaced in Revolutionary-era Philadelphia and other American cities.[21]

Franklin's experience and identity as a craftsman informed a political radicalism that predated the Revolutionary era. The advent of King George's war against Spain and France, bringing with it the possibility of naval and privateering attacks on Philadelphia, provided the seemingly unlikely occasion for Franklin to articulate these beliefs. He took action by writing and then printing and distributing a pamphlet entitled *Plain Truth*, in which he proposed to bypass the recalcitrant Quaker assembly, which had long resisted the creation of an official colonial militia, by forming "a voluntary Association of the People."[22] The author of *Plain Truth* identified himself as "A TRADESMAN of Philadelphia," and class politics informed his argument as he railed against "the Rich [who] may shift for themselves," as "The Means of speedy Flight are ready in their Hands." In contrast "Tradesmen, Shopkeepers, and Farmers" were "most unhappily circumstanced indeed," for "We cannot all fly with our Families; and if we could, how shall we subsist? No; we and they, and what little we have gained by hard Labour and Industry, must bear the Brunt."[23]

In his autobiography Franklin recalled that *Plain Truth* had "a sudden and surprizing Effect," and he immediately drafted "the Instrument of Association." At a meeting of a large number of Philadelphians, Franklin presented the terms of this voluntary militia association, and some twelve hundred men signed the printed copies that he had prepared. Further copies were distributed throughout the colony, eventually attracting some ten thousand signatures. The class politics of Franklin's argument for a militia influenced his organization of the Association: volunteers "form'd themselves into Companies, and Regiments, [and] chose their own Officers."[24] The Association envisioned by "A Tradesman of Philadelphia" not only gave workingmen the power to elect their own officers but in fact also allowed them access to these ranks themselves. In positions of authority within companies of as many as one hundred men each were such Philadelphians as Richard Swan, a hatter; Plunket Fleeson and Abraham Jones, both of whom were upholsterers; and Francis Garrigues, a house carpenter.[25] The Association was "a symbol in Philadelphia of artisan strength and unity." Its members "never engaged the enemy, but conferred among themselves, nonetheless, an enormous collective strength."[26]

Franklin enjoyed an enduring popularity among his fellow craftsmen and workingmen, not just because he acknowledged their rights to choose their own political—and in this case military—leaders, but also because he recognized their need for regular work. Following his organization of the militia, Franklin "propos'd a Lottery to defray the Expence of Building a Battery below the Town."[27] While war with Spain and France threatened Pennsylvanian commerce, the immediate dangers to the city of Philadelphia were relatively minor, and what followed was in many ways a major public works project, giving occasional employment to workers who were suffering during the interruption of Atlantic trade and thus bringing relief to their families. With characteristic precision Franklin recorded and then published the Philadelphia lottery accounts for the period between April 1748 and May 1751.[28] While some money was spent on the cannon for the battery, most of the thousands of pounds raised and disbursed found their way into the pockets of ordinary workingmen.

On many occasions the accounts are vague, recording the payment of one pound and seven shillings "to 3 Men, 3 Days Work each," or miscellaneous payments "to a Labourer" or "to the Workmen," but more often the information is far more specific. A "Labourer" was paid one pound and thirteen shillings "for 11 Days Work, levelling the ground"; Tobias Griscome earned eleven shillings "for Work at the upper Battery"; and Edward Turner received five pounds and seven shillings "for Ditching."[29] Craftsmen, too, benefitted from the lottery's largess. John Beezly received three pounds and twelve shillings "for nine Days Work on the Carriages"; George Kelly was paid twelve shillings "for Smith's Work"; James Catteer made one pound and one shilling "for jointing Shingles"; the bricks made by John Coates earned him two pounds and fourteen shillings; and other craftsmen and workers employed on the public project included gunsmiths, stone masons, painters, glaziers, carpenters, woodsmen, hauliers, blacksmiths, carters, joiners, turners, and nail-makers.[30] At least one hundred eleven unskilled workers were paid on an individual basis, some twenty-six of whom were identified by name. Numerous references to payments to "the Workmen," "sundry Workmen," and "the Men at the Battery" suggest that the total unskilled workforce was considerably larger. Seventy-nine craftsmen were identified in Franklin's accounts, and almost one-third of these were paid on more than one occasion. Given that skilled craftsmen employed journeymen and apprentices, it is clear that this constituted one of the largest public works projects in the city's history.

When military threats receded, the new Pennsylvania militias faded with them, but Franklin was instrumental in the revival of a militia force in the wake of General Edward Braddock's defeat at the beginning of the Seven Years' War. He drafted a bill to establish a militia and prepared the ground by composing a dialogue "stating and answering all the Objections I could think of to such a Militia," which appeared in the *Pennsylvania Gazette*.[31] True to form, Franklin's Militia Act placed power in the hands of "the Freemen of this Province," who would "form themselves into Companies, as heretofore they have used in Time of War without Law, and for each Company, by Majority of Votes, in the Way of Ballot, to chuse its own Officers, to wit, a Captain, Lieutenant and Ensign."[32] The popularly elected officers would then in turn elect a colonel, lieutenant-colonel, and major to command the regiment. While these officers and the colonial authorities enjoyed authority over the soldiers of Pennsylvania's new militia, the ordinary workingmen they commanded enjoyed significant control over the terms of their service. The militia could not be "led more than three Days March beyond the inhabited Parts of the Province; nor detained longer than three weeks in any Garrison, without an express Engagement for that Purpose first voluntarily entered into and subscribed by every Man so to march or remain in Garrison."[33]

Franklin's contrived dialogue in defence of the new militia dealt with objections to popular election of officers, and he began by noting that "if all Officers appointed by Governors were always Men of Merit and fully qualified for their Posts," then this would not be a problem. More significantly, "it seems likely that the People will engage more readily in the Service, and face Danger with more Intrepidity, when they are commanded by a Man they know and esteem."[34] Franklin was a man who was thus esteemed by his fellow Philadelphians, and he was elected Colonel of the Regiment. "The first Time I review'd my Regiment," he recalled with obvious relish, the twelve hundred or so men "accompanied me to my House, and would salute me with some Rounds fired before my Door, which shook down and broke several Glasses of my Electrical Apparatus."[35]

Increasing wealth and genteel status did not prevent Franklin from persisting in identifying with working craftsmen, and Philadelphia's artisans and workingmen continued to celebrate the man who was proud of his own artisanal roots, and who respected the civic and political rights of workingmen and craftsmen. The actions of the professional organization of ships carpenters who protected Franklin's Philadelphia home and possessions during the Stamp Act Crisis provide a revealing insight into Franklin's status among the craftsmen whose lives and work he celebrated.[36] Shipwrights and ship carpenters were often highly skilled and relatively affluent artisans, and the leading members of an array of craftsmen involved in shipbuilding including blockmakers, caulkers, joiners, sailmakers, blacksmiths, and rope makers.[37] Few records remain of their organization, the White Oaks, named for the strongest and best of the woods from which they constructed ships, and it may have been a typical craftsmen's social and mutual aid association.[38] While ships carpenters were, like Franklin, relatively elite and successful craftsmen, their trade depended upon a wide range of Philadelphia's skilled, semiskilled, and unskilled labor force, and contemporary reports suggest that a good many Philadelphia workers joined with the White Oaks in celebration or defense of Franklin. Echoing the salutes to Franklin by the popularly elected militia officers, the White Oaks serenaded Franklin as they rowed him to his ship when he left for London in 1764; they mobilized craftsmen and workers to defend his home against Stamp Act rioters in 1765; and they celebrated the repeal of that law by launching their new smack, which they named the *Franklin*. Samuel Wharton wrote to Franklin describing how Stamp Act rioters' plans to destroy Franklin's home had "roused Our Friends," including "every Mechanick, Who rowed you from Chester to the Ship."[39] Some eight hundred mechanics mobilized to protect Franklin's family and home, including many "hones[t] good traidesmen" who supplemented the core of ships' carpenters to form "a private army of Franklin's artisan supporters."[40]

This was one of the few instances when a crowd of American working-men banished the Sons of Liberty, whose members generally controlled American urban space from the mid-1760s. In virtually every other major urban area, craftsmen and workers united with the Sons of Liberty to oppose the Stamp Act: that this group of Philadelphia's craftsmen and workers over-came their own opposition to the law in order to defend Franklin's home and reputation is particularly telling.[41] Few American gentlemen were able to count on mechanics as such steadfast friends. Perhaps Franklin's creation of a militia in the preceding decade, a militia in which working men and crafts-men elected their own officers, had helped to consolidate his popularity. But it seems equally likely that the former apprentice, runaway, journeyman, and craftsman who throughout his life celebrated work and craftsmanship, was readily identified by workingmen as one of their own.[42]

It is perhaps in the lessons learned from the upbringing and education of his son William Franklin, and the way in which Franklin tried again with his grandson Benjamin Franklin Bache, that we can see how Franklin regarded respectable labor. Franklin recalled, somewhat wistfully, that he had wanted William to become an artisan, but that his son had become infatuated with English titles and was too ashamed to emulate his father, preferring the life and title of a gentleman. After Franklin's death those who had known both father and son even wondered whether William might suppress "the humble details" of his father's early life as chronicled in the *Autobiography*, complete with remarkably detailed memoirs of wages and the cost of living, the kind of fiscal details that were very familiar to working people.[43]

Regretful of the way that he had raised William, Franklin advised his son-in-law Richard Bache to raise his own son as a workingman.[44] Franklin then helped make this possible by taking Benjamin Franklin Bache with him to Europe and training him as a printer. Only seven years old when he accompa-nied his grandfather to France in 1776, Bache was educated in France and Switzerland until he began his apprenticeship in Franklin's Passy printing works. With evident delight Franklin wrote to his son-in-law that Bache is a very sensible and a very good Lad, and I love him much. I had Thoughts of . . . fitting him for Public Business, thinking he might be of Service hereafter to his Country; but being now convinc'd that *Service is no Inheritance*, as the Proverb says, I have determin'd to give him a Trade that he may have something to depend on, and not be oblig'd to ask Favours or Offices of any body. And I flatter my self he will make his way good in the World with God's Blessing. He has already begun to learn his Business from Masters who come to my House, and is very diligent in working and quick in learning.[45]

Franklin employed the best master craftsmen to supervise Bache's apprenticeship, and the young man even learned type casting and typefounding with the renowned Didot family.[46]

In his will Franklin bequeathed "to my grandson, Benjamin Franklin Bache, all the types and printing materials, which I now have in Philadelphia, with the complete letter foundry." Bache subsequently became one of the new republic's most successful newspaper printers, and one of the most politically radical Jeffersonian Republican printers of the 1790s. In the codicil to his will Franklin noted that he had been "bred to a manual art, printing," and asserted that "among artisans, good apprentices are most likely to make good citizens." Acknowledging that "all the utility in life that may be ascribed to me" had come from his success as a craftsman and the people who had aided him in that work, Franklin hoped to help other workingmen to follow the path he had traveled. He left one thousand pounds each to the cities of Boston and Philadelphia, to be loaned at low interest "to such young married artificers, under the age of twenty-five years, as have served an apprenticeship in the said town, and faithfully fulfilled the duties required in their indentures." Franklin's will also acknowledged the early education he had received in Boston, and left money for the free schools of that city.[47]

It is sometimes quite hard to recognize Gordon Wood's Franklin in the man who celebrated his own working past and the nobility of all who worked with their hands. Wood looks back from the nineteenth-century's refashioning of Franklin as a liberal capitalist hero and presents the printer as a somewhat typical self-made man who while revelling in his newfound wealth and power, was eager to enhance his status and was somewhat uncomfortable with his lower-sort origins. According to Wood, Franklin "believed in the power of a few reasonable men," and he "regarded the common people with a certain patronizing amusement, unless, of course, they rioted," in which case he reacted "with disgust."[48]

Whether a proud subject of the British Empire or a radical American revolutionary, Franklin in fact retained a comfortable pride in his working-class origins and a healthy respect for those who lived by their own labor. It was only after his death, in the nineteenth century, according to Wood, that "many middling Americans—tradesmen, artisans, farmers, proto-businessmen of all sorts—found in . . . [Franklin's] popular writings a middling hero they could relate to."[49] This sells both Franklin and his contemporaries short, for he was known and respected as a friend of workingmen throughout his public career. The advent of Revolutionary politics encouraged the politicization of Franklin's long-standing artisanal beliefs. Thus he built upon his earlier organization of the militia when he championed the Pennsylvania Constitution of 1776, premised upon the principle that freedom rather than property was the criterion for male suffrage. Only months before his death Franklin contributed to the debate over revision of this constitution, defiantly affirming the democratic politics that were, at least in part, the political articulation of his enduring respect for workingmen. A proposal to allow only men of property to elect members of a new upper chamber enraged the old printer who asked what "the great Majority of the Freemen" had done "to forfeit so great a Portion of their Rights in Elections?" He continued:

> Why is this Power of Controul, contrary to the Spirit of all Democracies, to be vested in a Minority, instead of a Majority? . . . Is it supposed that Wisdom is the necessary Concomitant of Riches . . . ? And why is Property to be represented at all? . . . [T]he important Ends of Civil Society are the personal Securities of Life and Liberty; these remain the same in every Member of the Society, and the poorest continues to have an equal Claim to them with the most opulent, whatever Difference Time, Chance or Industry may occasion in their Circumstances.[50]

Much of Franklin's lifelong commitment to public service had been informed by pride in his own working roots, a strong desire to help workingmen improve themselves and their situation, and a fierce belief in their political rights. Franklin had recorded with evident pride his role in creating a "HOSPITAL for the Relief of the Sick Poor," which rested on his belief that "saving and restoring useful and laborious Members to a Community, is a Work of Public Service." He had fashioned the rules for the creation of Pennsylvania's first militia, including the election of their officers by the ordinary men who comprised each company, with commissions from the governor dependent on the votes of workingmen, thus creating an "an Army of FREEMEN." And between July and September of 1776, Franklin had presided over the interim government of Pennsylvania, which drafted the most radical state constitution of the entire Revolutionary era. Franklin's carefully amended copy of the Declaration of Rights that preceded the Frame of Government illustrated his role in the creation of this document, which decreed "That all elections ought to be free; and that all free men having a sufficient evident common interest with, and attachment to the community, have a right to elect officers, or to be elected into office."[51] Franklin championed a polity in which a leather-apron man like his own youthful self and his printer grandson were the equal of any other man. Lauding this singular achievement were the great many of Philadelphia's workers and craftsmen, together with their wives and children, who swelled the ranks of the twenty thousand people who attended Franklin's funeral, as they bid farewell to one of their own.[52]

NOTES

1. *Autobiography*, 125. The most comprehensive biographical study of Franklin is the as-yet unfinished multivolume work by J. A. Leo Lemay. See Lemay, *The Life of Benjamin Franklin: Volume 1, Journalist, 1706-1730*; *Volume 2, Printer and Publisher, 1730-1747*; and *Volume 3, Soldier, Scientist, and Politician, 1748-1757* (Philadelphia: University of Pennsylvania Press, 2006-8). This chapter was first published in the *Journal of American Studies* 43 (2009): 161–75. It is reprinted here by permission of Cambridge University Press.

2. Edmund S. Morgan, *Benjamin Franklin* (New Haven, CT: Yale University Press, 2002); Gordon S. Wood, *The Americanization of Benjamin Franklin* (New York: Penguin, 2004); David Waldstreicher, *Runaway America: Benjamin Franklin, Slavery, and the American Revolution* (New York: Hill and Wang, 2004).

3. Morgan, *Benjamin Franklin*, 304.

4. Wood, *Americanization of Benjamin Franklin*, x. The best discussion of Franklin's pride in his working origins is Billy G. Smith, "Benjamin Franklin, Civic Improver," in *Benjamin Franklin: In Search of a Better World*, ed. Page Talbot (New Haven, CT: Yale University Press, 2005), 91–123.

5. "NEW-YORK, July 8," *American Minerva, and the New-York (Evening) Advertiser* (New York City), 8 July 1795.

6. *Autobiography*, 46.

7. *Autobiography*, 57.

8. The reference to an "excellent Craftsman" is drawn from Richard Saunders, *Poor Richard Improved: Being an Almanack and Ephemeris . . . for the Year of our Lord 1751* (Philadelphia: Franklin and Hall, 1751), in *Papers* 4:86. Examples of workers described by Franklin as "ingenious" include his uncle Benjamin, Aquila Rose, and Matthew Adams. See James N. Green and Peter Stallybrass, *Benjamin Franklin, Writer and Printer* (New Castle, DE: Oak Knoll Press, 2006), 9.

9. Here I take issue with the argument presented in Paul W. Connor, *Poor Richard's Politicks: Benjamin Franklin and His New American Order* (New York: Oxford University Press, 1965), 40–47.

10. *Autobiography*, 69.

11. Silence Dogood, *The New England Courant* (Boston), 2 April 1722, in *Papers* 1:9. For further discussion of Franklin's tendency to obscure his identity as an author and present himself as a printer, see Green and Stallybrass, *Benjamin Franklin*, 5–9.

12. I am indebted to James Green for this observation.

13. Lemay, *Life of Franklin*, 1:11.

14. Ibid., 1:5–211.

15. Ibid., 1:335, 334–36.

16. Smith, "Benjamin Franklin," 100.

17. Karl Marx, *A Contribution to the Critique of Political Economy* (New York: International Publishers, 1970), 55; Marx, *Capital: Volume 1*, transl. Ben Fowkes (Harmondsworth, UK: Penguin, 1990), 142, 286.

18. Franklin, *A Modest Enquiry into the Nature and Necessity of a Paper-Currency* (Philadelphia, 1729), in *Papers* 1:144, 148.

19. Ronald Schultz, *The Republic of Labor: Philadelphia Artisans and the Politics of Class, 1720–1830* (New York: Oxford University Press, 1993), 4–5.

20. *Autobiography*, 124.

21. For a discussion of these trends in Philadelphia see Schultz, *The Republic of Labor*, and Billy G. Smith, *The "Lower Sort": Philadelphia's Laboring People, 1750–1800* (Ithaca, NY: Cornell University Press, 1990).

22. *Autobiography*, 182; A Tradesman of Philadelphia, *Plain Truth: Or, Serious Consider-ations On the Present State of the City of Philadelphia, and the Province of Pennsylvania* (Philadelphia, 1747), in *Papers* 3:180–204.

23. A Tradesman of Philadelphia, *Plain Truth*, in *Papers* 3:198, 199, 198–199, 199.

24. *Autobiography*, 183.

25. "Philadelphia, January 5," *Pennsylvania Gazette* (Philadelphia), 5 January 1748. It is possible that Franklin's democratic ideas about militia organization were drawn from his youth in Massachusetts, where "over half the [militia] company officers identified themselves with manual occupations, and in fact followed the same livelihoods as private soldiers." See Fred Anderson, *A People's Army: Massachusetts Soldiers and Society in the Seven Years' War* (New York: W.W. Norton & Company, 1984), 55. I am grateful to Alan Houston, who has traced the occupations of many of the officers recorded as serving in the eleven Philadelphia companies listed in the *Pennsylvania Gazette* article. See Alan Houston, *Benjamin Franklin and the Politics of Improvement* (New Haven, CT: Yale University Press, 2008), 85–92.

26. Gary B. Nash, *The Urban Crucible: Social Change, Political Consciousness, and the Origins of the American Revolution* (Cambridge, MA: Harvard University Press, 1979), 232.

27. *Autobiography*, 183.

28. *Philadelphia Lottery Accounts* (Philadelphia: Franklin and Hall, 1752). For discussion of the ways in which the lottery scheme worked, and how it benefited Philadelphia's working men and their families, see Houston, *Franklin and the Politics of Improvement*, 92–100.

29. *Philadelphia Lottery Accounts*, 6, 11, 7, 11.

30. Ibid., 7, 11, 12.

31. *Autobiography*, 230; "A Dialogue between X, Y, and Z, concerning the present State of Affairs in Pennsylvania," *Pennsylvania Gazette*, 18 December 1755, in *Papers* 6:295–306.

32. "Militia Act," 25 November 1755, in *Papers* 6:270.

33. Ibid., 272–73.

34. "A Dialogue between X, Y, and Z," in *Papers* 6:298.

35. *Autobiography*, 238.

36. James H. Hutson, "An Investigation of the Inarticulate: Philadelphia's White Oaks," *William and Mary Quarterly*, 3d. ser., 28 (1971): 3–25; Jesse Lemisch and John K. Alexander, "The White Oaks, Jack Tar, and the Concept of the 'Inarticulate,'" *William and Mary Quarterly*, 3d. ser., 29 (1972): 109–34; Simeon J. Crowther, "A Note on the Economic Position of Philadelphia's White Oaks," ibid., 134–36.

37. Crowther, "The Economic Position of Philadelphia's White Oaks," 134–35.

38. Hutson argued that the White Oaks were "typical of the ordinary Philadelphia working-man": in Hutson, "An Investigation of the Inarticulate," 25. Lemisch and Alexander, and then Crowther disagreed, providing compelling evidence that many ships carpenters, and presum-ably many members of the White Oaks, were relatively successful craftsmen of middling rank. (Lemisch and Alexander, "The White Oaks," and Crowther, "The Economic Position of Phila-delphia's White Oaks.")

39. Samuel Wharton to Benjamin Franklin, Philadelphia, 13 October 1765, in *Papers* 12:316.

40. Deborah Franklin to Benjamin Franklin, Philadelphia, 22 September 1765, and 3 No-vember 1765, in *Papers* 12:271, 353; Nash, *Urban Crucible*, 305–6.

41. For examples of popular reactions to the Stamp Act see Alfred F. Young, *The Shoemak-er and the Tea Party: Memory and the American Revolution* (Boston: Beacon Press, 1999); Nash, *Urban Crucible*, 292–338; Simon P. Newman, *Parades and the Politics of the Street: Festive Culture in the Early American Republic* (Philadelphia: University of Pennsylvania Press, 1997), 11–44.

42. Hutson, "Philadelphia's White Oaks," 11–12.

43. Jacques Gibelin, *Mémoires de la Privée de Benjamin Franklin, Ecrits par Lui-même* (Paris: Chez Buisson, 1791), 110, as quoted in Green and Stallybrass, *Benjamin Franklin*, 154. See also Smith, "Benjamin Franklin," 113.

44. Pierre Jean Georges Cabanis, *Oeuvres Complètes de Cabanis* (Paris: Bossange Frères, 1825), 5:222–23.

45. Franklin to Richard Bache, Passy, 11 November 1784, in *Papers: Digital Edition*.

46. See James Tagg, *Benjamin Franklin Bache and the Philadelphia Aurora* (Philadelphia: University of Pennsylvania Press, 1991), especially 23–55, and Jeffrey A. Smith, *Franklin and Bache: Envisioning the Enlightened Republic* (New York: Oxford University Press, 1990), 67–82.

47. Franklin, Will and Codicil, 17 July 1788, in *Papers: Digital Edition.*

48. Wood, *Americanization of Benjamin Franklin*, 10.

49. Ibid., 235.

50. Franklin, "Queries and Remarks on *Hints for the Members of Pennsylvania Convention*," November 1789, in *Papers: Digital Edition.*

51. "Some Account of the Pennsylvania Hospital," 28 May 1754, in *Papers* 5:287; "FORM of the ASSOCIATION *into which Numbers are daily entering, for the Defence of this City and Province*," *Pennsylvania Gazette*, 3 December 1747; Franklin's amended copy of the first draft of the Pennsylvania Declaration of Rights is reprinted in *Papers* 22:531.

52. For Franklin's funeral see "Philadelphia, April 28," *Pennsylvania Gazette*, 28 April 1791.

Chapter Seven

Recasting Franklin as Printer

A Note on Recent Historiography

Douglas B. Thomas

The Body of
B. Franklin
Printer;
Like the Cover of an old Book,
Its Contents torn out,
And stript of its Lettering and Gilding,
Lies here, Food for Worms.
But the Work shall not be wholly lost;
For it will, as he believ'd, appear once more,
In a new and more perfect Edition
Corrected and amended
By the Author.[1]

At age twenty-two Benjamin Franklin composed an epitaph that styled himself "B. Franklin, Printer." By the time he wrote it, he had already worked as an apprentice for six years and had recently established his own print shop. In spite of the epitaph's metaphors of printed works, for most of Franklin's life it circulated in manuscript form; the epitaph was only printed near the end of his life when enterprising competitors had it printed.[2] Although it might be dismissed as a simple youthful vision of his career trajectory, Franklin distributed it throughout his life. Late in life, he signed his name "B. Franklin, Printer"[3] on various documents even though his life achievements could have warranted any number of titles or self-descriptions.

Whether or not Franklin intended it for public consumption, the self-description "printer" was still important to him. Yet Franklin's substantial accomplishments in public life have meant that his printing career has often been presented as a mere prologue. This is especially true since Franklin's own description of his printing career was in part presented to note his impressive rise to riches from his tradesman beginnings. With good reason, later Franklin historians treat his printing career as an epiphenomenon—in their hands his rise from meager beginnings to a place of prominence in society as a printer is a symbol of economic genius, personal ingenuity, and American capitalism.[4] Although economic and other interpretations of his printing career are important and understandable, recent scholarship uncovers the impact of Franklin's printing as central to our understanding of Franklin, not just as the beginnings of his future career.

Any effort to understand Franklin's "intellectual world," as this volume attempts, must take seriously the recent scholarship on Benjamin Franklin as printer. This chapter reasserts the importance of Benjamin Franklin's printing career as a subject of interest beyond bibliographic study or use as a prototypical allegory. Drawing primarily on works by Michael Warner, Ralph Frasca, David Waldstreicher, Peter Stallybrass, and James Green, this chapter highlights recent moves in the historiography of recasting Franklin as printer.[5] It illuminates two aspects of Benjamin Franklin's printing career that should influence any interpretation of his entire life. The first notes Franklin's establishment of an extensive information network through his printing to distribute his ideas on civic virtue. The second explores the way Franklin's understanding of printing composition affected his construction of his public image. Together they suggest that printing powerfully shaped his sense of self and community, and that Franklin's influence as a printer had a dramatic impact on the character of the American printing industry and helped establish an autonomous public sphere.

Michael Warner's treatment of Franklin in his *Letters of the Republic: Publications and the Public Sphere in Eighteenth-Century America* argues that Franklin's work as a printer and bookseller was pivotal in creating a public sphere, and this appears to be where the understanding of Franklin as printer has generally remained. Recently, however, two assessments of Franklin have emerged on the subject of Franklin as printer. In the first, the printer is key to understanding the distribution of larger cultural values (such as virtue, republicanism, or sensibility) in the Atlantic World. The printer becomes both a conduit in a larger network and the key figure in establishing new networks to distribute values and ideas. This view casts Franklin as *distributive printer*. In the second assessment, Franklin as printer is a primary metaphor for constructing his own identity. In this view, the role of a printer and its function in society is crucial to understanding the nature of the printer himself. This view could be called the *metaphorical printer*. The *distributive printer* is exemplified in Ralph Frasca's *Benjamin Franklin's Printing Network: Disseminating Virtue in Early America*; a darker reality of these same networks is critically examined in David Waldstreicher's *Runaway America*.

The *metaphorical printer* approach is explored in James N. Green and Peter Stallybrass's *Benjamin Franklin: Writer and Printer*.

These two approaches to Franklin as printer are not the only moves in recent Franklin historiography to examine Franklin's early career as a printer. Leo Lemay's important volumes on Franklin's life give scholars a comprehensive review of the documents and factual evidence of Franklin's printing career. Although central to any study of Franklin as printer, Lemay's comprehensive approach masks larger interpretive questions about the relative merits of various stages of Franklin's life.[6] Other recent volumes that comment on Franklin's printing career, such as Gordon Wood's *Americanization of Benjamin Franklin* or Alan Houston's *Benjamin Franklin and the Politics of Improvement*, only do so in order to treat larger concerns.[7] Although these and other approaches provide a coterie of contexts and consequences for Franklin's time as a printer, the following approaches investigate Franklin's inherent interest in printing itself. Franklin's printing, when shorn from allegorical necessity, uncovers "printer" as essential to Franklin's self-understanding.

I. THE PRINTER AND THE PUBLIC SPHERE

Warner's reading of Franklin centers on texts from Franklin's life that illuminate Franklin's relationship to printing. The first is the epitaph's poetic description of Franklin's body as a discarded book whose works will not be lost because it will reappear as a "new and more perfect Edition, Corrected and amended by the Author." Beyond the metaphoric description of death and resurrection, Warner, (like Green and Stallybrass) finds the epitaph emblematic of Franklin's larger connection to printing. In Warner's eyes the epitaph "equates print and life in equivalent terms: to live is to be published."[8] The epitaph is thus a metaphor for the printed life of Franklin rather than his death. Franklin's *Autobiography* complements this reading by noting the extent to which Franklin's life can be identified through the printed medium: Franklin identifies his life's mistakes as "errata" that cannot be fully corrected in life. His faults *can* be corrected, however, through the written recollection of that life, like typographic errors are corrected in a second edition of a book.[9] For Warner, Franklin's life is fundamentally mediated through printing.

The unique mediating element of print means that Franklin is famous both as a writer and printer and as subject, written and printed. Franklin is the first prominent American man of letters who did not achieve prominence as an orator, as other famous men of letters did (mainly preachers).[10] For this reason, Franklin, more than the famous preachers of the day, embodies the written subject within the public sphere. His plethora of pseudonyms and anonymous articles (including, most famously, Poor Richard) dialogue with each other; each article stands as testament to Franklin's knowing manipulation of the dichotomy between writer and written subject. Warner regards an example of Poor Richard admitting in his *Almanack* to have authored a text by Titan Leeds by controlling Leeds's dead hand as a literal sort of ghost-writing and notes the distinction between "the man of *letters* (the Hand written) and the *man* of letters (Richard's fleshy, manipulated hand)." [11]

In fact, Franklin's willful use of pseudonyms to engage in anonymous print discourse is important to the evolution of the colonial public sphere. Franklin exhibits each of the critical facets of Warner's idea of a republican public discourse: the ability to write to a large audience, to do so anonymously, and to write in the context of a circulating community newspaper. Franklin's printing becomes more than a financial success; his manner of printed discourse is transformative to the public sphere. Warner rejects previous narratives that simply privilege the rise of printing as the primary causal agent in changing discourse. [12] Such technological determinism misses key facts, such as the longer history of presses and printing in the colonies. Instead, Warner posits a "reciprocal determination" between printing technology and culture. For Warner, printed objects can only be understood through comprehension of the public sphere. Even though there had been newspapers in the colonies, they did not thrive until they adopted features enabling a local political discourse—including, crucially, anonymous writing. Before then, the newspaper was little more than a source for foreign news. [13] Instead of asking which came first, republicanism or a prospering print culture, Warner examines the way that both work to change each other. As he says about his book, "[it] does not explain changes in political culture by pointing to some noncultural version of reality; it tries to show that changes in political culture (republicanism, the Enlightenment, nationalism) in important ways refashioned the textuality of print." [14]

Warner's argument that Franklin's role as a printer and bookseller was pivotal in creating the public sphere begs an analysis of Franklin as Printer. Taking cues from both literary and bibliographic scholarship, scholars examining Franklin as Printer uncover Franklin by comparing editions and variants of his writing, and his publishing records, with those of his contemporaries, to situate his writing and publishing in their cultural context. Importantly, this methodology reveals Franklin's awareness of his own printed public presentation. [15]

Throughout his career Franklin placed himself at the center of the public sphere by collecting and disseminating information, first as a printer, then later in an enlarged way as a printer, bookseller, and postmaster. He realized the importance of receiving as much information as possible when he started his first printing shop in Philadelphia under competition from Andrew Bradford, who was also the postmaster. As postmaster, Bradford culled information from private correspondence, official government packets, and gossip from the inevitable foot traffic in and out of the post office. As a printer, Bradford relied on these sources for the most current and tantalizing information to sell to the public in his newspapers; he could also reduce the postage cost for sending his own papers. The advantages of both inhabiting a nexus of circulated information and having a publishing outlet were clear: only when Franklin attained the position of postmaster himself did his newspaper achieve financial success.[16]

Franklin attempted to craft public perception throughout his printing career by publishing his own ideas (often under pseudonyms) and even occasionally distributing the private correspondence of others. The reach, but also the limits, of Franklin's ability to shape public opinion were made explicit by a scandal that ultimately led to Franklin losing his appointment as postmaster. In 1772, in an attempt to influence members of the Massachusetts House, Franklin gave letters to the Speaker of the House that revealed designs between the governor and the lieutenant governor to gain firmer control over Commonwealth affairs from London. Without Franklin's knowledge, the Speaker circulated the letters to other House members, who then published the letters in newspapers to call attention to the perceived plot against their liberties. The leak was traced back to Franklin and he was dismissed as postmaster and as an agent of the Crown in the colonies.[17]

A historiographic turn investigating Franklin as Printer reveals a Franklin that was more aware of his printed words than most of his contemporaries. Scholarship on Franklin's ability, through his printing networks, to distribute cultural ideas is analyzed in the next section, Franklin as a *distributive printer*. The effects of Franklin's printing will then be turned inward to uncover how printing shaped Franklin's self-understanding, or a view of the *metaphorical printer*. An accurate picture of Franklin's life and writings is impossible without the full context of his attempts to control his own image as it was distributed publically through his printing networks and the metaphors he used to describe himself.

II. DISTRIBUTIVE PRINTER

In the *distributive printer* view, the printer's ideology and ideas are essential to understand what passes through his printing and print network. Of course, this view builds on a much larger history of American printing that has long been covered in bibliographic circles, as James Green has shown.[18] Because of Franklin's skill and prominence as a printer, his specific abilities are essential subjects for understanding the history of American printing. His early skill as a type compositor, his ability as a pressman, and his publishing talent (both writing and finding material to print) were essential to his rise.

His early success as a printer also allowed him to establish trade associations with other printers throughout the colonies for reciprocal benefit.[19]

By tracking these associations, Ralph Frasca's recent research finds Franklin's desire to inculcate public virtue an indispensible motive for expanding his printing network.[20] For Frasca, the personality and preferences of Franklin (and printers generally) determined the character of printed materials from newspapers to books across the colonies. Of course, this sort of analysis is usually done on a document-by-document basis and often compares various editions of competing sources. In contrast, Frasca analyzes the printer and his network as an ideological source itself. Similarly, cultural historian Sarah Knott describes booksellers as "the main transatlantic conduit" in her concept of the expansion of sensibility in general and specifically describes Philadelphia printer and publisher Robert Bell as one of the key figures in promoting it.[21] However, unlike Knott, Frasca is interested in Franklin's development of a particular morality of virtue and its influence on contemporaneous printing. As such, Frasca follows Franklin from the beginning of his printing experience, marking the development of his moral sense and also his connections to other printers. In many cases they develop simultaneously, as Franklin's formative experiences working in print shops exposed him to a variety of behaviors. It is his revulsion toward lazy fellow workers in London print shops that helps form Franklin's description of industry, likewise his observance of scandal in Philadelphia and London that informs his public virtue. While much of Frasca's analysis begins with the traditional printing narrative provided by Franklin's memoirs, it branches out to describe each extension of his network and the distribution of Franklin's brand of virtue across it.

The Franklin that emerges from Frasca's study is a veritable media mogul who at his apex in 1755 had established a network of associates that included eight out of the fifteen newspapers in North America and the West Indies.[22] In part, Franklin benefited from good timing—there was only a single North American newspaper in 1704—and his career corresponded with a period of growth in American printing.[23] Yet the *Pennsylvania Gazette* and Franklin's other publications owe their success to more than good timing. One of Franklin's key advantages in Philadelphia was that he combined his ability to run the mechanics of a press, his economic savvy to run the business, and his writing skill to provide top-notch content—he was far more involved than those who sneered at Franklin as a "*meer* Printer."[24] Indeed, Franklin's reach eventually extended to create an almost complete vertical integration of all the elements of information collection and dissemination. For example, Franklin quickly realized that his competitor Bradford enjoyed a tremendous privilege as postmaster and official colonial printer. As postmaster, Bradford controlled the distribution network and most of the newsgathering from letters and foreign packets. While Franklin found ways to circumvent Bradford's privileges, he also worked studiously to acquire them. Of course, this is well established in Franklin's *Autobiography*; Frasca elaborates on this familiar history by giving Franklin's competitors depth, thereby establishing broad contexts for the printing of the era.

Franklin demonstrated that in printing—as in so many other fields—he could successfully develop friendships and build communities. His keen judgment of character enabled him to build a business network where others failed; he started by establishing journeymen throughout the colonies in new print shops (such as his faithful worker Thomas Whitemarsh in Charleston, South Carolina, in 1731). Franklin's business empire culminated with making David Hall his full partner in 1748, allowing Franklin to turn to other civic activities beyond printing. [25] Even after Franklin's partnerships eventually split off to form their own private enterprises, Franklin's alliance was still the most successful throughout North America. [26] While Frasca focuses his attention on the American networks, Franklin was also connected to leading European printers. It was his association with them that helped Franklin demonstrate superior craftsmanship and innovate his business practices. After becoming the first American printer to use typefaces from the London type founder William Caslon in 1738, he continued to purchase almost exclusively from Caslon for his entire network throughout his life. [27] Franklin's use of Caslon's type had practical reasons beyond business loyalty. Because each print shop had the same set of typefaces, Franklin's network could print portions of large projects at different presses to be combined later in one binding—allowing Franklin to tackle bigger printing jobs than his competitors. The uniformity of type also allowed Franklin to print the same job across various print shops in the colonies—including his famous almanacs. [28] Beyond simple uniformity of look, the superior cut of Caslon's typefaces ensured that Franklin (and his network of allied printers) had better-quality printed books, newspapers, and advertisements—they looked more beautiful and were easier to read than his competitors—thanks to crisp letters and fewer blotched words. [29]

Franklin's use of Caslon, however, did not make him the only printer connected to Europe, since colonial printers did not develop their own type foundry or native built press until 1769. Nor was Caslon Franklin's only connection to Europe. Although he was a leading consumer and proponent of Caslon's typefaces, Franklin maintained correspondence with the innovative printer and type founder in Birmingham, John Baskerville. Baskerville's editions of Virgil, the Book of Common Prayer, and his Cambridge Bible are now viewed as masterpieces in English printing. [30] As printer for the University of Cambridge, Baskerville was one of the chief printers in the world. [31] Later, while Franklin lived in France he became well acquainted with printers there, as he made good use of French printers to publish pro-American tracts. Beyond making use of the French printing industry to publish, Frank-

lin was intimately acquainted with the leading printers and type founders of
Paris. French type founder Simon Pierre Fournier designed a typeface in
Franklin's honor.[32] Franklin also worked with, and sent his grandson to work
with, the famous Didot family which included François-Ambroise, the inventor of a standardized metric point system for measuring type (still used today), and his son Firmin, the inventor of stereographic printing and his famous typeface designs (known as "Didot") which would become emblematic
of French neoclassical printing.[33] Eager to establish American autonomy,
however, Franklin also developed his own type at his own press in Passy,
outside of Paris.[34] Franklin's friendships with Baskerville, Caslon, Fournier,
and Didot situate him in the orbit of the leading book publishers of his age,
not just in the colonies.

In stark contrast to Frasca's positive view of Franklin's printing networks,
David Waldstreicher's *Runaway America* underscores that American printing, like much of the colonial economy, was established by slaves and servants: the "labor of the unfree."[35] Like Frasca, Waldstreicher catalogs Franklin's rise to prominence and establishment of an extensive printing network,
but in view of slavery and servitude the network takes on a darker hue. For
Waldstreicher, Franklin himself straddled the world of unfree and free from
his earliest experiences as a printer. Franklin learned the trade as an inden-
tured servant to his older brother, while he helped establish the financial
well-being of the same brother's paper, *The New England Courant.* Like
every other paper, the *Courant* was dependent on the cheap labor of servants
or slaves. Even on a superficial level, the newspapers themselves extended
the reach of enforcement and sale of indentures and slaves—even after
Franklin's own experience, fully one-quarter of his own *Philadelphia Gazette* contained ads fostering the slave trade.[36]

For the "unfree" servants and slaves, anonymous self-fashioning in society through disguise and deceit was the only way to find freedom as run-
aways. Franklin himself was a runaway whose anonymous self-fashioning in
the pages of the *Courant* preceded his flight. This was true even though the
legal troubles of Franklin's brother limited his ability to enforce Ben's
contract (legally, Ben was a runaway). For Waldstreicher, printing itself
mediates the contradictions in establishing freedom. His freedom, like many
others, "was another's misfortune, even ruin."[37]

The distribution of ideas, from Franklin's notion of virtue to the continua-
tion of unfree labor, through Franklin's printing network also includes the
perpetuation of Franklin's own unique brand of public engagement through
the press. As a printer at the center of the public sphere, Franklin's influence
can be glimpsed by the number of concurrent job titles our age would assign
to him: reporter, editor, publisher, bookseller, and owner. In effect: a media
empire of one. In the age of Rupert Murdoch, Facebook, and Google, per-

haps we owe Franklin's media acumen and ability to control the flow of information a second look.[38]

III. METAPHORICAL PRINTER

Where the distributive view seems to focus on Franklin's idea of what the public square needed to hear, the metaphorical view turns the same evidence inward to analyze Franklin himself. In *Benjamin Franklin: Writer and Printer*, two experts focus on key elements of Franklin's world of print and identity. James N. Green, the librarian at Franklin's Library Company of Philadelphia, and Peter Stallybrass, professor of English and director of the History of the Book program at the University of Pennsylvania, analyze the construction of several key texts to understand Franklin himself. Rather than make Franklin the printer an ideal type for a larger phenomenon, the mechanical details of printing provide insights into Franklin's character. Originally conceived as a catalog to accompany an exhibition in celebration of Franklin's tercentenary, *Benjamin Franklin: Writer and Printer* evolved into a longer book and incorporated additional scholarship from both Green and Stallybrass. Its origin as a catalog, however, works to the advantage of the scholarship in the book, since the numerous full-color examples of Franklin's actual printed artifacts highlight the nature of Franklin's public image mediated through print. By exploring the material qualities of Franklin's editions compared with Franklin's account in his *Autobiography*, Green and Stallybrass provide in-depth scholarship about specific incidents of his life, and more essentially, the print-constructed nature of Franklin's life itself.[39]

This is their important insight: Franklin's role as a printer is crucial to understanding Franklin's identity, not merely his printing. For them "most of [Franklin's] writing was not only *for* print, but in one way or another *about* print."[40] This simple observation defines their approach to Franklin's self-fashioning in their exploration of Franklin as an author. The epitaph quoted at the top of this chapter, for example, is important to their analysis—Franklin continually saw himself as a printer. His identity as a printer helps make sense of the endeavors Franklin made to "erase authorship." For a printer, used to composing material from a variety of sources, the final product was more important than the originality of the material. This certainly helped Franklin recognize the possibility of anonymity—especially to overcome the editorial prejudice of his older brother James. Green and Stallybrass note that "anonymity and pseudonymity served many purposes for Franklin, and avoiding censorship was by no means the most important one. Above all, they enabled him to construct experimental selves, who argue on any and every side of a question."[41] For them, the print shop helps drive Franklin's understanding of authorship from his first published works. Franklin demonstrated dogged will in constructing various personas and writing styles, including mimicking that of Joseph Addison and helping to spark a recrudescence of satire in colonial America.[42] Although Franklin mentions his attempts to create pseudonyms in his memoirs, the author of Silence Dogood, for example, was not fully established as Franklin until 1868.[43] Even pieces supposedly authored by Franklin require scrutiny. Ironically, Ben Franklin's name was first published as a pseudonym for his brother James in his publication *The New England Courant*.[44] Franklin maintained the façade of "Poor" Richard Saunders's authorship throughout the publication of the *Almanac*, in part, to be able to attack himself, Benjamin Franklin, publisher, through Poor Richard, the writer. In fact, although Franklin is regarded as a "man of letters" for his contributions as a writer, the vast majority of his writing was done anonymously such that Ben Franklin could simply remain a printer in the public mind, or at least in Franklin's conception of the public mind.[45]

In addition to the widely published questions of authorship in the public eye, such as the Silence Dogood letters or Poor Richard, Franklin played with authorship to fight prejudice in small private groups too. As part of a writing group in Philadelphia, Franklin exchanged his writing with his friend James Ralph as an experiment. Ralph's work was thus presented to the group as Franklin's. Although his work was usually criticized when presented as Franklin's, it was also celebrated. In turn, Franklin's work, disguised as Ralph's, received more criticism than usual.[46] Perhaps remembering this example, Franklin highlighted a similar prejudice in typography. His printing friend John Baskerville's innovative, new typefaces were regarded as harder to read than prevailing styles (such as Caslon). Franklin took delight in sending Baskerville an amusing anecdote where he presented a critic with a type specimen sheet of Caslon as if it were Baskerville's. Franklin described the reaction:

> He went over the several founts, shewing me everywhere what he thought Instances of that Disproportion; and declared, that he could not then read the Specimen without feeling very strongly the Pain he had mentioned to me. I spared him that time the Confusion of being told, that these were the Types he had been reading all his Life, with so much Ease to his Eyes; the Types his adored Newton is printed with, on which he has pored not a little; nay, the very Types his own Book is printed with, for he is himself an Author; and yet never discovered this painful Disproportion in them, till he thought they were yours.[47]

Both anecdotes demonstrate Franklin's willingness to defend a friend against prejudice without need for financial or public advantage. For example, Franklin consistently used Caslon for the majority of his printing, not Baskerville.[48] For Franklin, the truth of a work should not depend on the authority or originality of the writer.

In fact, it was an anonymous guise that Franklin donned to develop his best-selling *Way to Wealth*. He invented a new character, Father Abraham, to use in the introduction to *Poor Richard Improved* as a device to quote liberally from Poor Richard. Quoting as an aspect of authorship is, in fact, the first subject of the preface. "I have heard that nothing gives an Author so great Pleasure, as to find his Works respectfully quoted by other learned Authors. This Pleasure I have seldom enjoyed," says Franklin.[49] In some sense this grandstanding is odd since an almanac is ephemeral and is primarily a compilation of the work of others—a feature that makes Franklin's preface a stunning critique of authorship in general.[50] The popularity of the 1758 preface led to it being printed separately as *Father Abraham's Speech to a Great Number of People* and later *The Way to Wealth*, which went on to become widely reprinted and disseminated. Only later editions by other printers would proclaim the actual author as Ben Franklin.[51] Green and Stallybrass demonstrate the variety of titles and authorial attributions with fourteen scans of various editions (including foreign editions), with Franklin's image and authorship shown to increase with time.[52]

Finally turning to the composition of the *Autobiography* itself, Green and Stallybrass note that printing is the book's major subject. Following the detailed bibliographic history of the *Autobiography*,[53] and the extensive biography by Leo Lemay,[54] their decision to include images from the various editions makes it unusually clear that the printed perception of Franklin constantly changed, as with his *Way to Wealth*, throughout the evolution of his memoirs.[55] Green and Stallybrass's innovative consideration of the visual aspect of the books should be duly noted because often such images are seen as ornamental, but in this case they have demonstrated how important they are to understanding reception history.[56] Franklin's description of his tradesman beginnings is not the simple story of everyday working life but a sophisticated recounting of the "model of what a working life should be" and that "the self-education of a tradesman could be at least as important as the Lives of Plutarch."[57] Franklin became the Franklin whom we read about in his memoir as he developed the skills of a printer. Reading books from a young age led to writing them in his old age; imitating the great writing of the *Spectator* leads to becoming a successful newspaperman. Franklin's epitaph, conceived at the beginning of his career, emerges as a manifesto of self-improvement, with each publication by Franklin demonstrating his own life as a "new and more perfect Edition Corrected and amended By the Author."[58] Each "corrected and amended" edition of Franklin's life was more sterling—if only in public perception. The importance, however, of interpreting Franklin as a printer throughout his life is that it was as a printer that Franklin developed his sense of self-fashioning and self-improvement.

Franklin is the model example of an interconnected discourse between print and politics. Before becoming an assemblyman himself, Franklin had been both printer and clerk for the Assembly, making him well aware of the "connection between public discourse and representative polity."[59] Because of his involvement in the expansion of printing in Philadelphia, and later in making a network of allied printers, Franklin's personal history is indivisible from any larger arguments about the republican discourse. Warner's analytical vantage point simultaneously celebrates the heroics of Franklin, as well as smaller forgotten printers across the colonies, that help prove his larger point in disseminating republican rhetoric and creating a genuine public sphere through print discourse. Of course, the printed public discourse, while a powerful agent for change, also reaffirmed long-standing power structures. White property-holding males had better access to the press organs. Yet, even if the new technology reified structures of power, Franklin offers a slight corrective as a tradesman whose first published words were as an old woman, Silence Dogood.

Frasca's analysis of Franklin's media network or Warner's use of Franklin to define an American public sphere both draw on Franklin as printer to achieve their aims, but these aims are largely extrinsic to Franklin (to define the public sphere or illuminate aspects of republicanism or the Atlantic World networks). It is Green and Stallybrass who help us to understand how Franklin as printer is essential to understanding Franklin himself, as well as the outlines of an aspect of American culture—the land of "second chances," a place where one's self may be recreated. Franklin's self-fashioning and continual constructed image-making seem to be acquired from his intimate understanding of print and its composed nature. The ability to see words composed in the printed columns of type improved Franklin's ability to frame issues on several sides of the debate—sometimes as author of each of the sides himself. Green and Stallybrass help highlight how Franklin's work as a printer was essential to his self-construction, if not self-understanding, and is not merely one of Franklin's jobs and hobbies or an interesting footnote in the history of print culture. Although much of Franklin scholarship continues to treat Franklin's printing as prologue or allegory, this quiet and perhaps overlooked movement in Franklin historiography asserts the primacy of printing to any interpretation of Franklin's life, writings, and intellectual world. To see Franklin as printer is to begin to uncover Franklin as he saw himself.

NOTES

1. J. A. Leo Lemay, *The Life of Benjamin Franklin*, vol. 1, *Journalist, 1706–1730* (Philadelphia: University of Pennsylvania Press, 2005), 320–23. I acknowledge gratefully the

thoughtful encouragement I received on this topic from Professors Paul Cheney and Eric Slauter, both of the University of Chicago.

2. James N. Green and Peter Stallybrass, *Benjamin Franklin: Writer and Printer* (New Castle, DE: Oak Knoll Press, 2006), 17–18. The various manuscripts of the epitaph are worded slightly differently but they create the same metaphoric image. See also Michael Warner, *The Letters of the Republic: Publication and the Public Sphere in Eighteenth-Century America* (Cambridge, MA: Harvard University Press, 1992), 73–75; Lemay, *Life of Benjamin Franklin* 1:321.

3. Stephen Carl Arch, "Benjamin Franklin's Autobiography, Then and Now," in *The Cambridge Companion to Benjamin Franklin*, ed. Carla Mulford (Cambridge: Cambridge University Press, 2008), 159.

4. John R. Aiken, "Benjamin Franklin, Karl Marx, and the Labor Theory of Value," *The Pennsylvania Magazine of History and Biography* 90, no. 3 (July 1966): 378–84; Karl Marx, *Capital: Volume 1: A Critique of Political Economy*, trans. Ben Fowkes (Harmondsworth, UK: Penguin Classics, 1992), 142; Max Weber, *The Protestant Ethic and the Spirit of Capitalism*, trans. Talcott Parsons, 2nd ed. (London: Routledge, 2001), 16–42.

5. Ralph Frasca, *Benjamin Franklin's Printing Network: Disseminating Virtue in Early America*, 1st ed. (Columbia: University of Missouri, 2006); Green and Stallybrass, *Benjamin Franklin*; Warner, *The Letters of the Republic*; David Waldstreicher, *Runaway America: Benjamin Franklin, Slavery, and the American Revolution* (New York: Hill and Wang, 2004).

6. See Lemay, *Life of Benjamin Franklin*, 1:320–23. Although volume 3, *Soldier, Scientist, and Politician* was published in 2008, the completion of the larger project stalled with Lemay's untimely passing later the same year.

7. Gordon S. Wood, *The Americanization of Benjamin Franklin* (London: Penguin, 2005); Alan Houston, *Benjamin Franklin and the Politics of Improvement* (New Haven, CT: Yale University Press, 2008).

8. Warner, *Letters of the Republic*, 74–75.

9. Ibid., 75; citing Benjamin Franklin's, *Autobiography*, in the Franklin volume of Library of America: *Benjamin Franklin: Writings; Autobiography, Poor Richard's Almanack, Bagatelles, Pamphlets, Essays & Letters*, ed. J. A. Leo Lemay (New York: Library of America, 1987), 1307.

10. Ibid., 76.

11. Ibid., 75.

12. For example, Warner cites the work of Harold Innis, Elizabeth Eisenstein, and Walter Ong as taking a "McLuhanite cast" that overly valorizes technological change. See also Marshall McLuhan and Quentin Fiore, *The Medium Is the Massage: An Inventory of Effects* (New York: Random House, 1967).

13. Warner, *The Letters of the Republic*, 34–43.

14. Ibid., xii.

15. Eric Slauter's recent analysis of the cultural origins of the Constitution demonstrates the power of this methodology toward a larger end. See Slauter, *The State as a Work of Art: The Cultural Origins of the Constitution* (Chicago: University of Chicago Press, 2009).

16. Lemay, *Life of Benjamin Franklin*,vol. 2, *Printer and Publisher, 1730–1747* (Philadelphia: University of Pennsylvania Press, 2006), 380–81.

17. Neil L. York, *Turning the World Upside Down* (Westport, CT: Praeger, 2003), 111–12. Both York and Wood cite this moment as key in shifting Franklin's allegiance away from being a subject of the British Empire. See Wood, *Americanization of Benjamin Franklin*, 91, 124, 141. Also see Lemay, *Life of Benjamin Franklin*,vol. 3, *Soldier, Scientist, and Politician, 1748–1757* (Philadelphia: University of Pennsylvania Press, 2008), 635–36.

18. See James N. Green, "English Books and Printing in the Age of Franklin," in *The Colonial Book in the Atlantic World*, vol. 1 of A History of the Book in America, ed. Hugh Armory and David D. Hall (Cambridge: Cambridge University Press; American Antiquarian Society, 2000), 248–98.

19. Frasca, *Benjamin Franklin's Printing Network*, 6–7.

20. Ibid., 66.

21. Sarah Knott, *Sensibility and the American Revolution* (Chapel Hill: University of North Carolina Press, 2009), 27–37.

22. Frasca, *Benjamin Franklin's Printing Network*, 196.

23. Ibid., 52.

24. A Philadelphia lawyer denigrated Franklin in *American Weekly Mercury*, 20 November 1740. Quoted in Bernard Bailyn and John B. Hench, *The Press & the American Revolution* (Boston: Northeastern University Press, 1981), 18, italics from Bailyn and Hench.

25. Frasca, *Benjamin Franklin's Printing Network*, 65–67.

26. Ibid., 123.

27. Prior to 1838, Franklin ordered from other London type foundries. Clarence William Miller, *Benjamin Franklin's Philadelphia Printing, 1728–1766: A Descriptive Bibliography*, Memoirs of the American Philosophical Society 102 (Philadelphia: American Philosophical Society, 1974), xxxiv.

28. Ibid., xxviv.

29. Miller demonstrates this observation in *Benjamin Franklin's Philadelphia Printing*, where he details the bibliographic information of Franklin's printing, including his type and paper choices.

30. See Philip Gaskell, *John Baskerville: A Bibliography* (Cambridge: Cambridge University Press, 1959) for a complete overview of Baskerville's editions.

31. Josiah Henry Benton, *John Baskerville, Type-Founder and Printer 1706–1775* (New York: Burt Franklin, 1968), 10–15.

32. Luther S. Livingston, *Franklin and His Press at Passy* (New York: Grolier, 1914), 176–77.

33. Ibid., 126 and 190–91.

34. Frasca, *Benjamin Franklin's Printing Network*, 177–78.

35. Waldstreicher, *Runaway America*, xiii.

36. Ibid., 23.

37. Ibid., 17.

38. Recent historiography of journalism has begun to take greater note of Franklin's printing networks and legacy. See David Paul Nord's "Benjamin Franklin and Journalism," in *A Companion to Benjamin Franklin*, ed. David Waldstreicher (Malden, MA: Wiley-Blackwell, 2011), 290–307, esp. 298. See also Lemay, *Life of Benjamin Franklin*, 1:455–56.

39. Green and Stallybrass, *Benjamin Franklin*.

40. Ibid., vii–viii.

41. Ibid., 6.

42. Paul E. Kerry, "Benjamin Franklin's Satiric Vein," in *The Cambridge Companion to Benjamin Franklin*, ed. Carla Mulford (Cambridge: Cambridge University Press, 2008), 37–49.

43. Green and Stallybrass, *Benjamin Franklin*.

44. Ibid., 7.

45. Ibid., 124.

46. Benjamin Franklin, *Benjamin Franklin: Autobiography, Poor Richard, and Later Writings* (New York: Library of America, 2005), 600–603.

47. Letter from Franklin to Baskerville, [1760], in *Papers* 9:260. William Bennett, *John Baskerville: The Birmingham Printer*, vol. 1, *His Press, Relations, and Friends* (Birmingham, UK: City of Birmingham School of Printing, 1937), 107.

48. Franklin purchased some of Baskerville's fine printed books and some of his type, but this did not replace Caslon as the typeface used in Franklin's printing network. See David Farrell, "John Baskerville," in *Encyclopedia of Library and Information Science*, ed. Allen Kent (New York: Marcell Decker, 1986), 40:11–22. See also Miller, *Benjamin Franklin's Philadelphia Printing* for an investigatioin of Franklin's type choices. Caslon's types remained popular throughout the nineteenth century. Early twentieth-century printers quipped "when in doubt, use Caslon." As such, popular concepts of the legibility of Caslon may extend beyond simple name recognition or prejudice. See Ellis Fulton, "Which Typefaces Are Most Useful?" *Inland Printer* 81 (April 1928): 101.

49. Preface to Franklin, *Poor Richard Improved (Way to Wealth),* 1758, quoted in Green and Stallybrass, *Benjamin Franklin,* 125–26.

50. Ibid., 126.

51. Ibid., 129–30.

52. Ibid., 133–45.

53. See Benjamin Franklin, *The Autobiography of Benjamin Franklin: A Genetic Text*, ed. J. A. Leo Lemay, and Paul M. Zall (Knoxville: University of Tennessee Press, 1979); Arch, "Benjamin Franklin's Autobiography."

54. Lemay, *The Life of Benjamin Franklin*, 3 vols. (Philadelphia: University of Pennsylvania Press, 2006–8).

55. Green and Stallybrass, *Benjamin Franklin*, 149–66.

56. See Ludmilla Jordanova on the importance of using images to understand the past and their neglect by historians in *History in Practice* (London: Hodder and Stoughton, 2006).

57. Green and Stallybrass, *Benjamin Franklin*, 151.

58. Lemay, *Life of Benjamin Franklin*, 1:320–23.

59. Ibid., 76.

Chapter Eight

Benjamin Franklin, Richard Price, and the Division of Sacred and Secular in the Age of Revolutions

Benjamin E. Park

The latter part of the 1780s found the esteemed philosophers Benjamin Franklin and Richard Price in ill health, succumbing to the physical infirmities that accompany old age, yet nonetheless still vibrant in their republican ideals that helped drive political change during the period. On 18 May 1787, Franklin wrote to Price that his "malady," though it "does not grow perceptibly worse," would likely remain until his death, which he imagined "cannot now be far distant."[1] However, though ill, Franklin continued participating in his many projects, including acting as president of the Pennsylvania Society for the Abolition of Slavery—a platform he felt crucial to America's future. In June, he wrote to Price concerning the society, including copies of its constitution and pamphlets, and asked permission to list Price as a corresponding member of the institution due to his having "long and successfully defended the rights of mankind," referring to Price's abolitionist efforts particularly but his radical republican views in general. "For in this business," Franklin continued, "the friends of humanity in every country are of one Nation and Religion."[2]

Price, who had spent the previous few months sea bathing to alleviate his ailments, was honored. Even if, due to geographical and health restrictions, he could not make many contributions to the society, he wished them well and sympathized with their cause. Then, reflecting on the overall impact of the American Revolution—which both he and Franklin devoutly supported—Price gleefully wrote of the "Spirit rising which must in time produce great effects" throughout the world: starting in America, it was destined to lead to "a State of Society more favourable to peace, virtue, Science, and liberty (and consequently to human happiness and dignity) than has ever yet been known, infinite good will be done." This "general fermentation . . . taking place thro' Europe" transcended national boundaries and local affinities, challenged despotism and dated traditions, and promised happiness to a world heretofore plagued with war, strife, and bondage.[3] Franklin likely agreed with the sentiment, similarly believing America's ascending importance on the international stage.

Taking a step back, owing to the two individuals' radically different backgrounds and overarching mind-sets, it seems remarkable that Franklin and Price agreed on so many political ideas. Franklin, often regarded as a secular humanist, saw in religion not much more than a social tool to maintain, appease, and at times even improve the populace; Price, a dissenting minister, based his politics on religious ideals that governed his overall worldview. Such dissimilarities are often dismissed merely by pointing out Franklin's pragmatism, as well as arguing that people of many different religious and philosophical backgrounds have worked together in similar causes. Such may very well be the case. Yet within this tension—first, a secular perspective completely devoid of supernatural purpose and, second, a theistic viewpoint tethered to a belief in divine intervention and intuition— reveals much about the heterogeneity of the Age of Revolutions, a period where formidable thinkers interpreted different promises for the future of Western democracy. These individuals elude traditional and simplistic classifications, highlight the heterodoxy of an intellectual movement often regarded as coherent, and offer glimpses into the major issues that would dominate political debates in the coming years.

Further, contradictions at the heart of both Price's and Franklin's politics reveal the tensions that would influence and shape America's democratic tradition. Most especially, they display the persistent paradox of sacred and secular elements that have pervaded conceptions of American identity. On the one hand, citizens and politicians constantly emphasized America breaking away from the previous blending of religion and government; this motivation demonstrates itself in proclaiming the separation of church and state, as well as grounding political discourse on Enlightenment reason rather than biblical revelation. On the other hand, Americans have long still held room for God within democracy, a providential strain that posits divine intervention and purpose for the nation. These competing principles cannot be easily—if at all—reconciled, yet each has played a continuing role in American conceptions of democracy from the beginnings of the republic to the present. Contrasting the political thought of Franklin and Price, then, serves to examine what these divergences mean and how elements from both sides shaped and influenced their conception of the world.

NATURAL PHILOSOPHY AND CONTRASTING WORLDVIEWS

Benjamin Franklin and Richard Price first met at organized intellectual gatherings in London during the late 1750s. Franklin had recently been enshrined as a leading thinker in Britain due to his work with electricity, and Price was heralded for his work on probability and editing the works of philosopher Thomas Bayle. Franklin was in London lobbying for colonial representation, soaking in the broad range of acquaintances and experiences it afforded him; Price lived only a short distance outside of the city and served as a dissenting clergyman. At that time both the Philadelphian printer and Newington Green minister understood themselves as safely within the boundaries of British loyalty.[4]

The clubs Price and Franklin attended are keys to understanding their overall worldviews. Though some of the groups appear primarily political, the discussions of those gatherings were far from limited to Whiggish policies. Indeed, patterned after London's Royal Society, the group touched on all philosophies: moral, natural, religious, and political.[5] This is important, for both Price and Franklin worked within an ideological framework that unified within the eclectic umbrella of "natural philosophy" aspects of varying intellectual disciplines. To be a "man of letters" meant being a Renaissance man possessing eclectic interests that included many subjects. To separate their different intellectual strains into distinct frameworks of understanding means introducing artificial boundaries never meant to exist in the first place; to distinguish moral philosophies from political views would be akin to bifurcating a message meant to be unified.

But intellectual bifurcating has dominated a large amount of scholarship on thinkers in the long eighteenth century, particularly individuals like Benjamin Franklin and Richard Price. Both thinkers began their careers musing on a broad range of philosophical subjects, writing important texts on moral philosophy that should be read as the foundations for their later thought. However, many historians interpret their later political writings as part of a different intellectual framework than their earlier moral writings. With Price, though he remained a minister, historians write as if he tabled many of his moral and religious focuses as part of a secular turn to radical republican politics; though cautioning against a complete "secularization" of his ideology, most modern-day scholars place Price's later political writings in a different paradigm than his early moral texts.[6] Price the theologian and moral philosopher was not the same man as Price the radical republican.

This interpretive inconsistency hints to the larger problem of categorizations during the Enlightenment. Earlier scholarship on eighteenth-century thought emphasized the secularism of the Enlightenment and posited the intellectual movement as taking place against traditional religion.[7] Though recent historiographical trends have emphasized how much these intellectual debates took place within a religious worldview,[8] there remains a desire to separate movements that were either sympathetic to or arguing against religious belief, contrasting a "radical Enlightenment" with an "Enlightenment contested."[9] Such a dualistic approach, however, while accurate in classifying certain historical figures, fails to account for enigmatic thinkers like Richard Price. Price understood his radical republicanism as stemming directly from his religious and moral beliefs. Interpreting his philosophical corpus as two unrelated efforts—religious belief on one hand and enlightened politics on the other—distorts the overall message he intended.

Things are even more complex with Franklin, but for different reasons. It is often noted how Franklin was "never very revealing of himself," always hesitant to give his full opinion, making him the toughest character to gauge among America's founders.[10] Many of his publications were written under pseudonyms—he utilized forty-two different signatures during his London time alone—meant not only to hide his true identity but also to offer diverging opinions from different, sometimes contrasting, points of view. While some of his earliest writings were more forthright, his later writings make him appear detached, reticent, and never completely committed.

Added to this difficulty is Franklin's outstanding success at creating a specific image of himself during his later life that continues to dominate interpretation two centuries later. Epitomized in his *Autobiography*, Franklin was exceptionally careful of how he was to be represented and understood once he became a national figure. He learned early on that, pragmatically, it was impractical to present views that might drive an ideological wedge between potential allies. This was especially the case when Franklin considered his earliest writings that, though in reality undergirded his entire natural philosophy, had the latent potential to draw scorn and disagreement. Learning his lesson, he described those earlier activities as an "erratum" in his memoirs and thereafter avoided thorny issues.[11] Most historians have succumbed to this image, and even noted historian Gordon Wood described Franklin's early statements as "sophomoric" as a way to dismiss them as inconsequential.[12] Yet such simplistic dismissal not only plays into Franklin's identity game but is also problematic due to his continued—if subtle—dependence on a materialistic ideology closer to humanism than orthodox Christianity.[13]

Indeed, both Price and Franklin were complex thinkers, and as such their complexity eludes simplistic categorization. Yet this difficulty is compounded by the fact that both individuals are grouped together within broader umbrellas like republican revolution and cosmopolitan reform. With these political links comes the desire to link many of the major figures of the period together into a cohesive whole meant to form the foundation for modernity.[14] Yet in many of these intellectual groupings, similarities are emphasized and divergences overlooked. Only when approaching enigmatic figures like Price and Franklin on their own terms, considering their larger corpus as a systematic whole, can their individual worldviews be better delineated and the vast heterogeneity of those associated with the Age of Revolutions be more fully understood and the complex legacy of early American democracy better comprehended.

MORAL AND RELIGIOUS UNDERPINNINGS

At the heart of their political divergences was profound disagreement in religious views. Price, though a Dissenter and staunch proponent for the separation between church and state, was a pious minister devout in his faith; Franklin, though he spoke different things to different people, carried a deep frustration with superstition and spiritually oriented mindsets. Price's science of politics stemmed from devotion to a Platonic sense of an a priori knowledge, divinely inspired human agency, and an assurance of future retribution in a millennial state—the very types of principles Franklin appeared apathetic toward. Though their differing outlooks perceivably placed them on similar political ground—they were, after all, in favor of the same revolutions—a closer analysis demonstrates different paths that led them to political agreement.

Though Benjamin Franklin identified himself as a "thorough Deist" early in his life, it was not until he moved to London in his early twenties that he was introduced to the varying strands of Deism and broader themes of philosophy.[15] In London, through both the print shop he was employed at as well as the reading circles he took part in, Franklin absorbed the learned society and culture, was introduced to the important intellectual topics of the day, and eventually published—albeit anonymously—his contribution to those debates.[16] It was here that he likely encountered thinkers like Thomas Hobbes and Bernard Mandeville, whose controversial outlook on the sociability of man had deep impact on his own worldview.[17] It was also here that Franklin began developing his own moral philosophy. Working for the printer Samuel Palmer, Franklin set type for an edition of William Wollaston's *The Religion of Nature Delineated*, a work that attempted to marry Christianity with natural religion by reconciling the idea of an intervening God and emerging philosophical principles.[18] Though the work was popular and was well received among many Deists of the period, Franklin felt it defective, and wrote an anonymous pamphlet in response that challenged moderate Deism and revealed his naturalistic outlook on humanity.

Titled *A Dissertation on Liberty and Necessity, Pleasure and Pain*, Franklin contested Wollaston on a number of points. First was Wollaston's insistence that there was a divinely decreed system of order that explained all aspects of nature and action. Such an outlook infringed upon agency and implied that humans "can have no such Thing as Liberty, Free-will or Power to do or refrain an Action." A deity could have no hand in the day-to-day actions of the world if humankind was to be truly free. Further, and more importantly, Franklin denounced the notion that individuals could be driven by spiritual impulses. It was impossible and incoherent for an immaterial spirit to be the source for thoughts, he reasoned, because all actions derived from physical sensations. There could only be one source for any thought or exertion: "uneasiness"—or, more succinctly, pain. "We are first mov'd by *Pain*," he wrote, "and the whole succeeding Course of our Lives is but one continu'd Series of Action with a View to be freed from it." When understood this way, "the natural Principle of *Self-Love* is the only and the irresistible Motive" for action. Religious sensibility could never serve as the foundation for natural philosophy because it wrongly depended on a supernatural source for knowledge. Franklin empirically believed that humankind was much more natural and crude than that—it was merely a "Machine set on work; this is Life."[19]

The pamphlet refused to shy away from the radical implications of these ideas. Hobbes and Mandeville had previously proposed similar proposals on the natural state of humankind and were decried as too naturalistic. Franklin expected a similar response and thus closed his anonymous work with a preemptive—and, characteristically, satiric and witty—strike that demonstrated the lengths his natural philosophy was willing to embrace:

> Whatever sooths our Pride, and tends to exalt our Species above the rest of the Creation, we are pleas'd with and easily believe, when ungrateful Truths shall be with the utmost Indignation rejected. 'What! bring ourselves down to an Equality with the Beasts of the Field! with the *meanest* part of Creation! 'Tis insufferable!' But, (to use a Piece of *common* Sense) our *Geese* are but *Geese* tho' we may think 'em *Swans*; and Truth will be Truth tho' it sometimes prove mortifying and distasteful.[20]

In a brief moment of candidness in his *Autobiography*, Franklin noted with glee that this pamphlet gained him introduction into Mandeville's own social club.[21]

Franklin later regretted publishing his controversial ideas. He came to learn that exposing his radical beliefs to more orthodox thinkers led to alienation and limited collaboration possibilities. He also grew to understand that revealed religion served an important communal function by encouraging individuals to live morally and treat others with respect. He embodied his own counsel given in *Poor Richard* to "let all men know thee, but no man know thee thoroughly."[22] Yet even if he ceased from proclaiming it, his naturalistic outlook continued to shape his personal philosophy. His Whiggish republicanism stemmed from his belief that all humans are to be considered equal because all are fellow "beasts" fleeing from the same pain and yearning for the same pleasure. Even during America's Constitutional Convention, he reminded his fellow Americans, "there are two Passions which have a powerful Influence in the Affairs of Men. These are *Ambition* and *Avarice*; the Love of Power, and the Love of Money."[23] Though subtle, this impulse undergirded his political beliefs, as his naturalistic outlook placed all human beings on the same social standing and requiring the same liberty.[24]

Richard Price, on the other hand, though writing nearly three decades after Franklin's *Dissertation*, took the very position Franklin tried to disprove. Published in 1858, his *Review of the Principal Questions and Difficulties in Morals* addressed many of the same questions as Franklin, with drastically different conclusions. Deeply influenced by the resurgent idealist tradition, Price's rejection of the extremes of Lockean empiricism led him to not only object to Hobbes and Mandeville but moderate Scottish ministers like Francis Hutcheson. Price objected to Hutcheson's placement of moral sense among the passions due to the possible subjectivity of such a classification. Rather, Price argued for a moral sense that was objective, everlasting, dependable, and capable of being the standard for moral philosophy. Ideas and impulses stemmed not from "sensation and reflection" but from a "higher original" that is placed outside human experience and passions. By differentiating an individual's "sense," which Price described as the ability to deduce particulars from provided universals, from "knowledge" (or "understanding"), which he described as ideas placed in the human mind, Price offered a divinely appointed moral tool that transcended the limits of human reasoning and experience.[25]

Price's attempt to provide a rationalist theory for objective truths originated from the influence of thinkers like Anglican Bishop Joseph Butler. From Butler he learned a useful framework in which to present human moral sense in a credible way beyond the reach of skepticism.[26] But it also depended on a revival of the dualistic Platonism of Ralph Cudworth and other Cambridge Platonists that emphasized spiritual truths, revelatory knowledge, and intuitive impressions.[27] He credited "our Maker" for imprinting on the human mind ideas of right and wrong, providing a mental structure based on virtue through which to then deduce particular truths. Human sociality was centered on intrinsic knowledge, and the abstract notions of truth were to be the basis for human societies.[28] Indeed, Price's early texts demonstrated his deep commitment to a theistic and providential philosophy of universal truths.

Price continued these themes in his central theological work *Four Dissertations*, reinforcing his belief in a providential society as the basis for human improvement. "The doctrine of Providence," he wrote, "is plainly of the highest importance" when considering human society. Life and government merely provided schools of virtue—settings for God to provide opportunities to accept or reject divine truths. Further, all major events that took place, whether on a local, national, or international level, stemmed from a divine will that was both omniscient and omnipresent in human actions. "The Deity cannot be an indifferent spectator of the series of events," Price reasoned, "in that world to which he has been given." He scoffed at the belief in a God who took no active hand in the world, noting that belief in a God without "providence" was an outright "contradiction."[29] It was only God that could "bringeth down one nation, and that exalteth another."[30] Price may have been a Unitarian Dissenter, but his worldview was not only tinged by but also dependent upon a staunch providentialist outlook.

Where Franklin saw a restriction of agency, Price saw the only framework in which agency could fully blossom. "Where can be the difficulty of believing an invisible hand, an universal and ever-attentive Providence, which guides all things agreeably to perfect rectitude and wisdom," he queried, and "at the same time that the general laws of the world are left unviolated, and the liberty of moral agents is preserved?"[31] Only in a providential setting, under the direction of God's will, could humankind make correct choices and fulfill their destinies. Where faith faltered and divinity was ignored, darkness and tyranny reigned. Reliance on human wisdom, reason, and deductive reasoning could only lead to slavery. Thus, the revolutions of the late eighteenth century were part and parcel with God's plan, dependent on revelatory inspiration, and served the purpose of spreading the truth of Christianity, Price determined. All human beings were equal because everyone was taking part in the same deific test and progressing to the same religious goal. Such moral and religious underpinnings not only provided the foundation for Price's political thought, but also filled the intermediary particulars and endgame of his ideological vision.

CITIZENS OF THE WORLD—BUT WHAT WORLD?

When such differences in the moral and religious views of Benjamin Franklin and Richard Price are juxtaposed with their seemingly similar political positions, the temptation to separate and classify the different aspects of their ideologies grows. Even the two individuals' friendship and support of each other's work seems to point to a compartmentalization of their political views from moral beliefs. Yet mistaking pragmatism for agreement only simplifies their philosophies and succumbs to Franklin's self-perpetuated caricature. Both Price and Franklin were significant thinkers due to their political imaginations, and any simplification of those imaginations through bifurcation distorts their overall visions. At the heart of their philosophies were imagined communities that provided equal laws and possibilities for individuals, but differences between those dreamed societies reveal how their dissimilar religious and moral foundations resulted in diverging political views.

Theorist Benedict Anderson notes how the eighteenth century gave rise to "imagined political communities" as the first modern nations were developed.[32] A large part of this change came with the realization that governments were manmade institutions. Both Price and Franklin were vocal proponents of this position, noting the distinctly human responsibility of creating civil governments.[33] In the place of what was previously contrived as divinely oriented perimeters, political thinkers began to imagine elastic boundaries with nations "conceived as a deep, horizontal comradeship."[34] These new boundaries were based on what were considered natural laws and moral foundations. Nation-making, then, was an endeavor that revealed an individual's deeper worldview, particularly an understanding of humanity. Previous conceptions of what nations and empires entailed were now questioned, and a host of pluralistic interpretations of law and civilization were presented as possible answers.[35]

Benjamin Franklin epitomized what Anderson defines as the "rationalist secularism" that pervaded the Enlightenment and introduced "the dusk of religious modes of thought."[36] Building on his moral theory that humankind was in constant pursuit of pleasure and avoidance of pain, Franklin imagined a government that would provide natural rights and encourage upward mobility, while still checking self-interestedness in favor of the whole population. Like many others of the period, he sought a system that provided justice and rewards in the present life. His cosmopolitanism posited that all human beings, no matter in what nation, deserved a government that focused on the present rather than the murky hereafter; rights were due to all nations and nationalities because liberty in this world was all that could be assured. The imagined political "world" Franklin embraced was firmly planted in temporary justice, immediate liberty, and terrestrial pleasures.

Although Franklin's democratic revolution aimed to bring sufficient happiness and recompense to mankind in their current, temporal existence, Price's was based on a diverging mental structure. To Price, the duty of civil government was to provide sufficient liberty for mankind to exercise the agency necessary in preparation for a future state. As rational as his political rhetoric was, it was still saturated with millennial fervor. "It is impossible that irregularities so inconsistent with our ideas of distributive justice should be suffered to pass without redress under the divine government," he preached in a sermon in 1781. "Since the present world is not the seat of adequate retribution, it must be reserved for another, and a future state appears to be as certain as the existence of a wise and righteous Deity."[37] Mortal existence and temporal governments were probationary, preparing individuals for the real moment of retribution. While civilization had progressed—and would continue to progress—throughout countless generations toward more liberties and further light, completion could only be accomplished through the "operations of Providence" in the final days, a moment government could only anticipate and emulate.[38] Franklin was apathetic to such a future; Price rested his entire philosophical system upon it.

Price insisted on a cosmopolitan society that transcended national borders because, in the end, there was only one political structure that one could be solely dedicated to: the Kingdom of God as promised in the Bible. He wrote that Christianity "makes us the subjects of a kingdom that is not of this world, and requires us to elevate our minds above temporal emoluments and to look forwards to a state beyond the grave where a government of perfect virtue will be erected under that Messiah."[39] In his famous *Discourse on the Love of our Country*—the pamphlet famous for inspiring Edmund Burke's *Reflections on the French Revolution* and igniting the republican pamphlet wars of the early 1790s—Price urged his audience to temper their national exceptionalism. "We should love [our nation] ardently but not exclusively," he argued, and that though individuals must keep allegiance to our local government, "at the same time we ought to consider ourselves as citizens of the world," because Christian loyalty trumped national allegiance.[40] Progress was made through Christian enlightenment, not through a secular political order. The Kingdom of God—the "heavenly Jerusalem"—was the preeminent community to be a citizen of. National governments were merely designed to provide a free environment for it to develop in. Price's ideology challenges both the common caricature of the Enlightenment as purely secularist and the recent caricature of a counter-Enlightenment that opposed secular provisions. Price's political and religious mindsets intermingled in a way that refutes simplistic categorization and urges a much more nuanced interpretation.

That both Price and Franklin urged for the complete separation between church and state masks their drastically different interpretations of how religion related to democracy. For Franklin, religion was, at its best, a societal safeguard that helped protect a nation against anarchy and selfishness; for Price, the nation was a safeguard to provide religion a chance for preparation for the coming millennium. Franklin's focus was on providing humankind the chance to achieve temporal success and standard principles of liberty; Price's goal was a Christian society free to practice and build virtue while emphasizing allegiance to a kingdom that extended beyond and above a merely temporal government. The Philadelphian sage's imagined community was intrinsically earth-centric; the English minister's was otherworldly.

Though both of their politics could be defined as "cosmopolitan," their cosmopolitanisms implied varying meanings, especially when considering what imagined community they claimed allegiance to. Their diverging views brought different outlooks on justice and expectations. Franklin's political outlook—and indeed, his personal religious views—emphasized temporal happiness and immediate justice. The purpose of this life, he reasoned, was to gain enjoyment in this world without focusing on the world to come.

Price's political ideology transformed this world into a pretext for the next. Government enabled human beings to prepare for divine retribution and government. Further, Franklin's loyalty was to a common bond of fallible human beings trying to achieve as much success and joy as possible, whereas Price's allegiance was to divine truths and Christ's celestial order. That both of their intellectual foundations led them to support a common cause was a pragmatic consequence, not a predetermined conclusion, yet both strands of thought continued in American political discourse.

DEFINING DEMOCRACY

Most of the difficulty in differentiating the political ideologies of thinkers like Price and Franklin is rooted in the fact that both employed much of the same political language.[41] Republican dialogue was so common in eighteenth-century discourse and so central to the Age of Revolution that popular phrases became political tropes that covered a wide range of ideals and even wider range of ideologies. Yet if these rhetorically charged words served to reveal similarities and common themes, they just as often worked to conceal differences.

Historian Daniel Rodgers has demonstrated how "political words" were used as "tools" as often as they were "signs of hidden intellectual systems."[42] Popular words of the age were not always invoked because they were consistent as much as they were effective. Merely because they became part of the public discourse does not mean they always had a shared meaning. Intellectual paradigms did not merge as easily as their languages seemed to imply. This is especially the case with Price and Franklin, whose shared political language feigns ideological agreement but in reality signifies a pragmatic alliance and willingness to take part in a collaborative community of discourse that emphasized universal rights and individual liberties.[43] To present a united front of opposition against outmoded governmental systems, cosmopolitan thinkers disguised disunity behind a shared language. Once this shared language is dissected, however, underlying tensions are revealed.

Most importantly, at the heart of the differences between Price and Franklin are the central complexities of defining democracy in the Western tradition. Both individuals turned to "democracy" as the solution for government, but their conceptions of democracy were birthed out of diverging intellectual tensions and depended on competing worldviews. Franklin's humanism was a product of skeptical thought, and he urged for a deliberate democracy that emphasized the limits of knowledge and the necessity of dialogue. Price's foundationalism grew from a Platonic understanding of universal truths and he emphasized an idealist possibility of absolute knowledge. Together they represent two of the most dominant strains of political thought in the American democratic tradition.

As Franklin grew older, he became more aware of his own intellectual fallibility. To his estranged son William he wrote that "our opinions are not in our power," implying that personal insights—even if obtained through perceived inspiration—put one at risk of foregoing alternative options. Rather, personal ideas "are form'd and govern'd much by Circumstances that are often as inexplicable as they are irresistible."[44] For Franklin, human knowledge is largely a product of culture, and most failings are a result of the refusal to admit as much. "I imagine a Man must have a good deal of Vanity who believes, and a good deal of Boldness who affirms, that all the doctrines he holds, are true, and all he rejects, are false," he wrote. "If I am wrong, I should not be displeas'd that another is right. If I am in the Right, 'tis my Happiness; and I should rather pity than blame him who is unfortunately in the wrong."[45] Such an antifoundationalist outlook was especially applicable in politics. Progress came from exposure, liberality, compromise, and an almost roguish attitude of constantly questioning the status quo.

Franklin's appeal for a deliberate democracy was nowhere more apparent than his participation in America's Constitutional Convention. Frustrated with the lack of compromise during the first month of debating, he announced their "small Progress" as "melancholy Proof of the Imperfection of the Human Understanding."[46] A few months later he mused, "[T]he older I grow the more apt I am to doubt my own Judgment, and to pay more respect to the Judgment of others." He welcomed many of the compromises in the constitution, positing that if participants were to cling to their ideas of government, then disagreement and discord would dominate. Franklin was, for the sake of democracy, willing to "sacrifice" his private opinions "to the Public Good."[47] The following summer, he compared an effective government to "a game of chess," reasoning that compromise—not merely principles—was the acme of democracy, as "ideas so different" and "prejudices so strong" battled against each other until a better "understanding" was achieved.[48] Thus with Franklin can be found the early roots of America's pragmatic philosophy, a political outlook for the skeptic that believed progress was a result of negotiation and experience rather than absolute truths. Indeed, the seeds of American pragmatism—which came to dominate American democratic discourse in the twentieth century—can be found in Benjamin Franklin's humanist political thought.

Richard Price, on the other hand, represented a competing tradition of democratic thought. While Franklin drew from his Puritan roots to craft an outlook of the depravity of man and the limited nature of human goodness, Price trumpeted an idealist tradition that placed greater authority on absolute truths, the potential of human understanding, and, most importantly, the divinely sanctioned value of human life.[49] His emphasis on the value of humankind centered on his belief that man was created in the image of God and worthy of temporal and eternal glory. Where Franklin's notion of government depended on humanity as depraved creatures, Price was insistent that there was a spark of holiness within the human race that divinized civilization. There was something sacred to human existence and human freedoms that validated humanity's value.

Further elements of this theistic belief were foundational to Price's political thought. Though still accepting the limits of human reason, Price defended the idea of universal principles and the importance of not yielding to false notions. In his earliest work, he painstakingly differentiated between an "understanding," which depended on universal truths, and a "sensation" (or "senses"), which was the mind trying to understand those truths. "It appears that the objects, employment, offices, and very notion of sense and understanding are, in all respects, different," he wrote. "The one conversant only about *particulars*; the other about *universals*: The one being incapable of determining any thing about truth or real existence; and the other employed entirely about this."[50] A democracy's success depended upon its leaders' ability to acquire this understanding through virtuous living and spiritual attunement.

Price was, of course, quick to explain that this inspiration could only provide "abstract ideas" and not concrete directions—few individuals were as wary of established religious voices making authoritative government claims as Price and his dissenting colleagues—but his notion on absolute truths and his optimism for human understanding played a major role in his political thought.[51] "Reason, as well as tradition and revelation," he wrote in 1785, "lead us to expect that a more improved and happy state of human affairs will take place before the consummation of all things."[52] Democracy was meant to give power to the people, but the framework in which that power was administered was both a product of and dependent upon both universal truths and a Platonic sense of understanding, and human progress was only achieved through devotion to absolute ideals.

Ironically, Price's foundationalism and theistic politics took root in Franklin's America more than his native England, and Franklin's skeptical pragmatism was soon alienated from the nation he helped establish. As the title of "American citizen" became increasingly synonymous with the label "believing Christian," especially at the popular level, universal truths and absolute principles dominated American political rhetoric. If Price's theistic undertones were subtle, the inheritors of the American Revolution were anything but. For much of the antebellum period, the skeptical philosophy of Franklin was deemed too dangerous for the pronouncedly Christian nation increasingly dominated by an Evangelical culture.

Yet the rising American democratic tradition was of a distinctly different tone than even Price envisioned. It was much more exclusive and uninterested in universal relations. It was much more dependent upon the Christian tradition rather than Platonic knowledge. Most importantly, though it claimed universal truths, its focus became increasingly parochial. With the declining support for the French Revolution came the rise of nationalism. Americans, once optimistic that their revolution was the beginning of a worldwide republican movement, became convinced that their nation was the last safe haven of pure democracy grounded in the boundaries of Christianity. The universal view of Franklin and Price gave way to the limited nationalism of American exceptionalism. That both Franklin and Price passed away before this intellectual shift spared them seeing their universal visions crumble. A revival of the democratic tradition of cosmopolitan sympathies, idealist perceptions of truth, and Platonic emphasis on universal brotherhood would not occur until Ralph Waldo Emerson and the Transcendentalist movement in the 1840s.

CONCLUSION

The cosmopolitan political movement during the Age of Revolutions was an important moment in the development of modern political thought, yet it is problematic to simplify the individuals within that movement as a single class of thinkers. The idea of new nations, the creation of new governments, and the hope for the spread of universal republicanism was a liberating ideal that spawned a myriad of responses. However, that very fact highlights the problem of trying to forcibly unify the ideologies of those involved. Benjamin Franklin and Richard Price were not strict intellectual bedfellows. It is important to understand the differences among seemingly similar thinkers, shifting the emphasis more on adaptability than commonality, or on the malleability rather than the outright agreement in intellectual movements. Such an interpretive shift promises not only to result in a better understanding of each individual figure, but also to help reconstruct the heterodox nature and varied expressions during an era of revolution and revolt.

Most importantly, the disagreements within this complex movement reveal many of the same tensions that came to dominate American political thought. The secular humanism of Franklin and the theist foundationalism of Price offered two models for politically understanding human nature and human government that are not easily reconcilable yet were equally influential in the development of American democracy. On the one hand, there is the skeptical strain that emphasized social contract and a depraved humanity; on the other is political reform based on the God-given nature of the human soul and the epistemological attachment to the divine. This paradox is still seen in the nation's emphasis on a separation between church and state while at the same time trumpeting its position as a Christian nation. Even if Franklin and

Price never debated the differences between their democratic worldviews, the tensions that would have highlighted their debate would eventually come to dominate America's democratic tradition.

NOTES

1. Franklin to Richard Price, 18 May 1787, in *Papers: Digital Edition.*
2. Franklin to Price, 9 June 1787, in *Papers: Digital Edition.*
3. Price to Franklin, 26 September 1787, in *Papers: Digital Edition.*
4. For Franklin's love of London during the period, see Gordon S. Wood, *The Americanization of Benjamin Franklin* (New York: Penguin, 2004), 84–88. For an overview of Price's life, see D. O. Thomas, *The Honest Mind: The Thought and Work of Richard Price* (New York: Oxford University Press, 1977).
5. For an overview of these meetings, see Verner W. Crane, "The Club of Honest Whigs: Friends of Science and Liberty," *William and Mary Quarterly*, 3rd ser., 23, no. 2 (1966): 210–33. For Franklin's infatuation with these clubs, see Wood, *Americanization of Benjamin Franklin*, 61–104.
6. See, for example, James E. Bradley, *Popular Politics and the American Revolution in England* (Macon, GA: Mercer University Press, 1986); Michael Henry Scrivener, *The Cosmopolitan Ideal in the Age of Revolution and Reaction, 1776–1832* (London: Pickering & Chatto, 2007), 85–86.
7. For a secular emphasis on the Enlightenment, the standard is Peter Gay's two-volume *The Enlightenment: An Interpretation*, rev. ed. (New York: W. W. Norton, 1995); a recent recapitulation is Louis Dupre, *The Enlightenment and the Intellectual Foundations of Modern Culture* (New Haven, CT: Yale University Press, 2005).
8. See David Sorkin, *The Religious Enlightenment: Protestants, Jews, and Catholics from London to Vienna* (Princeton, NJ: Princeton University Press, 2008); Jonathan Sheehan, "Enlightenment, Religion, and the Enigma of Secularization: A Review Essay," *American Historical Review* 108, no. 4 (October 2003): 1061–80.
9. Jonathan Israel, *Enlightenment Contested: Philosophy, Modernity, and the Emancipation of Man 1670–1752* (New York: Oxford University Press, 2006); see also his *Radical Enlightenment: Philosophy and the Making of Modernity* (New York: Oxford University Press, 2001).
10. Wood, *Americanization of Benjamin Franklin*, 13.
11. *Autobiography*, 96.
12. Ibid., 29.
13. See especially Joyce Chaplin, *Benjamin Franklin's Political Arithmetic: A Materialist View of Humanity* (Washington, DC: Smithsonian Libraries, 2008).
14. Most especially, see Thomas J. Schlereth, *The Cosmopolitan Ideal in Enlightenment Thought: Its Form and Function in the Ideas of Franklin*, Hume, and Voltaire, 1694–1790 (Notre Dame, IN: University of Notre Dame Press, 1977); Jack Fruchtman, Jr., *Atlantic Cousins: Benjamin Franklin and His Visionary Friends* (New York: Basic Books, 2007); Margaret C. Jacob, *Strangers Nowhere in the World: The Rise of Cosmopolitanism in Early Modern Europe* (Philadelphia: University of Pennsylvania Press, 2006); David M. Fitzsimons, "Thomas Paine's New World Order: Idealistic Internationalism in the Ideology of Early American Foreign Relations," *Diplomatic History* 19 (1995): 569–82.
15. *Autobiography*, 71, 113–14.
16. For an overview of Franklin's stay in London, see Julie Flavell, *When London Was Capital of America* (New Haven, CT: Yale University Press, 2010).
17. See *Autobiography*, 96–97.
18. William Wollaston, *The Religion of Nature Delineated* (London: Sam. Palmer, 1724).
19. [Benjamin Franklin], *A Dissertation on Liberty and Necessity, Pleasure and Pain* (London: Sam. Palmer, 1724), 10, 15, 17.
20. Ibid, 32, emphasis in original.

21. See Chaplin, *First Scientific American*, 29.

22. Franklin, "Poor Richard," 1743, in *Papers* 2:370.

23. Franklin to the Constitutional Convention, 2 June 1787, in *Papers: Digital Edition*.

24. For an overview of Franklin's pessimistic view of human nature, see Ronald A. Bosco, "'He That Best Understands the World, Least Likes It': The Dark Side of Benjamin Franklin," *Pennsylvania Magazine of History and Biography* 111 (October 1987): 525–54.

25. Richard Price, *A Review of the Principal Questions and Difficulties in Morals . . .* (London: A. Millar, 1758), 15–41 (quotes from 18, 29).

26. See John Stephens, "Conscience and the Epistemology of Morals: Richard Price's Debt to Joseph Butler," *Enlightenment and Dissent* 19 (2000): 133–46.

27. See Louise Hickman, "Godliness and Godlikeness: Cambridge Platonism in Richard Price's Religious Rationalism," *Enlightenment and Dissent* 24 (2008): 1–23; Martha K. Zebrowski, "We May Venture to Say, That the Number of Platonic Readers Is Considerable: Richard Price, Joseph Priestley, and the Platonic Strain in Eighteenth-Century British Thought," *Enlightenment and Dissent* 19 (2000): 193–213.

28. Price, *Review of the Principal Questions*, 100.

29. Price, *Four Dissertations*, 4–6.

30. Richard Price, *Britain's Happiness*, in *Price: Political Writings*, ed. D. O. Thomas (Cambridge: Cambridge University Press, 2009), 7–8.

31. Richard Price, *Four Dissertations*, 15.

32. Benedict Anderson, *Imagined Communities: Reflections on the Origins and Spread of Nationalism*, rev. ed. (New York: Verso, 1991), 6, 11–12.

33. See Richard Price, *Two Tracts*, in *Price: Political Writings*, 15; Franklin to Count Castiglione, 14 October 1787, in *Papers: Digital Edition*.

34. Anderson, *Imagined Communities*, 7.

35. For nation- and empire-building during this period, see Jack P. Greene, "The Alienation of Benjamin Franklin, British American," in *Understanding the American Revolution* (Charlottesville: University of Virginia Press, 1995); Eliga Gould, *The Persistence of Empire: British Political Culture in the Age of American Revolution* (Chapel Hill: University of North Carolina Press, 2000). See also Neil L. York, *Turning the World Upside Down: The War of American Independence and the Problem of Empire* (Westport, CT: Praeger, 2003).

36. Ibid., 11.

37. Richard Price, *A Discourse Addressed to a Congregation at Hackney*, in *Price: Political Writings*, 104.

38. Richard Price, *The Evidence for a Future Period of Improvement in the State of Mankind*, in *Price: Political Writings*, 163.

39. Richard Price, *Observations on the Importance of the American Revolution and the Means of Making it a benefit to the World*, in *Price: Political Writings*, 133.

40. Richard Price, *A Discourse on the Love of our Country*, in *Price: Political Writings*, 181.

41. Franklin, of course, expressed his political ideas in a range of genres, especially satire. See Paul E. Kerry, "Franklin's Satiric Vein," in *The Cambridge Companion to Benjamin Franklin*, ed. Carla Mulford (Cambridge: Cambridge University Press, 2008), 37–49.

42. See Daniel T. Rodgers, *Contested Truths: Keywords in American Politics since Independence* (New York: Basic Books, 1987), 4–10 (quote on p. 10).

43. For the literary elements of cosmopolitanism, see Sophia Rosenfeld, "Citizens of Nowhere in Particular: Cosmopolitanism, Writing, and Political Engagement in Eighteenth-Century Europe," *National Identities* 4 (2002): 25–43.

44. Franklin to William Franklin, 16 August 1784, in *Papers: Digital Edition*.

45. Franklin to Josiah and Abiah Franklin, 13 April 1738, in *Papers* 2:203.

46. Franklin, Speech to the Constitutional Convention, 28 June 1787, in *Papers: Digital Edition*. That this speech came in a motion to hold prayers in the Convention is an ideal example of Franklin's pragmatic religiosity: he did not himself believe that prayer would initiate divine inspiration, as some have interpreted, but realized that the sentiment of prayer would remind believers of the limits to their knowledge.

47. Franklin, Speech to the Constitutional Convention, 17 September 1787, in *Papers: Digital Edition.*

48. Benjamin Franklin to Pierre–Samuel du Pont de Nemours, 9 June 1788, in *Papers: Digital Edition.*

49. For Franklin's Congregationalist background, see William Pencak, "Benjamin Franklin's Autobiography, Cotton Mather, and a Puritan God," *Pennsylvania History* 53 (1986): 1–25.

50. Richard Price, *Review of the Principal Questions*, 25; emphasis in original.

51. Ibid., 42.

52. Price, *Observations on the Importance of the American Revolution*, in *Price: Political Writings*, 118.

Chapter Nine

Ben Franklin and Socrates

Lorraine Smith Pangle

Ben Franklin and Socrates were, in most respects, worlds apart. Socrates lived an uncompromisingly theoretical life, a life of endless questioning and apparent endless perplexity, a life of ten-thousand-fold poverty, as a gadfly on the fringes of society. Franklin lived a life of astonishing and versatile practicality, founding clubs and fire companies and newspapers, inventing stoves and lightning rods, moving in the highest circles of colonial, British, and Parisian society, and doing as much as anyone and more than anyone but Washington to pull America through the Revolutionary War. Socrates was deeply respectful of ancient republican life: he was in many ways an admirer of the austere, pious, aristocratic republic of Sparta with its scorn for money making, and often critical of the commercial, egalitarian, innovative spirit of Athens. Franklin could not have been more in sympathy with that spirit, as he poured his energies into spreading democracy, advancing religious freedom, championing economic growth, and instilling in his fellow citizens an enduring and sometimes intemperate love of progress.

Nonetheless, between these two men there run important threads of kinship, threads that actually go quite deep. Franklin read Xenophon's *Memorabilia* as a youth and was charmed by the portrait of Socrates he found there. As he explains in the *Autobiography*, he realized that the contentious mode of discourse that he had picked up from books of polemical theology was not winning him any friends or persuading many opponents. So he tried imitating Socrates and replacing his aggressive refutations and positive assertions with a modest, questioning approach. Like Xenophon's Socrates, he saw that in this way he could influence his companions to become more sober, moderate, and useful members of their community. But he admits that this new mode of discourse also brought advantages of a different kind: "I . . . grew very artful and expert in drawing People even of superior Knowledge into

Concessions the Consequences of which they did not foresee, entangling
them in Difficulties out of which they could not extricate themselves, and so
obtaining Victories that neither my self nor my Cause always deserved."[1]
Over time Franklin stopped laying traps for people and kept "only the Habit
of expressing myself in Terms of modest Diffidence," a habit that he immod-
estly reports won him many friendships and enormous influence.[2]

Franklin also shared with Socrates a wry wit and a love of concealment.
Both knew their own intellectual superiority to virtually everyone around
them and found in irony a useful tool for deflecting envy. Both also had a
remarkable capacity to rise above the fray, to keep emotionally detached
from the burning contests for honor and power that raged around them. They
even had a rare ability to step back and regard themselves with detachment.
And they found an ironic, self-concealing style of discourse useful for a
further reason: they were both deeply skeptical of the prevailing religious
orthodoxies of their day, and by avoiding proclaiming their own beliefs and
confining themselves instead to raising questions, they could avoid making
enemies.

However, if we follow the indications of Plato and Xenophon as to the
meaning of Socratic dialectic, we find that this important difference remains:
Franklin saw nothing deeply puzzling in justice and the other virtues Socrates was forever asking about; it never occurred to him that wisdom was to be
gained by listening carefully to and pondering the self-contradictions within
ordinary moral opinion. But is it possible that Franklin saw almost instinc-
tively the deeper lessons that Socrates labored to discover? There are hints, at
least, that he did.

One hint lies in Franklin's critical stance toward ordinary views of moral
responsibility. Already as a very young man he assailed the Christian notion
of free will, and for a time he entertained the hedonistic explanation of
human motivation that Socrates floats in the *Protagoras*. Soon Franklin realized that he had gone much too far in denying any significant difference
between virtue and vice, but his conclusion here, too, has a Socratic ring.
Virtue is not good because God commands it, he now saw, but is commanded
because it is good for us. (Whether it is in fact commanded by God or only
by men purporting to speak for God, Franklin does not quite say.[3]) He came
to see virtue as the essential foundation if not the substance of happiness,
which implies that all vice is folly. As he declares, echoing Socrates, "Wisdom and Vertue are the same thing."[4]

But what does Socrates mean by this counterintuitive claim that virtue is
wisdom? He expresses it in cryptic comments and often outrageous assertions throughout the dialogues, but the sober core of his argument is this:
Socrates prompts us to ponder the distinction we all make between what is
pleasant, what is good or beneficial, and what is noble or right or moral. He
observes that everyone is fairly clear about the distinction between the pleas-

ant and the good. We often disagree on how great a good pleasure is, but no one would deny that pleasure is as such a good thing. We also agree that things can be good without being pleasant, and many particular pleasant things can be so destructive that they are on balance bad. That is to say, the pleasant is clearly one part, and a qualified part, of the good. With the good and the noble, however, there is no such clear agreement as to how they fit together. Instead, we tend to see noble action as in one sense the greatest good, the thing in life most to be sought, and in another sense we see that same noble action as a sacrifice of what is good. For example, we say of the soldier who has died in battle for a just cause that he has made the ultimate sacrifice. But has he really suffered something terrible, like one who dies in a pointless accident? To the contrary, we tend to think that it is among the very best things to have such a soul and to do such deeds. In Plato's *Gorgias*, Socrates shows how much common opinion is of two minds about how the good and the noble fit together. People think with half of their minds that being noble is foolish because it is bad for oneself: the good and the noble seem simply opposed. But people think with the other half of their minds that it is really a splendid and attractive thing to be so noble.

Socrates escapes the self-contradiction he finds all his interlocutors mired in with one simple thought, a thought he carries so far that it changes his whole being and way of seeing everything: he refuses to allow any daylight ever to come between the noble and the good. If a thing is noble it is good, good all around, and that means it must be good above all for the soul of the one who does it. Virtue is human excellence, and excellence is altogether good to have, much better to have in one's soul than in one's body. Seen in this way, an act of courage or generosity or kindness is by no means a bad thing that needs a reward, so that without it the act is a pure loss, like prospecting for gold and coming up empty-handed. Rather, it is precisely the expression of a healthy, flourishing soul that is all that it was meant to be. It follows that anyone who understands virtue for what it is will want it as truly as we want good food and sound sleep, and he will recognize vice as the greatest of evils for himself. The failure to pursue virtue can only result from ignorance or confusion about what matters most, and this is a terrible condition of the soul, far worse than the worst cancer in the body. The proper remedy for that ignorance and confusion, Socrates argues, is not to pile evil upon evil by inflicting further suffering upon the man with the sick soul, but to attempt to cure him by teaching him the true nature of his condition and the true character of virtue. In sum, true virtue and its exercise are invariably good, true virtue rests on knowledge and vice on ignorance, and retributive punishment and the anger that demands it are both irrational.

Now if all of this sounds a little strange, there is an American version of the same thought that should seem quite familiar: the thought that honesty is the best policy, or that all virtue is really enlightened self-interest. Franklin tells the story about how he learned this lesson as a boy. One of his first public-spirited projects was to lead his friends in building a wharf on a muddy bank where they used to fish. Unfortunately, they constructed their wharf with stones stolen from a nearby construction site. The next day the builders missed the stones, inquiries were made, and the fathers were called in. Franklin reports that "several of us were corrected by our Fathers; and tho' I pleaded the Usefulness of the Work, mine convinc'd me that nothing was useful which was not honest."[5] It is not useful to get oneself a wharf and also come to be suspected as a shifty troublemaker by all the neighbors whose goodwill one needs. It is not useful to gain a narrow, short-term benefit and damage the social fabric of trust that everyone's happiness depends on.

This ethos of enlightened self-interest, developed by no one more than by Franklin, was so influential that by the 1830s Alexis de Tocqueville would portray it as the ethos of America itself. "In the United States it is almost never said that virtue is beautiful. They maintain that it is useful and they prove it every day. American moralists do not claim that one must sacrifice oneself to those like oneself because it is great to do it; but they say boldly that such sacrifices are as necessary to the one who imposes them on himself as to the one who profits from them."[6] Franklin not only regarded the practice of virtue as essential to happiness, but he seems to have drawn the Socratic corollary that anger is irrational. "A Man in a Passion rides a mad Horse," he warns, and "Anger is never without a Reason, but seldom with a good One."[7] Franklin never explicitly makes the Socratic argument against retribution, but he does show a remarkable freedom from both anger and feelings of guilt. His term in the *Autobiography* for his own misdeeds is errata, or printing errors.

Thus it seems possible that without the endless questioning and self-examination that demanded so much of Socrates's time and energy, Franklin was a Socratic almost by nature. Socrates says to Callicles in the *Gorgias* that unless Callicles refutes him, he is doomed to live his whole life in confusion and internal dissonance. Socrates implies that in this regard we are all Callicles, and that the life that is whole and wholly worth living requires hard self-examination, hard schooling to face the truth, and unrelenting self-control so as not to slip into tempting self-delusions. But Franklin's life suggests the possibility that this is not necessarily the case. Or are there important flaws in Franklin's sunny Socratism, and if so, what might these show us about the obstacles to living the life of pure rationality that he and Socrates both aspired to?

FREE WILL

Franklin first grappled with the problem of moral responsibility in an early essay on freedom of the will entitled *A Dissertation on Liberty and Necessity, Pleasure and Pain* (1725). Free will is a Christian notion that was fully developed only after Socrates' time, but one of the most important consequences of Socrates' arguments about moral responsibility is that, if he is right, free will as Christianity understands it does not exist. In this essay Franklin explicitly makes the same claim, and he never takes it back. But Socrates' and Franklin's arguments are different. Socrates' implicit denial of free will begins from his insistence that what is right is always good and never bad. When we choose, we are free in the limited sense that we really can choose what seems best to us; we are not automatons programmed by someone else's purposes. But by the same token, we *must* choose what seems best; we are not in fact free to choose what seems worst. The notion that we choose evil simply because it is evil Socrates does not discuss and clearly thinks does not describe any real human phenomena. When people speak of the freedom to choose evil, they generally have in mind the freedom to choose what is narrowly selfish or good for oneself instead of what is right or good for someone else. But Socrates, on the basis of years of listening carefully to what people say about right and wrong and questioning what they mean, argues that according to the only truly coherent account of virtue, virtue is always good for the virtuous person. We never in fact face a choice between what is right and what is best for *us* in the deepest sense and in the final analysis. Therefore there can be no freedom to make such a choice. Since any clear-sighted person will necessarily reject vice as bad for others and bad for himself, people can only choose it unfreely, out of ignorance.

In his essay *On Liberty and Necessity*, in contrast, Franklin rejects radical freedom on two very different grounds. First, he grants the common Christian premise that there exists an all-wise, all-good, and all-powerful God, and he draws from this premise the conclusion that everything that God does and allows to be done must be good, and that evil does not exist. Franklin finds the traditional distinction between what God does and what he permits unpersuasive. "If God permits an Action to be done, it is because he wants either *Power* or *Inclination* to hinder it; in saying he wants *Power*, we deny Him to be *almighty*; and if we say He wants *Inclination* or *Will*, it must be, either because he is not Good, or the Action is not *evil*."[8] Thus Franklin's first argument against free will is based on God's excellence: a wise God would no more allow free but ignorant beings to mar the order of his creation than a good watchmaker would build such beings into a watch. To claim that God designed the world with perfect wisdom and yet left his best creatures free to become evil is absurd, Franklin avers. But he denies not only the moral freedom to choose between good and evil that Christianity asserts but also the far more limited freedom, accepted by all ancient and most modern philosophers, to follow one's own judgment and to choose otherwise when one's judgment changes, for he describes all action as *mechanically* determined. Franklin concludes that "*If there is no such Thing as Free-Will in Creatures, there can be neither Merit nor Demerit in Creatures.*"[9]

Franklin's second argument against free will rests on no such religious presuppositions but merely on what he thinks he has observed of human psychology. We are moved in all that we do, he says, by pleasure and pain. And again he concludes that not only freedom and necessity but virtue and vice are meaningless terms.

> For since *Freedom from Uneasiness* is the End of all our Actions, how is it possible for us to do any Thing disinterested?—How can any Action be meritorious of Praise or Dispraise, Reward or Punishment, when the natural Principle of *Self-Love* is the only and the irresistible Motive to it?

Franklin ends the essay with the argument that "since every Action is the Effect of Self-Uneasiness, the Distinction of Virtue and Vice is excluded," and the denial of merit and demerit that was made on the basis of God's perfection "is again demonstrated."[10] As he suggests many years later in his *Autobiography*, this conclusion is the chief point the essay was designed to demonstrate. But Franklin fails here to distinguish two very different thoughts: the thought that no reward is earned by an act that is mechanistically determined or motivated only by an irresistible desire for pleasure—this seems correct—and the more radical and questionable claim that a sovereign God and a hedonistic account of human motivations both render meaningless all distinctions between virtue and vice, all judgments that courage is better than cowardice and self-control better than addiction and dissipation. Indeed, Franklin even denies any validity to the distinction between happiness and unhappiness. Claiming that all pleasure is the release from an equal and opposite pain, he maintains in the essay that every life—however cheerful and fortunate or however wretched and disappointing it may look—entails an exact balance between the two. Thus he can assert that no one gets any pleasure he does not deserve and no one deserves any suffering he has not already gotten—a further reason why heaven and hell make no sense.

The strained arguments of this essay suggest that the following may have been at work behind it. At a time in his life when he had twice run away from personal responsibilities and was living a carefree life in London, Franklin set out to prove by every means he could that the Puritan notion of sin and responsibility under which he had grown up was wholly unfounded. But he was uneasy; he could not absolutely refute the possibility that we are free and that heaven and hell await us; he went too far in constructing an argument about happiness that would make the afterlife unnecessary for justice; he went too far in denying the existence of virtue and vice when all that he had shown on his own premises is that no one merits rewards or punishments. Perhaps a part of him thought that he did have duties to others and that he ought to attend to them, and another part was intent on silencing this thought.

FRANKLIN'S RENEWED BELIEF IN MORALITY

Franklin tells us that not long after writing *On Liberty and Necessity*, he came to doubt the cleverness of the essay and of the "Deism" that inspired it. That Deism he does not define; perhaps it was a belief in the absolutely sovereign creator of the essay who micromanages everything, but it may also have been the common eighteenth-century view that God exists as at most a distant designer of the universe and not as ruler or judge or savior. The impetus for this reassessment seems to have been entirely pragmatic. Franklin's arguments for Deism, he says, caused both him and many of the friends he influenced to wrong one another without much compunction.

> I began to suspect that this Doctrine tho' it might be true, was not very Useful. My London Pamphlet, which . . . from the Attributes of God, his infinite Wisdom, Goodness and Power concluded that nothing could possibly be wrong in the world, and that Vice and Virtue were empty Distinctions, no such things existing: appear'd now not so clever a Performance as I once thought it, and I doubted whether some error had not insinuated itself unperceiv'd into my argument, so as to infect all that follow'd, as is common in metaphysical Reasonings. I grew convinced that *Truth, Sincerity and Integrity* in Dealings between Man and Man, were of the utmost Importance to the Felicity of Life, and I form'd written Resolutions, (which still remain in my Journal Book) to practice them ever while I lived. [11]

Franklin echoes this criticism of "Metaphysical Reasonings" in a letter to Benjamin Vaughan written near the end of Franklin's life. He tells of another early essay he wrote proving that everything must not be fated by God, because one of the things that God commands is prayer, and if everything were fated, prayer would be absurd. "The great uncertainty I found in metaphysical reasonings disgusted me, and I quitted that kind of reading and study for others more satisfactory." [12]

This chronology is important for our comparison of Franklin with Socrates. At the time in his life when he was thinking hardest about freedom and necessity, Franklin had not yet had the insight into the convergence of virtue and happiness that would later give decisive shape to his outlook. And his mature view of virtue developed only as he was rejecting the metaphysical speculations that had come to seem to him so uncertain and prone to error. Thus Franklin's theoretical critique of merit and retributive punishment is separated in time and thought from his embrace of virtue; he would grasp in a general way but never think through to the bottom the ramifications of the nature of true virtue, as he now understood it, for human responsibility.

Apart from the danger of stating certain views openly to others, what did Franklin come to realize about virtue and vice that made him reject his earlier position? Evidently he came to see at the least that even if we are simply motivated by pleasure and pain, there are qualities we can cultivate that make all the difference to our happiness and that of others, of which good sense is one of the most important. It is our own wise or foolish actions, not some inscrutable fate that drives us willy-nilly from without, that do most to determine how happy we are, and human lives do vary enormously in degrees of happiness. What is more, Franklin began to realize that his thesis that pleasure and pain determine everything we do was not right. Human benevolence exists and cannot be adequately explained on hedonistic grounds. A few years later, he wrote:

> It is the Opinion of some People, that Man is a Creature altogether selfish, and that all our Actions have at Bottom a View to private Interest; If we do good to others, it is, say they, because there is a certain Pleasure attending virtuous Actions. But how Pleasure comes to attend a virtuous Action, these Philosophers are puzzled to shew, without contradicting their first Principles, and acknowledging that Men are *naturally* benevolent as well as selfish. For whence can arise the Pleasure you feel after having done a good-natured Thing, if not hence, that you had *before* strong humane and kind Inclinations in your Nature, which are by such Actions in some Measure gratified? [13]

And this benevolence is no small matter. Friendship and trust are essential to happiness, and therefore a heartfelt concern for the welfare of others is to be encouraged not just in others but in ourselves. One who tried to get the benefits of virtue by merely feigning to have it would show that he had missed the great lesson that Franklin spent his life trying to teach: that doing real good is essential to happiness and self-respect, and thus that virtues like justice and honesty are not a sacrifice of self-interest but are integral to the richest happiness.

In a dialogue entitled "A Man of Sense," Franklin explores further the connection between enlightenment and virtue, pressing the question of whether a man who is dishonest can be called a man of sense. [14] The character "Socrates" quickly gets his interlocutor, "Crito," to agree that the knowledge that characterizes a man of sense is "the Knowledge of our *true Interest*; that is, of what is best to be done in all the Circumstances of Humane Life, in order to arrive at our main End in View, HAPPINESS." [15] Crito claims that one may know one's true interest and not do it, but Socrates replies that knowledge of virtue is like knowledge of shoemaking, and that one who speaks well about it but does not make good shoes really does not have the requisite knowledge. A man is virtuous only when he has "a thorough sense that what the other has said is true," and "knows how" to put it into practice. Those who "talk well of it" but "do not put it into practice "speak only by rote."[16] Most strikingly of all, Franklin has Socrates say that this lack of good sense is itself rooted in ignorance and not perverse willfulness, for the person who lacks an effective knowledge of virtue "is ignorant that the SCIENCE OF VIRTUE is of more worth, and of more consequence to his Happiness than all the rest put together."[17]

What remains, then, of the concept of deserving or merit? Franklin raises this question in an essay entitled "Self-Denial Not the Essence of Virtue."[18] In it he challenges the common notion "that without *Self-Denial* there is no Virtue, and that the greater the *Self-Denial* the greater the Virtue." It is possible, he argues in response, to have such a good nature or such good habits that one is never tempted by a given vice. A natural virtue is as much a virtue as one acquired through struggle, and a well-ingrained good habit is more of a virtue than a weak and frequently broken resolution. But does a virtue merit any reward, he allows a hypothetical objector to ask, if it never costs any pains? Franklin's response to this is radical. "We do not pretend to merit any thing of God, for he is above our Services; and the Benefits he confers on us, are the Effects of his Goodness and Bounty."[19] This unorthodox but reverent-sounding note is one that Franklin would strike throughout his life. He is silent on whether anyone merits divine punishment, but the suggestion is that God's kindness is given freely to all. Thus Franklin effectively removes God from his discussion of merit. God does not concern himself with assigning rewards and punishments, nor does justice require that he should. Instead, merit is nothing but the obligation one puts another under by rendering a good service. What matters is not the spirit in which an act is performed but simply how useful we really are to each other. Franklin does not even mind if the motive is mercenary or vain; the obligation to return it is the same. The superiority of true virtue lies not in its purity but in its consistency, for the good nature or habits that make virtue easy also make it reliable.

But what is the status of this indebtedness that Franklin speaks of? Is returning a favor anything more than a healthy soul's natural expression of gratitude and the dictate of prudence? Do we have here a duty of justice that the will is free to fulfill or violate? Or is the soul in this as in everything governed by an inner necessity of passions and judgments ultimately as inexorable as the necessities that govern the movements of the stars? Franklin never quite says. In concluding his autobiographical account of his turn to moral seriousness, he says he has realized that while nothing is bad *because* it has been forbidden by God or the Bible, certain actions "might be forbidden *because* they were bad for us." He concludes, "And this persuasion, with the kind hand of Providence, or some guardian Angel, or accidental favorable Circumstances and Situations, or all together, preserved me (thro' this dangerous Time of Youth . . .) without any willful gross Immorality or Injustice that might have been expected from my Want of Religion. I say willful, because the Instances I have mentioned, had something of Necessity in them, from my Youth, Inexperience, and the Knavery of others."[20] But this implies that these errors had something of freedom, too.

The same ambiguity appears again in the *Autobiography*, in the suggestive context of an account of the Socratic method of discourse. Franklin argues that a dogmatic style of conversation defeats the purposes of speech, which are mutual information and pleasure. Seconding Pope, he urges us instead "To speak tho' sure, with seeming Diffidence," and adds to it a line from another context, "For Want of Modesty is Want of Sense." This leads him to criticize the original couplet that contained the latter line:

> Immodest Words admit of *no* Defence,
> For Want of Modesty is Want of Sense.

Franklin observes,

> Now is not *Want of Sense* (where a Man is so unfortunate as to want it) some Apology for his *Want of Modesty?* and would not the Lines stand more justly thus?
>> Immodest Words admit *but this* Defence,
>> That Want of Modesty is Want of Sense.[21]

This is almost pure Socratism. But why does Franklin call this unfortunate want of sense only "some Apology," rather than the whole explanation, as Socrates would? Why does he suggest that the defense is still defective? He seems to be hedging, almost willing to grant that souls are governed by inner necessities that do not leave them free to be more sensible than they are, and yet still not prepared to rule out some modicum of freedom that he never explains.

The same ambiguity in fact pervades the *Autobiography*. Franklin shows great gentleness, great understanding of human faults, presenting his own as errata or inadvertent misprints, yet still holding himself to account for them; regarding those of others with the same generous understanding and equanimity, and holding them all up for gentle ridicule rather than hatred. After relating the way Governor Keith's duplicity left him stranded and penniless in London, he asks, "but what shall we think of a Governor's playing such pitiful Tricks, and imposing so grossly on a poor ignorant Boy! It was a Habit he had acquired. He wish'd to please every body; and having little to give, he gave Expectations. He was otherwise an ingenious sensible Man, a pretty good Writer, and a good Governor for the People. . . . Several of our best Laws were of his Planning, and pass'd during his Administration."[22] It is part of Franklin's charm that he shows such understanding; it belongs to the same charming, benevolent spirit to pass over with a light hand the metaphysical question of freedom and necessity and merit.

ANGER

But if the delightful *Autobiography* gives the impression of a wise, genial soul quite above the passion of anger, a careful reading of it reveals that Franklin was no such man by nature. This impression is in fact carefully cultivated, though by no means a sheer fabrication: it is a largely accurate reflection of the man Franklin schooled himself to become. Part of that schooling was a systematic self-training in thirteen virtues that Franklin set out to master, including moderation, which he defined as "forbear[ing] resenting injuries so much as you think they deserve."[23] When he wrote the *Autobiography*, with the advantage of time and distance, he was able to relate such stories as Governor Keith's betrayal with splendid, philosophic equanimity. But as he tells his story he gives many hints of the lively resentment he felt at the time at injustices. These include his responses to the violence of his brother James, but also to the colonial government that imprisoned James for his opposition; to the insults of his employer Keimer; to his rival Bradford, who as postmaster refused to let his newspaper be carried in the mail; to the family of a girl he courted, whose machinations provoked him to break off relations abruptly and irrevocably, despite a reportedly strong attachment; and to the Pennsylvania proprietors in their refusal to allow their massive dominions to be taxed.[24]

In these efforts to moderate his anger, Franklin had impressive success. We see him using his reason and sympathy to turn his resentment into constructive channels, as in his response to Bradford's injustice: "I thought so meanly of him for it, that when I afterwards came into his Situation, I took care never to imitate it."[25] We see him diffusing bitterness with humor, dining amicably with great political rivals, and helping them in causes on which they could agree. So habitually did Franklin adopt an unruffled spirit that a French friend would report, in awe, "His eyes reflect a perfect equanimity, and his lips a smile of unalterable serenity."[26] Despite the bitterness of his country's rupture with Great Britain, he preserved most of his personal friendships across the ocean. But he did not preserve all, and significantly not his friendship with his loyalist son William. Nor did Franklin demand of himself that he overcome all anger, but only that he give it less scope than he thought it deserved. He was certain that anger clouds the vision and drives people to irrational acts, but whether anger itself is irrational in every case he never said, and perhaps never made up his mind.

Franklin's inability to forgive his son William for taking the British side in the Revolution is the most revealing of his lapses regarding anger. In a wrenching letter of 1784 to William he wrote:

> I am glad to find that you desire to revive the affectionate Intercourse that formerly existed between us. It will be very agreeable to me; indeed nothing has ever hurt me so much and affected me with such keen Sensations, as to find myself deserted in my old Age by my only Son; and not only deserted, but to find him taking up Arms against me, in a Cause, wherein my good Fame, Fortune, and Life were all at Stake. You conceived, you say, that your Duty to your King and Regard for your Country requir'd this. I ought not to blame you for differing in Sentiment with me in Public Affairs. We are Men, all subject to Errors. Our Opinions are not in our own Power; they are form'd and govern'd much by Circumstances, that are often as inexplicable as they are irresistible. Your Situation was such that few would have censured your remaining Neuter, tho' there are Natural Duties which precede political ones, and cannot be extinguish'd by them. This is a disagreeable Subject. I drop it.

But the bitterness he could never really drop; the attempted reconciliation failed.[27]

Franklin still saw both the importance and the fallibility of human understanding, but he did not now press the insights of "A Man of Sense." He did not ask whether, if perceived interest and mistaken principle both seemed to recommend the loyalist side, anyone could really be blamed for taking it. He did not ask whether, if William's knowledge of his duty to his father was merely abstract, a truth known only "by rote," he could really be expected to follow it, or whether the failure to pursue a well-understood good would not reveal a lack of understanding of *how* to be good, like the theoretical shoemaker in Franklin's dialogue who does not know how to make shoes. Or again, if William was careless in thinking the whole matter through, would that not betray an ignorance "that the SCIENCE OF VIRTUE is of more worth, and of more consequence to his Happiness than all the rest put together"?[28] Nor, at this or any time, did Franklin seize upon such evident conflicts of duties as that between following one's own judgment and bowing to one's father as a challenge requiring us to rethink the question of whether commonsense notions of justice are wholly coherent. Lacking Socrates's doggedness in pursuing these questions, Franklin lacked the perfect equanimity of a philosopher in the face of bitter disappointment.

The same problem and the same bitterness pervaded Franklin's twenty-year effort to effect a reconciliation between Britain and her American colonies. Franklin was sure that free trade and extensive American autonomy within the empire were truly just and truly best for everyone involved, but this did not stop his outrage at the arrogance of the British ministry and press, the selfishness of British trade policies, or the unfairness of a system in which representatives of one part of the empire wielded unchecked power over all the rest.[29] Franklin's anger at these crucial junctures shows that in important ways he never persuaded himself of the complete convergence of virtue and happiness. He thought that William and the British merchants and ministry had a duty to curtail their interests in deference to him and to the just claims of the colonists. And surely such a perception is, after all, quite natural. This breakdown in Franklin's Socratism points us to an important problem: it simply is not clear that virtue is always in our interest, at least if we understand our interest in anything like the usual way, as a thriving life of comfort, influence, and success in the world for oneself and those one wishes to protect. Virtue really does leave us vulnerable to exploitation and terrible loss. The right thing is not so obviously best for everyone.

Franklin never faced this fact quite squarely, but I think Socrates did. Socrates, unlike Franklin, was fascinated by the problem of justice, the tensions within ordinary notions of justice, the extreme cases where honesty and lawfulness do not seem to be the best policy. Ultimately, he was able to hold consistently to his unusual view of justice only by virtue of his unusual way of life. He let himself care about none of the usual contests for honor and power and wealth that really are at many times zero-sum games. He embraced poverty and political obscurity and even opprobrium to enjoy the absolute clarity of thought that no one and no injustice could take from him. Socrates also reasoned that if virtue guaranteed happiness, happiness could not depend on having a long or secure life. He argued that to philosophize is to learn how to die, or to live each day in the clear knowledge that it could be one's last. Socrates thought that a few austere souls could follow him in such wisdom, but he never embraced the hope for universal enlightenment that Franklin did. In revealing contrast, Franklin declares, "It has always been my maxim to live on as if I was to live always. It is with such feeling only that we can be stimulated to the exertions necessary to effect any useful purpose."[30]

DEATH

What is at stake in this difference of perspective on death? Behind Franklin's faith in enlightenment lurks the sense that there are things we do best not to think about. The practical Franklin thinks of facing death as nothing you should have to waste any energy on until you really face it, and hopefully that happens only once. He tells in the *Autobiography* of a grave illness in his youth that almost carried him off. "I suffered a good deal, gave up the Point in my own mind, and was rather disappointed when I found my Self recovering; regretting in some degree that I must now some time or other have all that disagreeable Work to do over again."[31] But by not thinking about death until he absolutely must, Franklin also left himself open to a lingering, unexamined hope that death might not be the end after all. There are signs that this hope grew stronger in his later years, connected with a hope that good might still meet with some reward or at least divine assistance and evil with some punishment that Franklin's philosophy never quite explained the need for. One such hint comes in a 1782 letter in which Franklin reflects on the cruelties of George III's depredations in America.

> And yet this Man lives, enjoys all the good Things this World can afford, and is surrounded by Flatterers, who keep even his Conscience quiet, by telling him he is the best of Princes! I wonder at this, but I cannot therefore part with the comfortable Belief of a Divine Providence; and the more I see the Impossibility, from the number & extent of his Crimes of giving equivalent Punishment to a wicked Man in this Life, the more I am convinc'd of a future State, in which all that here appears to be wrong shall be set right, all that is crooked made straight. In this Faith let you & I, my dear Friend, comfort ourselves. It is the only Comfort, in the present dark Scene of Things, that is allow'd us.[32]

A second such hint contains a similarly intriguing interweaving of the themes of death and justice:

> But after all my dear Friend, do not imagine that I am vain enough to ascribe our Success to any superiority in any of those Points. I am too well acquainted with all the Springs and Levers of our Machine, not to see that our human means were unequal to our undertaking, and that, if it had not been for the Justice of our Cause, and the consequent Interposition of Providence in which we had Faith we must have been ruined. If I had ever before been an Atheist, I should now have been convinced of the Being and Government of a Deity. It is he who abases the Proud and favours the Humble! May we never forget his Goodness to us, and may our future Conduct manifest our Gratitude.[33]

In Socrates's analysis, ordinary, unreflective conventional morality necessarily contains a mixture of true insights into the intrinsic goodness of virtue and confused thoughts that virtue is a sacrifice: this mixture can leave us believing that we think of virtue as simply enlightened self-interest while we surreptitiously also think of virtue as noble sacrifice that needs a compensatory reward and think of vice as a profitable seizing of good things that ought to be taken away. Franklin's case suggests how enormously difficult it is to work ourselves free of this tangle and to embrace wholeheartedly the strange Socratic teaching that virtue is knowledge.

NOTES

1. *Autobiography*, 64–65.
2. Ibid., 65.

3. Ibid., 115.

4. "On Simplicity," *Pennsylvania Gazette*, 13 April 1732. This essay, like many pieces in the *Gazette* that are almost certainly by Franklin, is not included in the Yale edition of Franklin's papers, but it is reprinted in Benjamin Franklin, *Benjamin Franklin: Writings; Autobiography, Poor Richard's Almanack, Bagatelles, Pamphlets, Essays & Letters*, ed. J. A. Leo Lemay (New York: Library of America, 1987), 183. [Hereafter *Writings* (1987).]

5. *Autobiography*, 54; cf. 148: "It is in our Interest to be compleatly virtuous."

6. Alexis de Tocqueville, *Democracy in America*, trans. and ed. Harvey C. Mansfield and Delba Winthrop (Chicago: University of Chicago Press, 2000), 2:501. The editors add, "The name of Benjamin Franklin is so obvious among these 'American moralists' as to obscure all others."

7. Benjamin Franklin, *Poor Richard Improved: Being an Almanack and Ephemeris . . . for the Year of our Lord 1750 . . . By Richard Saunders, Philom* (Philadelphia: Printed and sold by B. Franklin and D. Hall, 1749 and 1753); and Franklin, *Writings* (1987), 1255 and 1277. Cf. "Articles of Belief and Acts of Religion," 20 November 1728, where Franklin calls anger a "momentary madness," in *Papers* 1:101–8, especially 108.

8. *Papers* 1:60.

9. Ibid., 1:63.

10. Ibid., 1:71.

11. *Autobiography*, 114.

12. Franklin to Benjamin Vaughan, 9 November 1779, in *Papers* 31:57–59; cf. Franklin to Thomas Hopkinson [16 October 1746], in *Papers* 3:84–88. The essay referred to is evidently "On the Providence of God in the Government of the World" [1732], written as a Junto exercise. Franklin's genuine interest in knowing the truth about metaphysical questions, an interest he abandoned only out of a failure to find solid footing here, distinguishes him from the shallower view of many of the later utilitarians, who cannot understand how we lost our way so badly as ever to concern ourselves with such impractical questions.

13. "Men are Naturally Benevolent as Well as Selfish," *Pennsylvania Gazette*, 30 November 1732, in Franklin, *Writings* (1987), 200–201.

14. "A Man of Sense," 11 February 1735, in *Papers* 2:15–19.

15. Ibid., 16.

16. Ibid., 17.

17. Ibid., 19.

18. "Self-Denial Not the Essence of Virtue," 18 February 1735, in *Papers* 2:19–21.

19. Ibid., 20.

20. *Autobiography*, 115.

21. Ibid., 66.

22. Ibid., 95.

23. Ibid., 150.

24. Ibid., 68–69, 110–11, 126–28, 214.

25. Ibid., 127.

26. David Levin makes the interesting suggestion that Franklin's equanimity is connected to his great curiosity in "Franklin: Experimenter in Life and Art," in *Benjamin Franklin: Statesman-Philosopher or Materialist?* ed. Wilbur R. Jacobs (New York: Holt, Reinhart and Winston, 1972), 58–62. For examples of Franklin's amicable relations with political rivals and even enemies, see *Autobiography*, 212–13, 239, 247–48. The French friend is Pierre-Samuel Du Pont de Nemours, quoted by Walter Isaacson in *Benjamin Franklin: An American Life* (New York: Simon and Schuster, 2005), 327.

27. Franklin to William Franklin, 16 August 1784, in *Papers: Digital Edition*. So bitter was Franklin in fact toward William and the other loyalists that in 1782 he threatened to scuttle the whole peace treaty with England rather than allow it to include American compensation for confiscated loyalist property. For a fascinating account of this aspect of the peace negotiations, see Isaacson, *Benjamin Franklin: An American Life*, 412–15. For an account of William's perspective and his efforts to undermine the independence movement and help the loyalists, see Sheila L. Skemp, *Benjamin and William Franklin: Father and Son, Patriot and Loyalist* (Boston: St. Martin's Press, 1994), 134–52.

28. "A Man of Sense," 11 February 1735, in *Papers* 2:15–19.
29. For examples of this anger, see "'N. N.' First Reply to Vindex Patriae," 28 December 1765, in *Papers* 12:413–16; "Homespun: Further Defense of Indian Corn" [15 January 1766], in *Papers* 13:44–49; "The Rise and Present State of Our Misunderstandings," 6–8 November 1770, in *Papers* 17:268–73; "Rules by which a Great Empire May be Reduced to a Small One," 11 September 1773, in *Papers* 20:389–99.
30. Quoted in John Epps, *Life of John Walker, M.D.* (London: Whittaker, Treacher, and Co., 1831), 143–44.
31. *Autobiography*, 107.
32. Franklin to James Hutton, 7 July 1782, in *Papers: Digital Edition.*
33. Franklin to William Strahan, 19 August 1784, in *Papers: Digital Edition.*

Chapter Ten

From Weimar, with Love

Benjamin Franklin's Influence on Johann Wolfgang von Goethe's Self-Fashioning

Paul E. Kerry

Nineteenth-century Bostonians, particularly those associated with Harvard University, took an active interest in German culture, German higher education, and Goethe. They were interested in his many achievements, but especially, like the Scottish historian Thomas Carlyle,[1] in the development of their own lives. They saw in Goethe a representative man, to use a famous phrase from Ralph Waldo Emerson, another Harvard scholar who looked to and learned from Goethe. George Bancroft, who after graduating from Harvard studied in Germany and afterward sought to introduce German educational ideas to the United States, made a pilgrimage to Weimar to meet Goethe in person. A former pupil of Bancroft's at the Round Hill School, John Lothrop Motley, wrote his Harvard senior exhibition essay on Goethe.[2] Margaret Fuller, the first woman allowed to conduct research in Harvard's libraries, wrote essays on Goethe's thought and wanted to write a biography of him.

Henry Wadsworth Longfellow, Smith Professor of Modern Languages at Harvard and translator of Goethe's "Wanderer's Night Song," intuited a connection between Goethe and Franklin. Wordsworth's novel *Hyperion* (1839) features two friends on a tour of Frankfurt am Main, Goethe's birthplace, conversing about Goethe: "Did it ever occur to you that [Goethe] was in some points like Ben Franklin,—a kind of rhymed Ben Franklin? The practical tendency of his mind was the same; his love of science was the same; his benignant, philosophic spirit was the same; and a vast number of his little poetic maxims and soothsayings seem nothing more than the world-

ly wisdom of Poor Richard, versified."[3] Later, James Parton, one of nineteenth-century America's foremost biographers, would describe Goethe as "a
man who had much in common with Franklin."[4]

Goethe was younger than Franklin and the two neither met nor corresponded. Yet had Goethe immigrated to the British Colonies in America in
1775, as he had fleetingly contemplated, it would not strain logic to suggest
that he would have sought out Franklin and sympathized with the cause of
the American Founders.[5] Ekkehart Krippendorff posited that Weimar was for
Goethe an "Ersatz-Amerika," meaning it was a place where he could be
engaged in social reform and direct his energies to the improvement of civic
institutions.[6] Even as late as 1819, while dining at home with several guests
including the young American, Joseph Green Cogswell, a former Harvard
student at the University of Göttingen who would cofound with Bancroft the
Round Hill School, Goethe declared that if he were twenty years younger, he
would have sailed to North America. As a man of eighty, Goethe revisited
the subject of immigration to America in *Wilhelm Meister's Journeyman
Years* (1821, 1829). It is not surprising that the destination of one of the
groups in this novel is apparently Pennsylvania. Goethe, like Voltaire, recognized Franklin's Philadelphia as a city that fostered Enlightenment ideals.

Franklin did in fact visit Germany and was well received there, as Jürgen
Overhoff's chapter in this volume attests. He toured key cities in the Empire
in 1766 and was introduced to many luminaries, especially in Göttingen,
which boasted one of Europe's finest universities, where he was inducted
into the Royal Society of Sciences, and also met Michaelis, Pütter, Achenwall, and Lichtenberg. His *Experiments and Observations on Electricity* had
been published in German translation in 1758, followed by a collection of his
political writings in 1780. In 1783 Johann Erich Biester published an essay
on Franklin in a well-known Berlin periodical, the *Berlinische Monatsschrift.*
Furthermore, Franklin's research on electricity had been praised by Lessing.[7]
Herder, a longtime associate of Goethe's, was effusive about Franklin: "You
know what I have ever thought of Franklin, how highly I have treasured his
healthy understanding, his bright and beautiful spirit, his Socratic method,
above all however his sense of humanity."[8]

Goethe had read about Benjamin Franklin's experiments and conducted
his own. Like Franklin he was involved in matters of state, in the duchy of
Saxe-Weimar. He supported the University of Jena and was director of
Duchess Anna Amalia's library, both of which mirror two Philadelphia institutions that Franklin was influential in founding, the University of Pennsylvania and the Library Company of Philadelphia. Goethe, who wrote an autobiography, read Franklin's with profit and pleasure. Franklin toured parts of
Germany, including Frankfurt am Main, and Goethe read Prince Carl Bernhard of Saxe-Weimar's account of his travels in the United States with eager-
ness. Goethe and Franklin were Free Masons. Both escaped the narrowness

of their northern lives, Goethe the distraction of Weimar politics and Franklin's puritanical Boston, and flourished in Italy and Philadelphia respectively. Both were interested in the federalist structure of the Empire.[9] Goethe and Franklin both witnessed revolutions: Franklin as a diplomat during the War of Independence and Goethe as an attaché to the Austro-Prussian armies as they engaged with French revolutionary armies. Franklin was feted in Paris and secured funds for the American cause. Goethe was honored by Napoleon, who spared his home from plundering French troops.

The goal here, however, is not to make a case for Plutarchian parallel lives. Nor is it an attempt to fathom Goethe's evolving perspective on republican America, which is how Goethe's scattered references to Benjamin Franklin have typically been interpreted.[10] Rather, the aim of this chapter is to show how Goethe drew on Franklin as a standard of reference for his own self-fashioning and achievements, scientific and literary.

Goethe's view of Franklin certainly stems to some degree from an admiration of his accomplishments. Yet, there is much more than blanket veneration on Goethe's part. Although Franklin did not occupy Goethe much, a pattern emerges from the contexts in which he did. Goethe, sensitive to his own image and legacy, was impressed with Franklin's care and success in fashioning himself, above all in his *Autobiography*.[11] Goethe was interested in his own self-fashioning and seems to have been aware that in Franklin's presence, although the disposition of their gifts and abilities was different, he was meeting a transatlantic kindred spirit. As Stephen Greenblatt has shown, the early moderns relied on external sources, such as conversation and courtesy manuals, as guidelines for fashioning their public selves, as does the young George Washington, who is famously associated with this tradition through his *Rules of Civility and Decent Behavior in Company and Conversation*.[12] Franklin boldly constructed his own rules, drawn from the Western tradition to be sure, and this attracted Goethe. More specifically, Goethe cited Franklin to mark and measure his own contributions, especially to science, and also to consider his own position as one creating an intellectual and cultural center in an evolving Germany, much as Franklin had done in an evolving colonial America.

One reason why these typically Goethean views have tended to be overlooked in relation to Franklin is that what Franklin has come to stand for is sometimes pressed into service by those wishing to make Goethe into a political liberal. Therefore, the tendency has been to focus on the following snippet in his own autobiography, *Poetry and Truth* (*Dichtung und Wahrheit*, 1811–1814, 1833) to illustrate that Goethe was indeed aware of the American Revolution and perhaps even sympathetic to its goals: "one wished the Americans every happiness and the names of Franklin and Washington began to glow and sparkle in the political and warlike firmament."[13]

This is not to say that Franklin held no political meaning for Goethe, as he did for other contemporary Germans.[14] Yet, this passage is disproportionately small when compared to Goethe's other references to Franklin, which appear in *Poetry and Truth*, his correspondence and conversations, and his scientific writings. Goethe's most detailed description of Franklin, in fact, speaks to his literary achievement and is fused with a high compliment to the historian Justus Möser:

> We find that the objects of his serious and jocular observations are the changes in manners and customs, clothing, diet, domestic life, and education. One would have to rubricate everything that happens in the civil and moral world if one wanted to make an exhaustive list of the subjects he treats. And his treatment is an admirable one. A perfect public official is speaking to the people in a weekly gazette, in order to explain to each individual, from the proper perspective, the things undertaken or executed by a reasonable, benevolent government. But this is by no means done in a didactic way; on the contrary, the forms are so varied they could be called poetic, and at any rate are to be classified as rhetorical, in the best sense of the word. He is always elevated above his subject and manages to give a cheerful view of the gravest matters. Half hidden behind one mask or another, or speaking in his own person, he is always complete and detailed, but at the same time lighthearted, somewhat ironical, absolutely thorough, upright, well meaning, and sometimes even blunt and vehement. All this is done so judiciously that one has to admire the author's wit, understanding, facility, skill, taste, and character, all at the same time. With regard to his choice of generally useful subject matter, deep insight, wide-ranging vision, felicitous treatment, and both genuine and joyous humor, I can compare him with none but Franklin.[15]

This description captures something of Franklin's persona and literary style in his *Autobiography*, which Goethe had read in 1810 as he was in the midst of writing his own, in which the description occurs.[16] Goethe might have felt attracted by another work of self-construction, written by a statesman-scientist, one that conveyed a "vivid portrait, etched with a disarming twinkle in the prose. . . . almost a picaresque novel,"[17] as he had turned sixty and was "above all concerned with the refashioning and interpretation of his recollections."[18] The mention of a periodical in conjunction with aspects of domestic life, customs, and commentary on society hints that Goethe might have been acquainted with *Poor Richard's Almanack*. Goethe's reference to "masks" is particularly intriguing because Franklin's satires, which were published throughout his life and appeared in periodicals both in the colonies and in Europe, employed them frequently.[19] Franklin's effective literary voice, its irony, wit, benevolence, and humor to which Goethe refers, have been long-standing descriptions of the *Autobiography*.[20]

Another internal reference to an obscure comment in Franklin's *Autobiography* provides further evidence that Goethe had done more than leaf through it. In a 28 February 1811 letter to his friend Carl Friedrich Zelter, whom Goethe compliments for reading *Theory of Color* (*Farbenlehre*, 1810) albeit "in small doses," Goethe brings up Franklin's aversion toward mathematicians in polite society and conversation. Franklin found unbearable their "pettiness and contrarian nature" (Kleinigkeits- und Widerspruchsgeist).[21] Indeed, Franklin listed the members of his Junto or "club of mutual improvement" and among them was "Thomas Godfrey, a self-taught Mathematician, great in his Way, and afterwards Inventor of what is now call'd Hadley's Quadrant. But he knew little out of his way, and was not a pleasing Companion, as, like most Great Mathematicians I have met with, he expected universal Precision in every thing said, or was forever denying or distinguishing upon Trifles, to the Disturbance of all Conversation. He soon left us."[22]

The description of Franklin's club resonated with Herder, who along with Goethe and others had organized the "Friday Society" (Freitagsgesellschaft) in 1791.[23] But Goethe's fixation on this obscure passage in Franklin's *Autobiography* illuminates a deeper concern. In his *Theory of Color* Goethe famously opposed a solely mathematical explanation of color in favor of a holistic theory that took into consideration subjective criteria. Goethe's book received a quiet reception, even a negative one in some quarters.[24] In this light, Goethe can be seen to be alluding to Franklin's observation to confirm Goethe's own view of some mathematicians as "mad fellows."[25]

In the historical section of *Theory of Color*, Goethe quotes from a German translation of Franklin's *Experiments and Observations on Electricity*. The quotation contains a summary of Franklin's assessment of how the eye responds to light and perceives color.[26] The historical section of *Theory of Color* conveys not only Goethe's commitment to self-understanding through history—he argues that the history of a discipline is nothing short of the discipline itself—but this section also serves to secure his place in the history and philosophy of science. The reference to Franklin occurs just prior to the "second epoch" of the eighteenth century that ushers in "our time."[27] Franklin is therefore implicitly the culmination of an epoch, a turning point and threshold figure, but not included in the final run-up to Goethe himself. The touch is delicate, yet undeniable: Goethe casts himself as one who builds on Franklin's insights, yet also surpasses him.

Nearly twenty years after the publication of *Theory of Color*, Goethe makes a similar move, one that demonstrates clearly how he deploys Franklin. He was still bitter about the lack of impact that the *Theory of Color* had had. In a 2 April 1829 letter of lament to Zelter, he complains of suppression and conspiracy. Franklin is again used as a key figure in Goethe's self-fashioning—Goethe's ignored work had answered a question that "trusty" (*wacker*) Franklin himself had asked. The implication is that if the great Franklin had asked the question and Goethe had answered it, why then was his *Theory of Color* ignored?[28] In fact, he makes a similar argument in the

Theory of Color itself, an effort to bring Franklin into his discursive orbit and show himself to be one who followed Franklin's questions, but then also found answers.[29]

The *Theory of Color* also contains a strong historical assumption. Goethe observes that scientific achievement in the Germanic lands begins in the court culture of the late seventeenth and early eighteenth centuries—the beginnings of German contributions to the science of optics and color theory.[30] Nevertheless, as mentioned above, Goethe's epoch improves on and goes beyond what came before.

Goethe was acutely aware of the uniqueness of his life. "In Goethe's case," writes Walter Wetzels, "his life not only is integrated into his work as a 'great confession' (in his words), it *is* a work in itself, closely observed, diligently documented and shaped into an illuminating narrative about himself and his time."[31] Thus, it is perhaps more than a coincidence that Goethe juxtaposes his birth with the name of Franklin, another figure of world-historical importance and one who was aware of it. Goethe sketches the cultural and scientific scene at his birth in the paralipomena of *Poetry and Truth*: "Constellation and horoscope at my birth. No talk of German literature. Great foreigners, Voltaire, Montesquieu. Preparation for the future fate of the world completely outside of Germany: Paoli, Franklin."[32] The "future fate of the world" rests in the hands of foreigners like statesman and scientist Benjamin Franklin. Goethe is once again using Franklin to establish his own historical significance. It is obvious that Goethe fostered a new age in German literature, and in selecting Franklin he appears to be making the parallel claim that he had done so in at least matters of science and perhaps by implication in matters of state, as one who "had more practical political experience than any writer of his age."[33] Perhaps he places his birth in Franklin's contrails because he, too, came of age in a land vexed with questions about political unity and that had not produced much notable literature or other cultural and scientific achievements.[34] Seeing his task as at least somewhat similar to that of Franklin places Goethe in the position of one who has created a cultural center in a land without a political one.

On 1 February 1827, after a lengthy discussion on *Theory of Color*, Goethe would tell Johann Peter Eckermann that he was fortunate that his life had occurred during the richest era of scientific discoveries—with Franklin being the only named scientist in the passage:

> If I have done anything with respect to the subjects that lay in my way, I had this advantage: that my life fell in a time richer than any other in great natural discoveries. As a child I became acquainted with Franklin's doctrine of electricity, the law of which he had just discovered. Thus through my whole life, down to the present hour, has one great discovery followed another; so that not only was I directed towards nature in my early years, but also my interest in it has been maintained ever since. Advances such as I could never have foreseen

are now made even on paths that I opened; and I feel like one who walks towards the dawn, and, when the sun rises, is astonished at its brilliancy.[35]

Goethe presents his younger self, however, not merely as a follower, but as one who had become a contributor, if not a leader: "Advances . . . are now made even on paths that I opened." Goethe's design is similar to that in *Theory of Color*. He inserts himself amid the most important scientific developments of the age, with Franklin as the key marker, and then highlights his own contributions.

In *Poetry and Truth* Goethe introduces his childhood fascination with electricity and implies that he was born not long after the time in which "electricity engaged everyone's intellect."[36] Certainly Goethe harbored a genuine interest in electricity and conducted his own electrical experiments.[37] He actively nurtured the image of one born "in the same year, even a few months after the discovery of the lightning rod," as one correspondent reported.[38] Heinz Otto Sibum asserted that Franklin did indeed represent a recognized transition, that his "work [was] out of time with the old doctrines of natural philosophy and exactly in time with the emerging thought style of enlightened science characterizing the scientific academies of Berlin and Paris."[39]

The lightning rod empowered individuals to not only describe nature but to control it—Franklin's *Poor Richard's Almanack* of 1752 contained instructions on how to install them—and this conceptual shift made a significant impact in Germany, where Franklin became known as the new "Prometheus," a title that seems to have originated with Immanuel Kant.[40] Indeed, the metaphor of the lightning rod competed with that of the earthquake as a way to effect rational political changes as opposed to violent upheavals. In Germany, Franklin's scientific and political roles were merged by Johann Christian Schmohl who published anonymously *On North America and Democracy* (*Ueber Nordamerika und Demokratie*, [1782]): "Franklin Prometheus, der du dem Himmel den Donner und den Tyrannen das Zepter entrissest,"[41] which echoed the famous phrase in a letter from the French finance minister Anne-Robert-Jacques Turgot: "Eripuit coelo, fulmen, sceptrumque tyrannis" [He snatched the lightning from the skies and the scepter from the tyrants].[42] In a 26 January 1798 letter to Schiller, Goethe summarized Erasmus Darwin's poem "The Botanic Garden," and included a description of the power of Franklin's lightning rod.[43]

Franklin's lightning rods contributed to the demythologization of lightning as a symbol of divine displeasure, a discourse in which Goethe's poem "Prometheus" (1774) fits. In some important ways, the poem anticipates Kant's formulation of Enlightenment: "Enlightenment is man's exit from his self-imposed immaturity."[44] The first commanding line of "Prometheus" is an abrupt dismissal of the god who wields the fearsome thunderbolt. It is doubly disrespectful for Zeus is reduced to the status of a child ("Knaben-gleich") and told to cover his heavens as if he were a boy being reprimanded for not making his bed: "Bedecke deinen Himmel Zeus / Mit Wolkendunst!" Rather than mankind fearing his lightning, Zeus is mocked for envying "my hearth" with its "glow," which implies the control and use of fire by mortals for their own ends. "Children and beggars" or in other words those who are immature and completely dependent, keep belief in the gods alive. To accept life's sorrows and joys, to affirm life rather than "flee into deserts," is a sign that one is not a "child" but a man. Prometheus tells Zeus that he "fashions humans" (forme Menschen), an affirmation of creative power.[45] The control of lightning, effected through Franklin's invention, is a symbol of self-fash-ioning as it represents a claim to lead one's own life and generate one's own meanings.

A famous image of Franklin in France was the 1777 print portrait by Augustin de Saint-Aubin, after Charles-Nicholas Cochin, featuring Franklin in his fur cap and spectacles in a slightly rumpled jacket. He wanted to be out of place "among the Powder'd Heads of Paris," consciously cultivating the image of virtue and simplicity; after all, his government was receiving two million livres in French aid and he would be asking for more.[46] This can be contrasted with an equally iconic image of Goethe, painted about ten years after the Franklin print: Johann Heinrich Wilhelm Tischbein's oil painting "Goethe in the Campagna." Goethe sports a large hat and lounges on Roman ruins, his right leg planted on the earth as the left one dangles over the edge of a stone block. His right hand is exposed and relaxed, and his left hand rests on his right knee. The scene is framed by soft hills in the distance in front of which stand large Roman architectural remains. Plants are beginning to over-grow the ruins in the foreground, including a relief featuring what appears to be a scene from *Iphigenia in Tauris* (1779), the scene which would set in motion the conflict between representatives of European civilization and supposed barbarians in Goethe's play, on which he was working at the time. The French print highlights a Franklin charmingly out of place in Europe as he sought solutions to American problems. Goethe is completely at home in a European landscape, amid European history and culture, working out En-lightenment solutions to European challenges of the kind he produced in *Iphigenia*.

It is on the level of those kinds of solutions that Franklin and Goethe come together again. Franklin's commitment to the processes and projects of the Enlightenment confirm Goethe's own investment. One of these projects was the fostering of religious tolerance. This is one context in which the American Founders learned about Goethe. John Adams wrote to Thomas Jefferson on 14 November 1813:

Among all of your researches in Hebrew History and Controversy have you ever met a book, the design of which is to prove, that the ten Commandments, as We have them in our Catechisms and hung up in our Churches were not the Ten Commandments written by the Finger of God upon tables, delivered to Moses on mount Sinai and broken by him in a passion with Aaron for his golden calf, nor those afterwards engraved by him on Tables of Stone, but a very different Sett of Commandments?
There is such a book by J. W. Goethens Schristen. Berlin 1775–1779. I wish you to see this Book. [47]

This is probably a reference to one of Goethe's essays on biblical criticism (*Zwo wichtige bisher unerörterte biblische Fragen*, 1773). [48] Jefferson, who had reworked the accounts of the Four Evangelists into a naturalistic narrative, responded that he was unaware of Goethe. Franklin, like the other Founders, wanted to avoid religious rancor in a society where religious liberty, of the kind initiated by Jefferson in the "Virginia Statute for Religious Freedom," was meant to prevail. Franklin donated building funds for various Christian and Jewish places of worship, believing that, in general, their teachings confirmed public "Morality." [49] Walter Isaacson summarizes Franklin's civic bent when it came to matters of religion:

When [Franklin] narrowly escaped a shipwreck as he neared the English coast in 1757, he had joked to [his wife] Debbie that "were I a Roman Catholic, perhaps I should on this occasion vow to build a chapel to some saint; but as I am not, if I were to vow at all, it would be to build a *lighthouse*." Likewise, when a town in Massachusetts named itself Franklin in 1785 and asked him to donate a church bell, he told them to forsake the steeple and build a library, for which he sent "books instead of a bell, sense being preferable to sound." [50]

Goethe read in Franklin's *Autobiography* again in December 1828 and January 1829, while he was working on *Wilhelm Meister's Journeyman Years.* [51] Franklin does not appear in the wide-ranging novel, but Philadelphia is held up as a model, as is its Quaker founder, William Penn, and, most significantly, "religious freedom" (Religionsfreiheit), likely the first time the concept as such appears in Goethe's writings. [52] At this time, as mentioned above, Prince Bernhard of Saxe-Weimar had recently returned from a significant tour of the American republic (he was received by John Adams and Thomas Jefferson) and kept a detailed travel journal that Goethe read with avid interest. Bernhard reported that there were twenty-two sects, including Jews, in Philadelphia, "And each of these sects co-exists peacefully." [53]

This view accords with Franklin's description of how religious denominations in Philadelphia worked together. He explains in his *Autobiography* that it was decided to create a charity school that would also be a civic building to allow a venue for occasional preachers "of any religious Persuasion, who might desire to say something to the People of Philadelphia." Although

Franklin may be exaggerating slightly when he added "even if the Mufti of Constantinople were to send a missionary to preach Mahometanism to us, he would find a Pulpit at his Service," the wide scope of his vision of religious pluralism is evident. A committee was established to raise funds for the building, consisting of members of diverse sects, "one Church of England-man, one Presbyterian, one Baptist, one Moravian, &c."[54] Goethe put forward a similar interfaith solution to the problems some foresaw when contemplating a sectarian celebration of Luther's tercentenary—and he seems in earnest about including "Mahometanern" or Muslims. Goethe considered such cooperation, especially about practical matters of manifest benefit to the entire community, of deep worth, as can be seen most clearly in his *Saint Roch Festival at Bingen* (1817).[55]

In 1829 an associate conversed with Goethe about heated theological controversies brewing in Germany. His reply is a reminder of how much Goethe valued religious pluralism, for he mentioned that he had recently read about a city in North America in which there were sixty different churches— "there one could be edified in a different confession on each Sunday of the year."[56] The American solution to the devastating problem of religious strife, of which Franklin's Philadelphia was a model, was compelling to Goethe, and he portrayed it flatteringly in *Wilhelm Meister's Journeyman Years*. Goethe wanted to achieve a similar broadness of sympathy in Weimar.[57]

In the paralipomena to *Poetry and Truth*, Goethe observed that writing an autobiographical confessional is risky because one could easily fall into the morose habit of focusing excessively on moral failings rather than one's virtues.[58] This was surely one reason he appreciated the *Autobiography* so much: Franklin was devoted to developing and confessing his virtues. He allowed himself to see his life as a work in progress, a perpetual construction zone. This would have appealed to Goethe and resonated deeply with his own idea of *Bildung*, which meant for him something akin to self-cultivation and the development of personal meaning. Although the obvious connection here is to self-creation, this was more than mere window dressing. Both Franklin and Goethe believed that industry was necessary to achieve any significant growth, but both held that self-transformation was possible.

Franklin writes of the "Virtue" of "Industry" that he had practiced throughout his life. Yet he also understood that it was important as a young entrepreneur in Philadelphia to be seen to be diligent by his potential customers, so that they would think: "the Industry of that Franklin, says he, is superior to any thing I ever saw of the kind: I see him at work when I go home from the Club; and he is at Work again before his Neighbours are out of bed."[59] He tells of how he would take his "Wheelbarrow" through the streets of Philadelphia, filled with paper he had purchased, "to show that I was not above my Business" and be "esteem'd an industrious thriving young Man."[60] "In order to secure my Credit and Character as a Tradesman," writes

Franklin, "I took care not only to be in *Reality* Industrious and frugal, but to avoid all *Appearances* of the Contrary."[61] There is a European tradition represented by Werner Sombart, Max Weber, and D. H. Lawrence that holds episodes such as this one to indicate that Franklin was merely a self-interested businessman who had introduced the "marriage of virtue and worldly prosperity" to a wide readership and "found a substitute for the confessional in self-examinations" such as Franklin's *Autobiography* contained.[62] This line of criticism misses the point that Franklin's sense of civic duty and practical contributions to the development and improvement of civic institutions were consonant with his sense of self-interest, as Michael Zuckerman has eloquently argued.[63]

W. H. Bruford's insight is all the more remarkable for seeing beyond this narrower view of Franklin at a time when it had reached its European high-water mark. He provided examples of middle-class young men in Germany, such as Werner in Goethe's *Wilhelm Meister's Apprenticeship* (1795–1796), who wanted, like Franklin, to "attain moral perfection, and worldly success as its reward." Furthermore, Bruford argued that German philosophers had already "propounded very similar rules to Franklin's, long before his time." So what set Franklin's *Autobiography* apart? Bruford suggests that the answer might lie in its emphasis on civic duty and responsibility, as well as its pragmatic contours, or as one historian has put it, "Franklin represented new habits of thinking about political and social problems," one for whom the "character of his natural science left its mark on his political science," a political science that could be summed up in one "devastating question"— "*Does it work well?*"[64]:

> But in justice to Franklin it should be added that he possessed qualities of mind and feeling that are recorded . . . between the lines of his autobiography and in his great public achievements. The natural wisdom of his mind enabled him to make good use of even the dry scraps of traditional morality, and the generosity of his temperament and his abounding public spirit made him a "citizen" in a sense which perhaps no German of that age deserved the name. Compared with him even the highest embodiments of German ideals, such as Lessing's *Nathan the Wise*, have something provincial and theoretical about them.[65]

In an entry of his extended autobiographical writings (*Tag- und Jahreshefte*), Goethe assesses "Das Leben *Franklins*," probably referring to the *Memoirs of the Life and Writings of Benjamin Franklin*, "as a monument to a glorious intellect" who had despite minimal formal education "developed himself nobly and powerfully through nature."[66] Goethe admired the unfolding self of Franklin, bodied forth in the *Autobiography*, which can be understood as a testament to *Bildung,* and he drew on Franklin's achievements, foremost in the realm of science, and the literary life he composed, to help situate and fashion his own.

NOTES

1. Paul E. Kerry, "Goethe and Carlyle: What Kind of Spiritual Inheritance?" *Occasional Papers of the Carlyle Society*, N.S. 17 (2004-5): 32–42. This chapter is a revised and expanded version of "Goethe and Franklin," in ФИЛОСОФСКИЙ ВЕК АЛЬМАНАХ [The Philosophical Age, Almanac 31] (St. Petersburg: St. Petersburg Center for the History of Ideas, 2006), 74–88.

2. "Essay on the Genius and Character of Goethe," HUC 6831, Harvard University Archives. Motley comments in particular on Goethe's "versatility," a description that could also be applied to Franklin.

3. Henry Wadsworth Longfellow, *Hyperion: A Romance* (Boston: Ticknor, Reed, and Fields, 1853), 159.

4. James Parton, *Life and Times of Benjamin Franklin* (Boston: Ticknor and Fields, 1867), 2:581.

5. Katharina Mommsen, *Goethe und unsere Zeit* (Frankfurt am Main: Suhrkamp, 1999), 39.

6. Ekkehart Krippendorff, *Jefferson und Goethe* (Hamburg: Europäische Verlagsanstalt, 2001), 19–42.

7. Jürgen Overhoff, *Benjamin Franklin: Erfinder, Freigeist, Staatenlenker* (Stuttgart: Klett-Cotta Verlag, 2006), 10–15, 223–30. See also Horst Dippel, "Franklin: An Idol of the Times," in *Critical Essays on Benjamin Franklin*, ed. Melvin H. Buxbaum (Boston: G. K. Hall, 1987), 202–10.

8. Johann Gottfried Herder, *Briefe zu Beförderung der Humanität*, ed. Hans Dietrich Irmscher (Frankfurt am Main: Suhrkamp, 1991), 14–15. All translations mine unless otherwise indicated.

9. See Overhoff, *Benjamin Franklin*, ch. 7, and Maiken Umbach, *Federalism and Enlightenment in Germany* (London: Hambledon Press, 2000).

10. Susan Gustafson, "The Religious Significance of Goethe's 'Amerikabild,'" *Eighteenth-Century Studies* 24 (1990): 69–91. Walter Hinderer has written an insightful essay on "Goethe und Amerika," in *Goethe und das Zeitalter der Romantik*, ed. Hinderer and Alexander van Borman, (Wurzburg: Verlag Königshausen, 2002), 489–506.

11. Jeff Osborne, "Benjamin Franklin and the Rhetoric of Virtuous Self-Fashioning in Eighteenth-Century America," *Literature and History* 17, no. 2 (2008): 14–30.

12. See Stephen Greenblatt, *Renaissance Self-Fashioning: From More to Shakespeare* (Chicago: University of Chicago Press, 1990). Although it could be argued that "self-fashioning" has existed in the Western tradition since classical times, Greenblatt galvanized the term with critical meaning in his landmark book.

13. Johann Wolfgang von Goethe, *Sämtliche Werke: Briefe, Tagebücher und Gespräche*, Frankfurter Ausgabe, ed. Friedmar Apel et al. (Frankfurt am Main: Deutscher Klassiker, 1987–99), I, iv, 770; see also Eduard Baumgarten, *Benjamin Franklin: Der Lehrmeister der amerikanischen Revolution* (Frankfurt am Main: Klisterman, 1936). Though several editions of the complete works of Goethe have been published, none is perfectly comprehensive. This chapter favors the Frankfurt edition (cited hereafter as FA) but also uses the Munich edition (MA) and the Weimar edition (WA) when necessary.

14. See M. C. Sprengel, *Allgemeines historisches Taschenbuch oder Abrisz der merkwürdigsten neun Welt-Begebenheiten: enthaltend für 1784, Die Geschichte der Revolution von Nord-America* (Berlin: Haude und Spener, [1783]).

15. FA, I, xiv, 649–50. English translation in Johann Wolfgang von Goethe, *From My Life: Poetry and Truth, Parts One to Three*, vol. 4 *of Goethe's Collected Works*, trans. Robert R. Heitner, ed. Thomas P. Saine, and Jeffrey L. Sammons (New York: Suhrkamp, 1987), 438–39.

16. FA, I, xxiii, 65, 1413.

17. Esmond Wright, "The *Autobiography*: Fact or Fiction?" in *The Intellectual World of Benjamin Franklin: An American Encyclopaedist at the University of Pennsylvania*, ed. Dilys Pegler Winegrad (Philadelphia: University of Pennsylvania Press, 1990), 31.

18. Dennis F. Mahoney, "Autobiographical Writings," in *The Cambridge Companion to Goethe*, ed. Lesley Sharpe (Cambridge: Cambridge University Press, 2002), 147.

19. Paul E. Kerry, "Franklin's Satiric Vein," in *The Cambridge Companion to Benjamin Franklin*, ed. Carla Mulford (Cambridge: Cambridge University Press, 2008), 37–49.

20. Stephen Carl Arch, "Benjamin Franklin's *Autobiography*, Then and Now," in ibid., 159–71.

21. Johann Wolfgang von Goethe, *Sämtliche Werke nach Epochen seines Schaffens*, Münchener Ausgabe, ed. Karl Richter (Munich: Hanser, 1985–98) xx/1:249. Hereafter MA.

22. *Autobiography*, 117. Part one of the *Autobiography* was first published in French translation in 1791 and is presumably the edition that Goethe used.

23. Herder, *Briefe zu Beförderung der Humanität*, 18–23.

24. See Felix Höpfner, "Wissenschaft wider die Zeit: Goethes Farbenlehre aus rezeptionsgeschichtlicher Sicht: Mit einer Bibliographie zur Farbenlehre," *Beiträge zur neueren Literaturgeschichte* 3 (Heidelberg: Winter, 1990).

25. MA, xx/1, 249.

26. FA, I, xxiii, 912.

27. FA, I, xxiii, 913.

28. MA, xx/2, 1215.

29. FA, I, xxiii, 1055.

30. FA, I, xxiii, 894–95.

31. Walter D. Wetzels, "Goethe's Belief in Himself: Talent as Gift and Obligation," *Literature and Belief: Special Issue on Goethe and Religion* 20, no. 2 (2000): 29.

32. FA, I, xiv, 931.

33. Gordon Craig, *The Politics of the Unpolitical: German Writers and the Problem of Power, 1770–1871* (Oxford: Clarendon Press, 1993), 3.

34. FA, I, xiv, 931.

35. MA, xix, 215. English translation in Johann Peter Eckermann, *Conversations of Goethe with Johann Peter Eckermann*, trans. John Oxenford, ed. J. K. Moorhead (1850, repr. Boston: Da Capo Press, 1998), 172.

36. FA, I, xiv, 132.

37. Rudolf Magnus, G*oethe as Scientist*, trans. Heinz Norden (New York: Henry Schuman, 1949), 12, 15, 25, 231.

38. A. E. Odyniec to J. Korsak, 25 August 1829, in FA, II, xxxviii, 158.

39. Heinz Otto Sibum, "The Bookkeeper of Nature: Benjamin Franklin's Electrical Research and the Development of Experimental Natural Philosophy in the Eighteenth Century," in *Reappraising Benjamin Franklin: A Bicentennial Perspective*, ed. J. A. Leo Lemay (Newark: University of Delaware Press, 1993), 221–46.

40. Aeka Ishihara, *Goethes Buch der Natur: Ein Beispiel der Rezeption naturwissenschaftlicher Erkenntnisse und Methoden in der Literatur seiner Zeit* (Würzburg: Königshausen & Neumann, 2005), 76–77. See Reiner Wild, "Prometheus-Franklin: Die Gestalt Benjamin Franklins in der deutschen Literatur des 18.Jahrhunderts," *Amerikastudien* 23, no. 1 (1978): 30–39.

41. Ishihara, *Goethes Buch der Natur*, 75–85.

42. J. A. Leo Lemay, "The Life of Benjamin Franklin," in *Benjamin Franklin: In Search of a Better World*, ed. Page Talbott (New Haven, CT: Yale University Press), 46.

43. MA, viii/1, 508.

44. Immanuel Kant, "Beantwortung der Frage: Was ist Aufklärung?" in *Schriften zur Anthropologie, Geschichtsphilosophie, Politik und Pädagogik*, ed. Wilhelm Weischedel, (Frankfurt am Main: Suhrkamp, 1996), 53.

45. All quotations from "Prometheus" are taken from FA, I, i, 203–4.

46. Lemay, "Life of Benjamin Franklin, " 45–46.

47. Lester J. Cappon, ed. *The Complete Correspondence between Thomas Jefferson and Abigail and John Adams* (Chapel Hill: University of North Carolina Press, 1987), 395. Adams has confused the word "Schriften" for "Schristen" and made it a part of Goethe's name. Jefferson responds on 24 January 1814.

48. Goethe can be placed in the tradition of higher biblical criticism emanating from the Germanic lands at this time. See Michael C. Legaspi, *The Death of Scripture and the Rise of Biblical Studies* (Oxford: Oxford University Press, 2010), 135.

49. *Autobiography*, 146.

50. Walter Isaacson, ed., *Benjamin Franklin Reader* (New York: Simon and Schuster, 2005), 376. Isaacson maintains that Franklin became more secure in his "amorphous faith in a benevolent God" as he grew older.

51. WA, III, xi, 322–23 and xii, 9. See also Goethe's diary entries from 30–31 December 1828 to 19 January 1829.

52. FA, I, x, 342–44.

53. Prince Carl Bernhard von Sachsen-Weimar-Eisenach, *Reise Sr. Hoheit des Herzogs Bernhard zu Sachsen-Weimar-Eisenach durch Nord-Amerika in den Jahren 1825 und 1826*, ed. Heinrich Luden (Weimar: Wilhelm Hoffman, 1828), 220–21 and 204–12.

54. *Autobiography*, 176.

55. See chapters four and seven of Paul E. Kerry, *Enlightenment Thought in the Writings of Goethe: A Contribution to the History of Ideas* (Rochester, NY: Camden House, 2009).

56. Conversation with L. Löw von und zu Steinfurt, 3 October 1829, in FA iii/2, 532.

57. "Weimaraner" ("Zahme Xenien V"). FA, I, ii, 661.

58. FA, I, xiv, 931.

59. *Autobiography*, 119.

60. Ibid., 126.

61. Ibid., 125.

62. W. H. Bruford, *Germany in the Eighteenth Century: The Social Background of the Literary Revival* (Cambridge: Cambridge University Press, 1965), 227–28. Subsequent quotations are to this source. Although not in the same way, Goethe, too, challenges the traditional confessional. See also Wilson J. Moses, "Protestant Ethic or Conspicuous Consumption? Benjamin Franklin and the Gilded Age," in *A Companion to Benjamin Franklin*, ed. David Waldstreicher (Malden, MA: Wiley-Blackwell, 2011), 132–44. Moses explores Franklin and the nineteenth-century philanthropists who modeled themselves on, for example, *The Way to Wealth* in the light of Thorstein Veblen's theories.

63. Michael Zuckerman, "Doing Good While Doing Well: Benevolence and Self-Interest in Franklin's *Autobiography*," in *Reappraising Benjamin Franklin: A Bicentennial Perspective*, edited by J. A. Leo Lemay (Newark, DE: University of Delaware Press, 1993), 441–51. Alan Houston, *Benjamin Franklin and the Politics of Improvement* (New Haven, CT: Yale University Press, 2008).

64. Clinton Rossiter, *Seedtime of the Republic: The Origin of the American Tradition of Political Liberty* (New York: Harcourt, Brace and Company, 1953), 311 and 294.

65. Bruford, *Germany in the Eighteenth Century*, 228.

66. FA, I, xvii, 285, 592. Similar to the earlier description of Justus Möser being applied to Franklin in *Dichtung und Wahrheit*, this summary of Franklin's *Memoirs* is Goethe's judgment of a biography by Joseph Adams, *Memoirs of the Life and Doctrines of the late John Hunter, Esq.* (London: J. Callow, 1817), that he applies to Franklin.

Afterword

Benjamin Franklin's Material Presence in a Digital Age and Popular Culture World

Roy E. Goodman

Benjamin Franklin wrote to his daughter Sally from Passy on 3 June 1779, in a lighter moment when he could think beyond the political intrigues that Neil York's chapter in this volume shows were pressing at precisely this time:

> The clay medallion of me you say you gave to Mr. Hopkinson was the first of the kind made in France. A variety of others have been made since of different sizes; some to be set in lids of snuff boxes, and some so small as to be worn in rings; and the numbers sold are incredible. These, with the pictures, busts, and prints, (of which copies upon copies are spread every where) have made your father's face as well known as that of the moon, so that he durst not do any thing that would oblige him to run away, as his phiz would discover him wherever he should venture to show it. It is said by learned etymologists that the name *Doll*, for the images children play with, is derived from the word IDOL; from the number of *dolls* now made of him, he may be truly said, *in that sense,* to be *i-doll-ized* in this country.[1]

This revealing eighteenth-century observation holds true today. Few Americans offer a window into the hearts and minds of a nation like Benjamin Franklin does. Although scholars have produced excellent work on the historical iconography of Franklin,[2] the daunting amount of video and print media, especially advertising literature, recordings, art, websites, and collectibles, is a task I have pursued. Similar to Paul Kerry's chapter in this volume, it is a way of showing how Benjamin Franklin's intellectual world continues to influence us and our paradigms. This influence is present not only in scholarly discussions about his political philosophy—and Lorraine Pangle

167

and Benjamin Park remind us that Franklin's thought can be considered in that rarified air—but it pervades our popular and material culture, the world not only of scholars but of Simon Newman's leather-apron men.

Collecting artifacts that reflect Franklin's humor, business acumen, networking skills, philanthropy, and scientific and civic values has been especially useful in monitoring contemporary America's sentiments about its history. Financial and educational institutions, plumbers and day planners, science institutes and craft stores, and much more have attempted to use his name and iconic image to tap into the American character that he is associated with creating, or at least projecting, for Franklin can be a "slippery customer" to define, as Jerry Weinberger observes. The hope is that their association with Franklin's now mythical reputation will project his values onto their goods and services in the eye of a consuming public. As Curator of Printed Materials at the American Philosophical Society, I work in an institution that Benjamin Franklin founded. I have curated and displayed these objects and online databases, including the Franklin Papers, in museums and elsewhere. The material engages new audiences of all ages and interests, a priority cultural institutions always appreciate.

Even Franklin bobblehead dolls are not out of place, for among the pantheon of Founding Fathers, this one is seen to have at least one foot firmly planted on the earth. In our mind's eye we can see him at the baseball park, cheering on the Philadelphia Phillies, sporting a team cap and enjoying a hot dog. Indeed, Franklin Field on the University of Pennsylvania campus (another Philadelphia institution where Franklin looms large as a founder) is where the famous Penn Relays have been held since the late nineteenth century. So much of Franklin is modern and updatable. We relate well to his strong belief in cooperation in the public square, and although we sometimes fall short in this regard, this kind of civil society remains an American ideal. Franklin, a Free Mason, was a prominent donor to the Mikveh Israel synagogue of the local Jewish congregation, and one could see him happily welcoming the National Museum of American Jewish History and the Mormon temple, two recent additions to the City of Brotherly Love, the former nestled near Constitution Hall, the Liberty Bell, and the city's colonial Christian churches, the latter along the beautiful boulevard between City Hall and the Philadelphia Museum of Art, adjacent to the Cathedral Basilica of Saints Peter and Paul. This commitment to fundamental liberties, such as religious liberty, represents Michael Zuckerman's Franklin, one who relished deeply his freedom and actively sought it for others. It is the mature political liberalism of which Carla Mulford writes.

The 300th anniversary of Franklin's birth sparked commemorations in 2006 and beyond. Numerous learned conferences, like the one Paul Kerry and Matthew Holland organized at the University of Cambridge, as well as a plethora of events, publications, and exhibits in the United States and abroad were held. And, I should add, staged: playwright Tim Slover's *Lightning Rod* made its world premiere. A different twist on Franklin was in order.

My eclectic, unorthodox assemblage of Franklin memorabilia was gathered from disparate sources and with the assistance of many people. Flea markets, souvenir shops, organizations with Franklin links, and the watchful eyes of colleagues have contributed to the protean growth of my collection. Certainly, eBay and the web have provided convenient means in expanding my Frankliniana, especially over the past ten years.

In a broader context, collections of any sort offer an opportunity to reflect on why one collects anything. Franklin's interest in supporting and contributing to the American Philosophical Society's "cabinet of curiosities" is a literal case in point. The APS artifacts are now available to view online. Franklin & Marshall College hosts a website on furniture, portraiture and other works of art relating to Franklin. Indeed, I had planned to contribute a Franklin timeline to this volume; however, through the wonders of technology under the auspices of the Franklin 300th celebration, a marvelous interactive "lifetime" exists for all to access. Everything I have just mentioned is available on www.benfranklin300.org.

I would be remiss in not citing the digital Papers of Benjamin Franklin (www.franklinpapers.org), produced by Yale University and cosponsored by the American Philosophical Society. This resource is the mother lode of Franklin correspondence and available for all to use. The print edition, which will be close to fifty volumes when completed, includes footnotes not present in the digital resource.

I must also mention here the recent passing of a great Franklin scholar: J. A. Leo Lemay (17 January 1935–15 October 2008). Leo Lemay was the du Pont Winterthur Professor of English at the University of Delaware and an early supporter in fostering Franklin scholarship in digital media through his website, Benjamin Franklin: A Documentary History, which can be found at www.english.udel.edu/lemay/franklin/. He will of course be gratefully remembered by scholars for coediting, with his friend the late Paul M. Zall a critical edition of *Benjamin Franklin's Autobiography* as well as for completing the first three volumes of a multivolume biography: *The Life of Benjamin Franklin*.

If Dr. Franklin could return years after his death, as he amusingly wrote in *A Bagatelle*, preserved in a barrel of Madeira wine, he would certainly be amazed with today's technology and the variety of media profusely producing iconography using his image and ideas. In the play *1776*, John Adams is seen to protest precisely this vision of future history and Franklin's place in it: "I won't appear in the history books, anyway—only you. [*He thinks about it.*] Franklin did this, Franklin did that, Franklin did some other damned thing. Franklin smote the ground, and out sprang George Washington, fully grown and on his horse. Franklin then electrified him with his miraculous

lightning rod, and the three of them—Franklin, Washington, *and* the horse—
conducted the entire Revolution all by themselves."[3] Franklin, however,
would be more than impressed; I suspect that he would be an innovator and
participant in the twenty-first century fusion of technology, creativity, and
communication, just as he was in eighteenth-century Philadelphia.

It does not take much imagination to consider Franklin, who as Douglas
Thomas reminds us in this volume was a man who understood communication networks, being on the ground floor of Wikipedia or Google to name but
two, maybe as an investor or founder (Franklin and Zuckerberg anyone?),
and using the emerging social media to full effect. A simple Google search of
"Benjamin Franklin" yields 29,200,000 hits. How many followers would
Ben's Tweets have?

It is this Franklin that has also remained with us, more pliant and more
usable in different socioeconomic and cultural contexts. George Lundeen's
well-known bronze of Benjamin Franklin, commissioned for the University
of Pennsylvania, features Franklin sitting on a park bench reading a copy of
the *Pennsylvania Gazette* with a pigeon looking on. Franklin blends into the
scenery of this bustling and leafy part of campus perfectly. In a similar way,
the Franklin image, brand, and ethos, as shown in the material, popular, and
digital culture of our day, blend into and continue to shape America's twen-
ty-first-century culture and society.

NOTES

1. *Papers: Digital Edition.* Print ed. in *Papers* 29:612.
2. See, for example, Megan Walsh, "Benjamin Franklin's Material Cultures," in *A Companion to Benjamin Franklin*, ed. David Waldstreicher (Malden, MA: Wiley-Blackwell, 2011),
412–29.
3. Peter Stone and Sherman Edwards, *1776: A Musical Play* (New York: Penguin, 1982),
74.

Bibliography

Abingdon, Earl of. *Thoughts on the Letter of Edmund Burke, Esq.; To the Sheriffs of Bristol, On the Affairs of America,* Oxford: W. Jackson, 1777.

Achenwall, Gottfried. "Einige Anmerkungen über Nord-Amerika und über dasige Großbrittanische Colonien. Aus mündlichen Nachrichten des Herrn D. Franklins [Some observations on North America and her British Colonies. From Oral Information by Dr. Franklin.]" *Hannoverisches Magazin 17tes, 18tes, 19tes, 31tes, 32tes Stück* (1767): 257–96, 482–508. Also published in Helmstedt: J. H. Kuhnlin, 1777.

Adams, John. *Diary and Autobiography of John Adams.* 4 vols. Edited by Lyman Butterfield. Cambridge, MA: Harvard University Press, 1961.

Adams, Joseph. *Memoirs of the Life and Doctrines of the late John Hunter,* Adams, Joseph. Memoirs of the Life and Doctrines of the late John Hunter, London: J. Callow, 1817.

Aiken, John R. "Benjamin Franklin, Karl Marx, and the Labor Theory of Value." *The Pennsylvania Magazine of History and Biography* 90, no. 3 (July 1966): 378–84.

Albemarle, Earl of. *Memoirs of the Marquis of Rockingham and His Contemporaries.* 2 vols. London: Richard Bentley, 1852.

Alden, John Richard. "Again, the American Revolution—Inevitable?" *Phi Kappa Phi Journal* 55 (1975): 3–10.

Aldridge, Alfred Owen. *Benjamin Franklin and Nature's God.* Durham, NC: Duke University Press, 1967.

Alstyne, Richard W. Van. *Empire and Independence.* New York: John Wiley & Sons, 1965.

Amory, Hugh, and David D. Hall, eds. *The Colonial Book in the Atlantic World.* 5 vols. A History of the Book in America. Cambridge: Cambridge University Press; American Antiquarian Society, 2000.

Anderson, Benedict. *Imagined Communities: Reflections on the Origins and Spread of Nationalism.* Revised edition. New York: Verso, 1991.

Anderson, Douglas. "The Art of Virtue." In Mulford, *Cambridge Companion to Benjamin Franklin,* 24–36.

———. *The Radical Enlightenments of Benjamin Franklin.* Baltimore: Johns Hopkins University Press, 1997.

Anderson, Fred. *A People's Army: Massachusetts Soldiers and Society in the Seven Years' War.* New York: W. W. Norton & Company, 1984.

Anderson, James. *The Interest of Great-Britain with Regard to Her American Colonies Considered.* London: T. Cadell, 1782.

Anson, Sir William R., ed. *Autobiography and Political Correspondence of Augustus Henry Third Duke of Grafton.* London: John Murray, 1898.

Appleby, Joyce. *Liberalism and Republicanism in the Historical Imagination.* Cambridge, MA: Harvard University Press, 1992.

Bailyn, Bernard, and John B. Hench. *The Press and the American Revolution.* Boston: Northeastern University Press, 1981.

Bancroft, George. *History of the United States from the Discovery of the American Continent.* 10 vols. Boston: Little, Brown and Company, 1866.

Barker, G. F. Russell, and Alan H. Stenning. *The Record of Old Westminsters.* 2 vols. London: Chiswick Press, 1928.

Baumgarten, Eduard. *Benjamin Franklin. Der Lehrmeister der amerikanischen Revolution.* Frankfurt am Main: Klisterman, 1936.

Beeman, Richard. "Benjamin Franklin and the American Enlightenment." The Benjamin Franklin Tercentary. www.benfranklin300.org/_etc.../Enlightenment_Richard_Beeman.pdf.

Bellot, Leland. *William Knox.* Austin: University of Texas Press, 1977.

Bemis, Samuel Flagg. "British Secret Service and the French-American Alliance." *American Historical Review* 29 (1924): 474–95.

———. *The Diplomacy of the American Revolution.* New York: D. Appleton-Century, 1935.

———. *The Hussey-Cumberland Mission and American Independence.* Princeton, NJ: Princeton University Press, 1931.

Bennett, William. *John Baskerville: The Birmingham Printer. Vol. 1: His Press, Relations, and Friends.* Birmingham, UK: City of Birmingham School of Printing, 1937.

Benton, Josiah Henry. *John Baskerville, Type-Founder and Printer 1706–1775.* New York: Burt Franklin, 1968.

Berger, Peter, and Richard John Neuhaus. "Mediating Structures and the Dilemmas of the Modern Welfare State." In *To Empower People: From State to Civil Society,* 157–64. Washington, DC: American Enterprise Institute, 1996.

Bernhard von Sachsen-Weimar-Eisenach, Prince Carl. Reise Sr. Hoheit des Herzogs Bernhard zu Sachsen-Weimar-Eisenach durch Nord-Amerika in den Jahren 1825 und 1826 . Edited by Heinrich Luden. Weimar: Wilhelm Hoffman, 1828.

Berthoff, Rowland. "Peasants and Artisans, Puritans and Republicans: Personal Liberty and Communal Equality in American History." *Journal of American History* 69 (December 1982): 579–98.

Bigelow, Jacob, ed. *The Complete Works of Benjamin Franklin.* 12 vols. New York: G. P. Putnam's Sons, 1887–96.

Black, Jeremy. *War for America.* New York: St. Martin's Press, 1991.

Bonwick, Colin. *English Radicals and the American Revolution.* Chapel Hill: University of North Carolina Press, 1977.

Bosco, Ronald A. "'He That Best Understands the World, Least Likes It': The Dark Side of Benjamin Franklin." *Pennsylvania Magazine of History and Biography* 111 (October 1987): 525–54.

Boudreau, George W. "The Philadelphia Years, 1723–1757." In Waldstreicher, *Companion to Benjamin Franklin*, 25–45.

Bowdoin, James. "Bowdoin and Temple Papers." *Massachusetts Historical Society. Collections* 9, sixth series (1897): 416–17.

Boyd, Julian, ed. *The Declaration of Independence.* Revised ed. Washington, DC: Library of Congress, 1999.

Bradley, James E. *Popular Politics and the American Revolution in England.* Macon, GA: Mercer University Press, 1986.

———. *Religion, Revolution, and English Radicalism: Nonconformity in Eighteenth-Century Politics and Society.* Cambridge: Cambridge University Press, 1990.

Brands, H. W. *The First American: The Life and Times of Benjamin Franklin.* New York: Doubleday, 2000.

Breitweiser, Mitchell. Review of *Becoming Benjamin Franklin: The Autobiography and the Life*, by Ormond Seavey. *William and Mary Quarterly,* 3rd ser., 46 (1989): 816–19.

Brown, Alan S. "The Impossible Dream: The North Ministry, the Structure of Politics, and Conciliation." In *The American Revolution and "A Candid World,"* edited by Lawrence S. Kaplan, 17–39. Kent, OH: Kent State University Press, 1977.

Brown, Alan S., and Forrest McDonald. "Letters to the Editor." *William and Mary Quarterly*, 3rd ser., 32 (1975): 179–82.

Brown, Gerald Saxon. *The American Secretary.* Ann Arbor: University of Michigan Press, 1963.

Brown, Wallace. *The Good Americans.* New York: William Morrow, 1969.

Brown, Weldon A. *Empire or Independence?* Baton Rouge: Louisiana State University Press, 1941.

Bruford, W. H. *Germany in the Eighteenth Century: The Social Background of the Literary Revival.* Cambridge: Cambridge University Press, 1965.

Bullock, Alan, and Maurice Shock. *The Liberal Tradition: From Fox to Keynes.* London: A. and C. Black, 1956.

Burnett, Edmund Cody. *The Continental Congress.* New York: Macmillan, 1941.

———, ed. *Letters of Members of the Continental Congress.* Washington, DC: Carnegie Institution of Washington, 1921.

Cabanis, Pierre Jean Georges. *Oeuvres Complètes de Cabanis.* 5 vols. Paris: Bossange Frères, 1825.

Campbell, James. "The Pragmatist in Franklin." In Mulford, *Cambridge Companion to Benjamin Franklin,* 104–16.

Cannon, John. "The Loss of America." In *Britain and the American Revolution,* by H. T. Dickinson, 233–57. London: Longman, 1998.

Cappon, Lester J., ed. *The Complete Correspondence between Thomas Jefferson and Abigail and John Adams.* Chapel Hill: University of North Carolina Press, 1987.

Carlisle, Earl of. *The Manuscripts of the Earl of Carlisle.* Historical Manuscripts Commission. London: Eyre and Spottiswoode, 1897.

Cartwright, John. *American Independence: The Interest and Glory of Great Britain. A New Edition.* London: H. S. Woodfall, 1775.

Chaplin, Joyce. *Benjamin Franklin's Political Arithmetic: A Materialist View of Humanity.* Washington, DC: Smithsonian Libraries, 2008.

———. *The First Scientific American: Benjamin Franklin and the Pursuit of Genius.* New York: Basic Books, 2006.

Christie, Ian. *The End of North's Ministry.* London: Macmillan, 1958.

Cobbett, William, ed. *The Parliamentary History of England.* 36 vols. London: T. C. Hansard, 1806–20.

Coffey, John. "Puritanism and Liberty Revisited: The Case for Toleration in the English Revolution." *Historical Journal* 41 (1998): 961–85.

Connor, Paul W. *Poor Richard's Politicks: Benjamin Franklin and His New American Order.* New York: Oxford University Press, 1965.

Conway, Steven. *The British Isles and the War of American Independence.* Oxford: Oxford University Press, 2000.

———. *The War of American Independence, 1775–1783.* London: Edward Arnold, 1995.

Copeland, Thomas W., ed. *The Correspondence of Edmund Burke.* 10 vols. Chicago: University of Chicago Press, 1958–78.

Craig, Gordon. *The Politics of the Unpolitical: German Writers and the Problem of Power, 770–1871.* Oxford: Clarendon Press, 1993.

Crane, Verner W. "The Club of Honest Whigs: Friends of Science and Liberty." *William and Mary Quarterly,* 3rd ser., 23 (1966): 210–33.

Crowther, Simeon J. "A Note on the Economic Position of Philadelphia's White Oaks." *William and Mary Quarterly,* 3rd ser., 29 (1972): 134–36.

Currey, Cecil. *Code Number 72.* Englewood Cliffs, NJ: Prentice Hall, 1972.

Dartmouth Papers, D (W) 1778/II/1750. Staffordshire Record Office, Staffordshire, England.

Dierks, Konstantin. "Benjamin Franklin and Colonial Society." In Waldstreicher, *Companion to Benjamin Franklin,* 83–103.

Dippel, Horst. "Franklin: An Idol of the Times." In *Critical Essays on Benjamin Franklin,* edited by Melvin H. Buxbaum, 202–10. Boston, G. K. Hall, 1987.

———. *The Secret History of the American Revolution.* New York: Viking Press, 1941.

Doyle, William. *Aristocracy and its Enemies in the Age of Revolution.* New York: Oxford University Press, 2009.

Dray, Philip. *Stealing God's Thunder: Benjamin Franklin's Lightning Rod and the Invention of America.* New York: Random House, 2005.

Dull, Jonathan R. *A Diplomatic History of the American Revolution.* New Haven, CT: Yale University Press, 1985.

———. *Franklin the Diplomat: The French Mission.* Philadelphia: American Philosophical Society, 1982.

Dupre, Louis. *The Enlightenment and the Intellectual Foundations of Modern Culture.* New Haven, CT: Yale University Press, 2005.

Ebel, Wilhelm. *Der Göttinger Professor Johann Stephan Pütter aus Iserlohn.* Göttingen: Verlag Otto Schwartz & Co, 1975.

Eckerman, Johann Peter. *Conversations of Goethe with Johann Peter Eckermann.* Translated by John Oxenford. Edited by J. K. Moorhead. 1850. Reprint, Boston: Da Capo Press, 1998.

Ellison, Ralph. "Change the Joke and Slip the Yoke." In *Shadow and Act,* 45–59. New York: Random House, 1964.

Elshtain, Jean Bethke. *Sovereignty: God, State, and Self.* New York: Basic Books, 2008.

Epps, John. *Life of John Walker, M.D.* London: Whittaker, Treacher, and Co., 1831.

Farrell, David. "John Baskerville." In *Encyclopedia of Library and Information Science,* edited by Allen Kent, 11–22. New York: Marcell Decker, 1986.

Fea, John. "Benjamin Franklin and Religion." In Waldstreicher, *Companion to Benjamin Franklin,* 129–45.

Fitzmaurice, Edmond. *Life of William, Earl of Shelburne.* 2 vols. London: Macmillan and Co., 1912.

Fitzsimons, David M. "Thomas Paine's New World Order: Idealistic Internationalism in the Ideology of Early American Foreign Relations." *Diplomatic History* 19 (1995): 569–82.

Flavell, Julie. *When London Was Capital of America.* New Haven, CT: Yale University Press, 2010.

Ford, Worthington C., ed. *Journals of the Continental Congress.* 34 vols. Washington, DC: Government Printing Office, 1904–37.

Fortescue, Sir John, ed. *The Correspondence of King George III, from 1760 to 1783.* 6 vols. London: Macmillan and Co., 1927–28.

Foster, Joseph, ed. *Alumni Oxoniensis.* 4 vols. London: Parker & Co., 1888.

Fowler, William M. Jr., *American Crisis.* New York: Walker & Company, 2011.

Franklin, Benjamin. *The Autobiography of Benjamin Franklin.* Edited by Leonard W. Labaree, Ralph L. Ketcham, Helen C. Boatfield, and Helene H. Fineman. New Haven, CT: Yale University Press, 1964. [First published in Paris: Buisson 1791 (French edition); first English publication in London: J. Parsons, 1793.]

———. *The Autobiography of Benjamin Franklin: A Genetic Text.* Edited by J. A. Leo Lemay and Paul M. Zall. Knoxville: University of Tennessee Press, 1979.

———. *Benjamin Franklin: Autobiography, Poor Richard, and Later Writings.* Edited by J. A. Leo Lemay. New York: Library of America, 2005.

———. *Benjamin Franklin: Writings; Autobiography, Poor Richard's Almanack, Bagatelles, Pamphlets, Essays & Letters.* Edited by J. A. Leo Lemay. New York: Library of America, 1987.

———. *A Dissertation on Liberty and Necessity, Pleasure and Pain.* London: Sam. Palmer, 1724.

———. *The Interest of Great Britain Considered, With Regard to her Colonies, And the Acquisitions of Canada and Guadaloupe. To which are added, Observations Concerning the Increase of Mankind, Peopling of Countries, &c.* London: T. Becket, 1760.

———. *The Papers of Benjamin Franklin.* 39 volumes to date. Edited by Leonard W. Labaree, et al. New Haven, CT: Yale University Press, 1959–. Digital edition, including forthcoming print volumes, published by the Packard Humanities Institute. http://franklinpapers.org/franklin/framedVolumes.jsp.

———. *Poor Richard Improved: Being an Almanack and Ephemeris . . . for the Year of our Lord 1750. . . . By Richard Saunders, Philom.* Philadelphia: B. Franklin and D. Hall, 1750.

Frasca, Ralph. *Benjamin Franklin's Printing Network: Disseminating Virtue in Early America.* Columbia: University of Missouri Press, 2006.

Fruchtman, Jack Jr. *Atlantic Cousins: Benjamin Franklin and his Visionary Friends.* New York: Basic Books, 2007.

Fulton, Ellis. "Which Typefaces Are Most Useful?" *Inland Printer* 81 (April 1928): 101.

Gaskell, Philip. *John Baskerville: A Bibliography.* Cambridge: Cambridge University Press, 1959.

Gaustad, Edwin. *Benjamin Franklin: Inventing America.* New York: Oxford University Press, 2004.

Gay, Peter. *The Enlightenment: An Interpretation.* 2 vols. Revised ed. New York: W. W. Norton, 1995.

Germain, George. Papers. William L. Clements Library. University of Michigan. Printed, with minor changes, in the Historical Manuscripts Commission, 1904 and 1910.

Gilbert, Felix. *To the Farewell Address.* Princeton, NJ: Princeton University Press, 1961.

Gipson, Lawrence H. "The Great Debate in the Committee of the Whole House of Commons on the Stamp Act, 1766, as Reported by Nathaniel Ryder." *Pennsylvania Magazine of History and Biography* 86 (1962): 10–41.

Goethe, Johann Wolfgang. *From My Life: Poetry and Truth, Parts One to Three.* Translated by Robert R. Heitner. Edited by Thomas P. Saine, and Jeffrey L. Sammons. Vol. 4 of *Goethe's Collected Works.* New York: Suhrkamp, 1987.

———. *Goethes Gespräche: Eine Sammlung zeitgenössischer Berichte aus seinem Umgang auf Grund der Ausgabe und des Nachlasses von Flodoard Freiherrn von Biedermann.* Edited by Wolfgang Herwig. Zurich: Artemis Verlag, 1965–1987.

———. *Goethes Werke.* Weimarer Ausgabe. Herausgegeben im Auftrage der Großherzogin Sophie von Sachsen. 143 vols. Weimar: Böhlau, 1887–1919. Cited as WA.

———. *Sämtliche Werke. Briefe, Tagebücher und Gespräche.* Frankfurter Ausgabe. Edited by Friedmar Apel, et al. 40 vols. Frankfurt am Main: Deutscher Klassiker, 1987–99. Cited as FA.

———. *Sämtliche Werke nach Epochen seines Schaffens.* Münchener Ausgabe. Edited by Karl Richter. 21 vols. Munich: Hanser, 1985–1998. Cited as MA.

Goldie, Mark, and Robert Wolker. *The Cambridge History of Eighteenth-Century Political Thought.* Cambridge: Cambridge University Press, 2006.

Gould, Eliga. "Empire and Nation." In Waldstreicher, *Companion to Benjamin Franklin,* 359–72.

———. *The Persistence of Empire: British Political Culture in the Age of American Revolution.* Chapel Hill: University of North Carolina Press, 2000.

[Granville, George.] *The Genuine Works in Verse and Prose of the Right Honourable George Granville, Baron Lansdowne.* 3 vols. London: J. and R. Tonson, 1736.

Green, James N. "Benjamin Franklin, Printer." In Talbott, *Benjamin Franklin: In Search of a Better World,* 55–89.

Green, James N., and Peter Stallybrass. *Benjamin Franklin, Writer and Printer.* New Castle, DE: Oak Knoll Press, 2006.

Greenblatt, Stephen. *Renaissance Self-Fashioning: From More to Shakespeare.* Chicago: University of Chicago Press, 1990.

Greene, Jack P. "The Alienation of Benjamin Franklin, British American." In *Understanding the American Revolution.* Charlottesville: University of Virginia Press, 1995.

———. *The Constitutional Origins of the American Revolution.* Cambridge: Cambridge University Press, 2010.

Grenville Papers. British Library.

Grinde, Donald A. Jr., and Bruce E. Johansen. *Exemplar of Liberty: Native America and the Evolution of Democracy.* Los Angeles: American Indian Studies Center, 1991.

Gruber, Ira D. "Britain's Southern Strategy." In *The Revolutionary War in the South,* edited by W. Robert Higgins, 205–38. Durham, NC: Duke University Press, 1979.

———. *The Howe Brothers and the American Revolution.* Chapel Hill: University of North Carolina Press, 1972.

Gustafson, Susan. "The Religious Significance of Goethe's 'Amerikabild.'" *Eighteenth-Century Studies* 24 (1990): 69–91.

Guttridge, George Herbert. *David Hartley, M. P.* Berkeley: University of California Press, 1926.

———. *English Whiggism and the American Revolution.* Berkeley: University of California Press, 1966.

———. "Thomas Pownall's *The Administration of the Colonies*: The Six Editions." *William and Mary Quarterly* 3rd ser., 26 (1969): 31–46.

Hamilton, Alexander, John Jay, and James Madison. *The Federalist.* 1788. Edited by Jacob C. Cooke. Middletown, CT: Wesleyan University Press, 1961.

Harlow, Vincent. *The Founding of the Second British Empire, 1763–1793.* 2 vols. London: Longmans, Green, 1953, 1964.

Hartley, David. *Letters on the American War.* London: J. Almon, 1778.

Hayes, Kevin J. "Benjamin Franklin's Library." In Mulford, *Cambridge Companion to Benjamin Franklin*, 11–23.

Herder, Johann Gottfried. *Briefe zu Beförderung der Humanität.* Edited by Hans Dietrich Irmscher. Frankfurt am Main: Suhrkamp, 1991.

Hickman, Louise. "Godliness and Godlikeness: Cambridge Platonism in Richard Price's Religious Rationalism." *Enlightenment and Dissent* 24 (2008): 1–23.

Higginbotham, Don. *The War of American Independence.* New York: Macmillan, 1971.

Hinderer, Walter. "Goethe und Amerika." In *Goethe und das Zeitalter der Romantik*, edited by Walter Hinderer and Alexander von Bormann, 489–506. Würzburg: Verlag Königshausen, 2002.

Hobbes, Thomas. *Leviathan.* Edited by Richard Tuck. Cambridge: Cambridge University Press, 1996.

Holland, Matthew S. *Bonds of Affection: Civic Charity and the Making of America—Winthrop, Jefferson, and Lincoln.* Washington, DC: Georgetown University Press, 2007.

Holmes, Stephen. *Passions and Constraint: On the Theory of Liberal Democracy.* Chicago: University of Chicago Press, 1995.

Höpfner, Felix. "Wissenschaft wider die Zeit: Goethes Farbenlehre aus rezeptionsgeschichtlicher Sicht: Mit einer Bibliographie zur Farbenlehre." *Beiträge zur neueren Literaturgeschichte* 3. Heidelberg: Winter, 1990.

Houston, Alan. *Benjamin Franklin and the Politics of Improvement.* New Haven, CT: Yale University Press, 2008.

Houston, Alan, and Steven Pincus, eds. *A Nation Transformed: England after the Restoration.* Cambridge, Cambridge University Press, 1991.

Huang, Nian-Sheng, and Carla Mulford. "Benjamin Franklin and the American Dream." In Mulford, *Cambridge Companion to Benjamin Franklin*, 145–58.

Hume, David. *Essays and Treatises on Several Subjects: A New Edition .* London: Millar, Kincaid, and Donaldson, 1758.

Hutson, James H. "An Investigation of the Inarticulate: Philadelphia's White Oaks." *William and Mary Quarterly* 3rd ser., 28 (1971): 3–25.

———. *John Adams and the Diplomacy of the American Revolution.* Lexington: University of Kentucky Press, 1980.

Isaacson, Walter. *Benjamin Franklin: An American Life.* New York: Simon & Schuster, 2003.

———, ed. *A Benjamin Franklin Reader.* New York: Simon and Schuster, 2005.

Ishihara, Aeka. *Goethes Buch der Natur: Ein Beispiel der Rezeption naturwissenschaftlicher Erkenntnisse und Methoden in der Literatur seiner Zeit.* Würzburg, Königshausen & Neumann, 2005.

Israel, Jonathan. *Enlightenment Contested: Philosophy, Modernity, and the Emancipation of Man 1670–1752.* New York: Oxford University Press, 2006.

———. *Radical Enlightenment: Philosophy and the Making of Modernity.* New York: Oxford University Press, 2001.

Jacob, Margaret C. *Strangers Nowhere in the World: The Rise of Cosmopolitanism in Early Modern Europe.* Philadelphia: University of Pennsylvania Press, 2006.

Jefferson, Thomas. *The Papers of Thomas Jefferson*. 38 volumes. Edited by Julian P. Boyd. Princeton, NJ: Princeton University Press.

Johansen, Bruce E. "Native American Societies and the Evolution of Democracy in America, 1600–1800." *Ethnohistory* 37 (1990): 279–97.

Johnson, Samuel. *Dictionary of the English Language*. London: William Strahan, 1755.

Jordan, John W. "Some Account of James Hutton's Visit to Franklin in December 1777." *Pennsylvania Magazine of History and Biography* 32 (1908): 223–32.

Jordanova, Ludmilla. *History in Practice*. London: Hodder and Stoughton, 2006.

Joy, Neill R. "Politics and Culture: The Dr. Franklin–Dr. Johnson Connection, with an Analogue." *Prospects* 23 (1998): 59–105.

Kant, Immanuel. "Beantwortung der Frage: Was ist Aufklärung?" In *Schriften zur Anthropologie, Geschichtsphilosophie, Politik und Pädagogik*, vol. 1, edited by Wilhelm Weischedel, 53–61. Frankfurt am Main: Suhrkamp, 1996.

Kelleter, Frank. "Franklin and the Enlightenment." In Mulford, *Cambridge Companion to Benjamin Franklin*, 77–90.

Kerry, Paul E. *Enlightenment Thought in the Writings of Goethe: A Contribution to the History of Ideas*. Rochester, NY: Camden House, 2009.

———. "Franklin's Satiric Vein." In Mulford, *Cambridge Companion to Benjamin Franklin*, 37–49.

———. "Goethe and Carlyle: What Kind of Spiritual Inheritance?" *Occasional Papers of the Carlyle Society*, N.S. 17 (2004-5): 32–42.

Kloppenberg, James T. "The Virtues of Liberalism: Christianity, Republicanism, and Ethics in Early American Political Discourse." *Journal of American History* 74 (June 1987): 9–33.

Knott, Sarah. *Sensibility and the American Revolution*. Chapel Hill: University of North Carolina Press, 2009.

Knox, William. Papers. William L. Clements Library, University of Michigan.

Kors, Alan Charles, ed. *Encyclopedia of the Enlightenment*. 4 vols. Oxford: Oxford University Press, 2003.

Korshin, Paul J. "Benjamin Franklin and Samuel Johnson: A Literary Relationship," in *Benjamin Franklin: An American Genius*, edited by Gianfranca Balestra and Luigi Sampietro, 33–49. Rome: Bulzoni Editore, 1993.

Koschnik, Albrecht. "Benjamin Franklin, Associations, and Civil Society." In Waldstreicher, *Companion to Benjamin Franklin*, 335–58.

Krider, E. Philip. "Benjamin Franklin's Science." In Talbott, *Benjamin Franklin: In Search of a Better World*, 163–97.

Krippendorff, Ekkehart. *Jefferson und Goethe*. Hamburg: Europäische Verlagsanstalt, 2001.

LaCroix, Alison. "Drawing and Redrawing the Line: The Pre-Revolutionary Origins of Federal Ideas of Sovereignty." In *Transformations in American Legal History*, edited by Daniel W. Hamilton and Alfred L. Brophy, 58–84. Cambridge, MA: Harvard Law School, 2009.

———. *The Ideological Origins of American Federalism*. Cambridge, MA: Harvard University Press, 2010.

Lawrence, D. H. "Benjamin Franklin." In *Benjamin Franklin and the American Character*, edited by Charles L. Sanford, 57–64. Boston: D.C. Heath, 1955.

Lee, Arthur. Papers. Houghton Library, Harvard University.

Lee, Richard Henry. *Life of Arthur Lee, LL.D.* 2 vols. Boston: Wells and Lilly, 1829.

Legaspi, Michael C. *The Death of Scripture and the Rise of Biblical Studies*. Oxford: Oxford University Press, 2010.

Lehmann, Hartmut. "Another Look at Federalism in the Holy Roman Empire." In *German and American Constitutional Thought: Contexts, Interaction, and Historical Realities*, edited by Hermann Wellenreuther, 80–85. New York: St. Martin's Press, 1990.

Lemay, J. A. Leo, ed. *Reappraising Benjamin Franklin. A Bicentennial Perspective*. Newark, DE: University of Delaware Press, 1993.

———. *The Life of Benjamin Franklin*. 3 vols. Philadelphia: University of Pennsylvania Press, 2005–2008.

Lemisch, Jesse, and John K. Alexander. "The White Oaks, Jack Tar, and the Concept of the Inarticulate." *William and Mary Quarterly* 3rd ser., 29 (1972): 109–34.

Levin, David. "Franklin: Experimenter in Life and Art." In *Benjamin Franklin: Statesman-Philosopher or Materialist?* edited by Wilbur R. Jacobs, 58–62. New York: Holt, Reinhart and Winston, 1972.

[Lind, John.] *An Answer to the Declaration of the American Congress.* London: T. Cadell, 1776.

———. *Remarks on the Principal Acts of the Thirteenth Parliament of Great Britain.* London: T. Payne, 1775.

Livingston, Luther S. *Franklin and His Press at Passy.* New York: Grolier, 1914.

Longfellow, Henry Wadsworth. *Hyperion: A Romance.* Boston: Ticknor, Reed, and Fields, 1853.

Mackesy, Piers. *Could the British Have Won the War of Independence?* Worcester, MA: Clark University Press, 1976.

———. *The War for America, 1775–1783.* London: Longmans, 1964.

Macpherson, C. B. *The Political Theory of Possessive Individualism: Hobbes to Locke.* Oxford: Clarendon Press, 1962.

Madden, A. F. M. "1066, 1776 and All That: The Relevance of English Medieval Experience of 'Empire' to Later Imperial Constitutional Issues." In *Perspectives of Empire,* edited by John E. Flint and Glyndr Williams, 9–26. London: Longmans, 1973.

Magnus, Rudolf. *Goethe as Scientist.* Translated by Heinz Norden. New York: Henry Schuman, 1949.

Mahoney, Dennis F. "Autobiographical Writings." In *The Cambridge Companion to Goethe,* edited by Lesley Sharpe, 147–59. Cambridge: Cambridge University Press, 2002.

Main, Jackson Turner. *The Sovereign States, 1775–1783.* New York: New Viewpoints, 1973.

Marston, Jennifer Greene. *King and Congress.* Princeton, NJ: Princeton University Press, 1987.

Marty, Martin E., and Jonathon Moore. *Politics, Religion, and the Common Good: Advancing a Distinctly American Conversation about Religion's Role in our Shared Life.* San Francisco, CA: Jossey-Bass, 2000.

Marx, Karl. *Capital.* Volume 1. Translated by Ben Fowkes. Harmondsworth, UK: Penguin, 1990.

———. *A Contribution to the Critique of Political Economy.* New York: International Publishers, 1970.

Matthew, H. C. G., and Brian Harrison, eds. *Oxford Dictionary of National Biography.* 60 vols. Oxford: Oxford University Press, 2004.

McConville, Brendan. *The King's Three Faces: The Rise and Fall of Royal America, 1688–1776.* Chapel Hill: University of North Carolina Press, 2006.

McLuhan, Marshall, and Quentin Fiore. *The Medium Is the Massage: An Inventory of Effects.* New York: Random House, 1967.

Middlekauff, Robert. "Benjamin Franklin, Pragmatic Visionary: Politician, Diplomat, Statesman." In Talbott, *Benjamin Franklin: In Search of a Better World,* 199–233.

Miller, Clarence William. *Benjamin Franklin's Philadelphia Printing, 1728–1766: A Descriptive Bibliography.* Memoirs of the American Philosophical Society 102. Philadelphia: American Philosophical Society, 1974.

Mommsen, Katharina. *Goethe und unsere Zeit.* Frankfurt am Main: Suhrkamp, 1999.

Morgan, Edmund S. *Benjamin Franklin.* New Haven, CT: Yale University Press, 2002.

Morgan, Edmund S., and Helen M. Morgan. *The Stamp Act Crisis: Prologue to Revolution.* Chapel Hill: University of North Carolina Press, 1953.

Morris, Richard B. *The Peacemakers.* New York: Harper & Row, 1965.

Moses, Wilson J. "Protestant Ethic or Conspicuous Consumption? Benjamin Franklin and the Gilded Age." In Mulford, *Cambridge Companion to Franklin,* 132–44.

Motley, John Lothrop. Senior Exhibition Essay. Harvard University Archives.

Mouffe, Chantal, ed. *Dimensions of Radical Democracy: Pluralism, Citizenship, Community.* London: Verso, 1992.

Mulford, Carla. "Benjamin Franklin, Traditions of Liberalism, and Women's Learning in Eighteenth-Century Philadelphia." In *"The Good Education of Youth": Worlds of Learning in the Age of Franklin,* edited by John Pollack, 100–121. New Castle, DE and Philadelphia: Oak Knoll Press and University of Pennsylvania Libraries, 2009.

————, ed. *The Cambridge Companion to Benjamin Franklin*. Cambridge: Cambridge University Press, 2008.

Namier, Lewis, and John Brooke. *The House of Commons*. 3 vols. New York: Oxford University Press, 1964.

Nash, Gary B. *The Urban Crucible: Social Change, Political Consciousness, and the Origins of the American Revolution*. Cambridge, MA: Harvard University Press, 1979.

Nelson, Paul David. *General Sir Guy Carleton, Lord Dorchester*. Madison, NJ: Fairleigh Dickinson University Press, 2000.

Neuhaus, Helmut. "The Federal Principle and the Holy Roman Empire." In *German and American Constitutional Thought: Contexts, Interaction, and Historical Realities*, edited by Hermann Wellenreuther, 27–49. New York: St. Martin's Press, 1990.

Newman, Simon P. *Parades and the Politics of the Street: Festive Culture in the Early American Republic*. Philadelphia: University of Pennsylvania Press, 1997.

Nord, David Paul. "Benjamin Franklin and Journalism." In Waldstreicher, *Companion to Benjamin Franklin*, 290–307.

Norris, John. *Shelburne and Reform*. London: Macmillan & Co., 1963.

Onuf, Peter S. *The Origins of the Federal Republic*. Philadelphia: University of Pennsylvania Press, 1983.

Osborne, Jeff. "Benjamin Franklin and the Rhetoric of Virtuous Self-Fashioning in Eighteenth-Century America." *Literature and History* 17, no. 2 (2008): 14–30.

O'Shaughnessy, Andrew Jackson. *An Empire Divided*. Philadelphia: University of Pennsylvania Press, 2000.

————. "If Others Will Not Be Active, I Must Drive." *Early American Studies* 2 (2004): 1–46.

Oswald, John Clyde. *Benjamin Franklin, Printer*. Garden City, NY: Doubleday, Page & Co., for the Associated Advertising Clubs of the World, 1917.

Overhoff, Jürgen. *Benjamin Franklin: Erfinder, Freigeist, Staatenlenker*. Stuttgart: Klett-Cotta Verlag, 2006.

Pagden, Anthony. *Lords of All the World*. New Haven, CT: Yale University Press, 1995.

Pangle, Lorraine Smith. *The Political Philosophy of Benjamin Franklin*. Baltimore: Johns Hopkins University Press, 2007.

Papers of the Continental Congress, 1774–1789. Washington, DC: Government Printing Office, 1959.

Parton, James. *Life and Times of Benjamin Franklin*. 2 vols. Boston: Ticknor and Fields, 1867.

Patterson, Annabel M. *Early Modern Liberalism*. Cambridge: Cambridge University Press, 1997.

Pencak, William. "Benjamin Franklin's Autobiography, Cotton Mather, and a Puritan God." *Pennsylvania History* 53 (1986): 1–25.

Philadelphia Lottery Accounts. Philadelphia: Franklin and Hall, 1752.

Pickering, Danby, ed. *The Statutes at Large*. 46 vols. Cambridge: Joseph Bentham, 1762–1807.

Pincus, Steven. "From Butterboxes to Wooden Shoes: The Shift in English Popular Sentiment from Anti-Dutch to Anti-French in the 1670s." *Historical Journal* 38 (1995): 333–61.

————. "Neither Machiavellian Moment nor Possessive Individualism: Commercial Society and the Defenders of the English Commonwealth." *American Historical Review* 103 (1998): 705–36.

————. "Popery, Trade and Universal Monarchy: The Ideological Context of the Outbreak of the Second Anglo-Dutch War." *English Historical Review*, no. 422 (January 1992): 1–29.

————. *Protestantism and Patriotism: Ideologies and the Making of English Foreign Policy, 1650–1668*. Cambridge: Cambridge University Press, 1996.

Pitt Papers. Public Record Office. Prerogative Court of Canterbury, England.

Pocock, J. G. A. "Contingency, Identity, Sovereignty." In *The Making of British History*, edited by Alexander Grant and Keith B. Stringer, 292–302. London; Routledge, 1995.

————. "Empire, State and Confederation: The War of American Independence as a Crisis in Multiple Monarchy." In *A Union for Empire*, edited by John Robertson, 318–48. Cambridge: Cambridge University Press, 1995.

————. *The Machiavellian Moment: Florentine Political Thought and the Atlantic Republican Tradition*. Princeton, NJ: Princeton University Press, 1975.

————, ed. *The Political Works of James Harrington*. Cambridge: Cambridge University Press, 1977.

Pollack, John H., ed. *The Good Education of Youth: Worlds of Learning in the Age of Franklin*. New Castle, DE and Philadelphia: Oak Knoll Press and the University of Pennsylvania Libraries, 2009.

Powell, Martyn, ed. *Oxford Dictionary of National Biography*. Oxford: Oxford University Press. 2008. www.oxforddnb.com.

[Pownall, Thomas.] *The Administration of the Colonies*. London: J. Wilkie, 1764.

————. *Administration of the British Colonies, Part the Second*. London: J. Wilkie, 1774.

————. *A Letter from Governor Pownall to Adam Smith*. London: J. Almon, 1776.

Price, Richard. *Four Dissertations. I. On Providence. II. On Prayers. III. On the Reasons for Expecting that Virtuous Men shall meet after Death in a State of Happiness. IV. On the Importance of Christianity, the Nature of historical Evidence, and Miracles*. Second Edition. London: A. Millar and T. Cadell, 1768.

————. *Price: Political Writings*. Edited by D. O. Thomas. Cambridge: Cambridge University Press, 2009.

————. *A Review of the Principal Questions and Difficulties in Morals; Particularly those Relating to the Original of our Ideas of Virtue, its Nature, Foundation, Reference to the Deity, Obligation, Subject-Matter, and Sanctions*. London: A. Millar, 1758.

Proposals for a Plan Towards a Reconciliation And Re-Union With the Thirteen Provinces of America. London: G. Kearsly, 1778.

Pulteney, William, Esq. *Thoughts on the Present State of Affairs with America*. 5th ed. London: J. Dodsley and T. Cadell, 1778.

Pütter, Johann Stephan. *Historisch-politisches Handbuch von den besonderen Teutschen Staaten*. Göttingen: Vandenhoeck, 1758.

————. *Kurzer Begriff des Teutschen Staatsrechts*. Göttingen: Vandenhoeck, 1764.

————. *Selbstbiographie*. 2 vols. Göttingen: Vandenhoeck, 1798.

Quinlan, Maurice J. "Dr. Franklin Meets Dr. Johnson," *Pennsylvania Magazine of History and Biography* 73 (1949): 34–44.

Reich, Jerome R. *British Friends of the American Revolution*. Armonk, NY: M. E. Sharpe, 1998.

Reill, Peter Hanns, and Ellen Judy Wilson. *Encyclopedia of the Enlightenment*. New York: Facts on File, 1996.

Report on the Manuscripts of Mrs. Stopford-Sackville. 2 vols. London: His Majesty's Stationery Office, 1904–1910.

Ritcheson, Charles R. *British Politics and the American Revolution*. Norman: University of Oklahoma Press, 1954.

Robbins, Caroline. *The Eighteenth-Century Commonwealthman: Studies in the Transmission, Development, and Circumstance of English Liberal Thought from the Restoration of Charles II until the War with the Thirteen Colonies*. Indianapolis, IN: Liberty Fund, 2004. First published 1959.

Robson, Eric. *The American Revolution*. London: The Batchworth Press, 1956.

Rodgers, Daniel T. "Republicanism: The Career of a Concept." *Journal of American History* 79 (June 1992): 11–38.

————. *Contested Truths: Keywords in American Politics Since Independence*. New York: Basic Books, 1987.

Rosenfeld, Sophia. "Citizens of Nowhere in Particular: Cosmopolitanism, Writing, and Political Engagement in Eighteenth-Century Europe." *National Identities* 4 (2002): 25–43.

Rossiter, Clinton. *Seedtime of the Republic: The Origin of the American Tradition of Political Liberty*. New York: Harcourt, Brace and Company, 1953.

Schaeper, Thomas J. *Edward Bancroft*. New Haven, CT: Yale University Press, 2011.

Schiff, Stacy. *A Great Improvisation. Franklin, France, and the Birth of America*. New York: Henry Holt and Company, 2006.

Schlereth, Thomas J. *The Cosmopolitan Ideal in Enlightenment Thought: Its Form and Function in the Ideas of Franklin, Hume, and Voltaire, 1694–1790*. Notre Dame, IN: University of Notre Dame Press, 1977.

Schlie, Ulrich. *Johann Stephan Pütters Reichsbegriff.* Göttingen: Schwartz, 1961.

Schocket, Andrew M. "Benjamin Franklin in Memory and Popular Culture." In Waldstreicher, *Companion to Benjamin Franklin*, 479–98.

Schultz, Ronald. *The Republic of Labor: Philadelphia Artisans and the Politics of Class, 1720–1830.* New York: Oxford University Press, 1993.

Schutz, John A. *Thomas Pownall, British Defender of American Liberty: A Study of Anglo-American Relations in the Eighteenth Century.* Glendale, CA: A. H. Clark, 1951.

Scott, H. M. *British Foreign Policy in the Age of the American Revolution.* Oxford: Clarendon Press, 1990.

Scrivener, Michael Henry. *The Cosmopolitan Ideal in the Age of Revolution and Reaction, 1776–1832.* London: Pickering & Chatto, 2007.

Shakespeare, William. *The Riverside Shakespeare: The Complete Works.* 2nd ed. Boston: Houghton Mifflin, 1997.

Shannon, Timothy J. *Indians and Colonists at the Crossroads of Empire: The Albany Congress of 1754.* Ithaca, NY: Cornell University Press, 2000.

Sheehan, Jonathan. "Enlightenment, Religion, and the Enigma of Secularization: A Review Essay." *The American Historical Review* 108, no. 4 (October 2003): 1061–80.

Shields, David. "Franklin in the Republic of Letters." In Mulford, *Cambridge Companion to Franklin*, 50–62.

Sibum, Heinz Otto. "The Bookkeeper of Nature: Benjamin Franklin's Electrical Research and the Development of Experimental Natural Philosophy in the Eighteenth Century." In *Reappraising Benjamin Franklin: A Bicentennial Perspective*, edited by J. A. Leo Lemay, 221–46. Newark: University of Delaware Press, 1993.

Simmons, R. C., and Peter David Gartner Thomas, eds., *Proceedings and Debates of the British Parliaments Respecting North America, 1754–1783.* 6 vols. Millwood, NY: Kraus International, 1982–1987.

Simms, Brendan. *Three Victories and a Defeat: The Rise and Fall of the British Empire, 1714–1783.* London: Allen Lane, 2007.

Skemp, Sheila L. *Benjamin and William Franklin: Father and Son, Patriot and Loyalist.* Boston: St. Martin's Press, 1994.

Slauter, Eric. *The State as a Work of Art: The Cultural Origins of the Constitution.* Chicago: University of Chicago Press, 2009.

Smith, Billy G. *The "Lower Sort": Philadelphia's Laboring People, 1750–1800.* Ithaca, NY: Cornell University Press, 1990.

Smith, Jeffrey A. *Franklin and Bache: Envisioning the Enlightened Republic.* New York: Oxford University Press, 1990.

Smith, Paul H. *Loyalists and Redcoats.* Chapel Hill: University of North Carolina Press, 1964.

Smith, Paul H., et al., eds., *Letters of Delegates to Congress, 1774–1789.* 26 vols. Washington, DC: Library of Congress, 1974–2000.

Soderlund, Jean, ed. *William Penn and the Founding of Pennsylvania, 1680–1684: A Documentary History.* Philadelphia: University of Pennsylvania Press, 1983.

Sorkin, David. *The Religious Enlightenment: Protestants, Jews, and Catholics from London to Vienna.* Princeton, NJ: Princeton University Press, 2008.

Sprengel, M. C. *Allgemeines historisches Taschenbuch oder Abrisz der merkwürdigsten neun Welt-Begebenheiten enthaltend für 1784.* Die Geschichte der Revolution von Nord-America. Berlin: Haude und Spener, 1784.

Spring, Matthew H. *With Zeal and with Bayonets Only.* Norman: University of Oklahoma Press, 2008.

Ssymank, Paul. "Benjamin Franklin und die erste Berührung deutscher und nordamerikanischer Wissenschaft." *Universitätsbund Göttingen. Mitteilungen* 15, no. 2 (1934), 1–16.

Stephens, John. "Conscience and the Epistemology of Morals: Richard Price's Debt to Joseph Butler." *Enlightenment and Dissent* 19 (2000): 133–46.

Stevens, Benjamin Franklin. *Facsimiles of Manuscripts in European Archives Relating to America, 1773–1783.* 25 vols. London: Charles Whittingham and Co., 1898.

Stevens, Jacqueline. "The Reasonableness of John Locke's Majority: Property Rights, Consent, and Resistance in the *Second Treatise*." *Political Theory* 24 (1996): 423–63.

Stone, Peter, and Sherman Edwards. *1776: A Musial Play.* New York: Penguin, 1982.

Tagg, James. *Benjamin Franklin Bache and the Philadelphia Aurora.* Philadelphia: University of Pennsylvania Press, 1991.

Talbott, Page, ed. *Benjamin Franklin: In Search of a Better World.* New Haven, CT: Yale University Press, 2005.

Taylor, Alan. *The Civil War of 1812.* New York: Alfred A. Knopf, 2010.

Taylor, William Stanhope, and John Henry Pringle, eds. *Correspondence of William Pitt, Earl of Chatham.* 4 vols. London: John Murray, 1838–1840.

Thomas, D. O. *The Honest Mind: The Thought and Work of Richard Price.* New York: Oxford University Press, 1977.

Thomas, Peter D. G. *From Tea Party to Independence.* Oxford: Clarendon Press, 1991.

Tocqueville, Alexis de. *Democracy in America.* Translated and edited by Harvey C. Mansfield and Delba Winthrop. Chicago: University of Chicago Press, 2000.

Tolles, Frederick B. "Franklin and the Pulteney Mission: An Episode in the Secret History of the American Revolution." *Huntington Library Quarterly* 17 (1954): 37–58.

Toohey, Robert. *Liberty and Empire.* Lexington: University of Kentucky Press, 1978.

Townshend, Thomas, 1st Viscount Sydney Papers 1665–1828. 3 vols. William L. Clements Library, University of Michigan.

Tucker, Josiah. *Four Tracts, together with Two Sermons on Political and Commercial Subjects.* Glocester: R. Raikes, 1774.

———. *Tract V.* Glocester: R. Raikes, 1775.

Tudda, Chris. "'A Messiah that Will Never Come': A New Look at Saratoga, Independence, and Revolutionary War Diplomacy." *Diplomatic History* 32 (2008): 779–810.

Umbach, Maiken. *Federalism and Enlightenment in Germany, 1740–1806.* London: Hambledon Press, 2000.

Van Doren, Carl. *Benjamin Franklin.* New York: Viking Press, 1938.

Van Horne, John C. "Collective Benevolence and the Common Good in Franklin's Philanthropy." In *Reappraising Benjamin Franklin: A Bicentennial Perspective*, edited by J. A. Leo Lemay, 425–40. Newark, DE: University of Delaware Press, 1993.

Vierhaus, Rudolf. "*Benjamin Franklin*: Rede anläßlich der Enthüllung einer Gedenktafel am 24. September 1981, Prinzenstraße 21 (Michaelishaus)." *Göttinger Jahrbuch* 30 (1982): 206–8.

Waldstreicher, David. *A Companion to Benjamin Franklin.* Malden, MA: Wiley-Blackwell, 2011.

———. *Runaway America: Benjamin Franklin, Slavery, and the American Revolution.* New York: Hill and Wang, 2004.

Walpole, Horace. *The Last Journals of Horace Walpole during the Reign of George III, from 1771–1783.* Edited by A. Francis Steuart. 2 vols. New York: J. Lane, 1910.

Walsh, Megan E. "Benjamin Franklin's Material Cultures." In Waldstreicher, *Companion to Benjamin Franklin,* 412–29.

Walters, Kerry S. *Benjamin Franklin and His Gods.* Urbana: University of Illinois Press, 1999.

Walz, Hans. "Benjamin Franklin in Hannover 1766." *Hannoverische Geschichtsblätter* 21 (1967): 61–65.

Ward, John William. "Franklin: His Masks and His Character." *American Scholar* 32 (1963): 541–53.

Warner, Michael. *The Letters of the Republic: Publication and the Public Sphere in Eighteenth-Century America.* Cambridge, MA: Harvard University Press, 1992.

Weber, Max. *The Protestant Ethic and the Spirit of Capitalism.* Translated by Talcott Parsons. New York: Charles Scribners, 1958.

———. *The Protestant Ethic and the Spirit of Capitalism.* 2nd ed. London: Routledge, 2001.

Weinberger, Jerry. "Benjamin Franklin and Political Theory." In Waldstreicher, *Companion to Benjamin Franklin,* 430–62.

———. *Benjamin Franklin Unmasked: On the Unity of His Moral, Religious, and Political Thought.* Lawrence: University Press of Kansas, 2005.

Wentworth Woodhouse Muniments. Sheffield Archives, England.

Wetzels, Walter D. "Goethe's Belief in Himself: Talent as Gift and Obligation." *Literature and Belief: Special Issue on Goethe and Religion* 20, no. 2 (2000): 27–36.

Wharton, Francis, ed. *The Revolutionary Diplomatic Correspondence of the United States.* 6 vols. Washington, DC: Government Printing Office, 1889.

Wheare, K. C. *The Statute of Westminster and Dominion Status.* [1938]. 5th ed. Oxford: Oxford University Press, 1953.

Wheatley, Henry B., ed. *The Historical and the Posthumous Memoirs of Sir Nathaniel William Wraxall, 1772–1784.* 5 vols. London: Bickers and Sons, 1884.

Wild, Reiner. "Prometheus-Franklin: Die Gestalt Benjamin Franklins in der deutschen Literatur des 18.Jahrhunderts." *Amerikastudien* 23, no. 1 (1978): 30–39.

Willcox, William B. "Why Did the British Lose the American Revolution." *Michigan Alumnus Quarterly Review* 62 (1956): 317–24.

Wollaston, William. *The Religion of Nature Delineated.* London: Sam. Palmer, 1724.

Wood, Gordon S. *The Americanization of Benjamin Franklin.* New York: Penguin, 2004.

Wootton, David, ed. *Republicanism, Liberty, and Commercial Society, 1649–1776.* Stanford, CA: Stanford University Press, 1994.

Wright, Esmond. "The *Autobiography*: Fact or Fiction?" In *The Intellectual World of Benjamin Franklin: An American Encyclopaedist at the University of Pennsylvania,* edited by Dilys Pegler Winegrad, 29–42. Philadelphia: University of Pennsylvania Press, 1990.

Wolf, Edwin 2nd, and Kevin J. Hayes. *The Library of Benjamin Franklin.* Philadelphia: American Philosophical Society and Library Company of Philadelphia, 2006.

Yolton, John W., Roy Porter, Pat Rogers, and Barbara Maria Stafford, eds. *The Blackwell Companion to the Enlightenment.* Oxford: Blackwell, 1993.

York, Neil L. "American Revolutionaries and the Illusion of Irish Empathy." *Eire-Ireland* 21 (1986): 13–30.

———. "Ending the War and Winning the Peace: The British in America and the Americans in Vietnam." *Soundings* 90 (1987): 444–74.

———. "The First Continental Congress and the Problem of American Rights." *Pennsylvania Magazine of History and Biography* 122 (1998): 353–83.

———. *Turning the World Upside Down: The War of American Independence and the Problem of Empire.* Westport, CT: Praeger, 2003.

Young, Alfred F. *The Shoemaker and the Tea Party: Memory and the American Revolution.* Boston: Beacon Press, 1999.

Zebrowski, Martha K. "We May Venture to Say, That the Number of Platonic Readers Is Considerable: Richard Price, Joseph Priestley, and the Platonic Strain in Eighteenth-Century British Thought." *Enlightenment and Dissent* 19 (2000): 193–213.

Zuckerman, Michael. "Founding Fathers: Franklin, Jefferson, and the Educability of Americans." In *"The Good Education of Youth": Worlds of Learning in the Age of Franklin,* edited by John Pollack, 36–53. New Castle, DE and Philadelphia: Oak Knoll Press and University of Pennsylvania Libraries, 2009.

Zuckerman, Michael. "Doing Good While Doing Well: Benevolence and Self-Interest in Franklin's *Autobiography.*" In *Reappraising Benjamin Franklin: A Bicentennial Perspective,* edited by J. A. Leo Lemay, 441–51. Newark, DE: University of Delaware Press, 1993.

———. "Founding Fathers: Franklin, Jefferson, and the Educability of Americans." In *"The Good Education of Youth": Worlds of Learning in the Age of Franklin,* edited by John Pollack, 36–53. New Castle, DE and Philadelphia: Oak Knoll Press and University of Pennsylvania Libraries, 2009.

Index

List of Contributors

Roy E. Goodman is assistant librarian and curator of printed materials at the American Philosophical Society, the country's first learned society, founded in 1743 by Benjamin Franklin. He is a director and past president of the Friends of Franklin located in Philadelphia.

Matthew S. Holland is president of Utah Valley University. Prior to that appointment he was an associate professor of Political Science at Brigham Young University. He has been a James Madison Program in American Ideals and Institutions visiting fellow at Princeton University and a Raoul Wallenberg scholar at the Hebrew University of Jerusalem. He is the author of *Bonds of Affection: Civic Charity and the Making of America.*

Paul E. Kerry is associate professor of history, associate dean of undergraduate education, and fellow of the Wheatley Institute at Brigham Young University. He is the author of *Enlightenment Thought in the Writings of Goethe* and has edited scholarly volumes on Goethe, Schiller, Mozart, and Carlyle. He has been a visiting fellow with Princeton University's James Madison Program in American Ideals and Institutions and the University of Cambridge's Centre for Research in the Arts, Sciences, and Humanities. He took his DPhil from the University of Oxford where he was a member of St. John's College. He is a fellow at the Royal Historical Society.

Carla Mulford is associate professor of English at Penn State University and is currently completing her book manuscript, *Benjamin Franklin and the Ends of Empire.* The recipient of grants in aid of research from the American Council of Learned Societies, the National Endowment for the Humanities, and the Andrew W. Mellon Foundation, Mulford has recently been honored by an award, the William L. Mitchell Prize, from the Bibliographical Society of America, for an essay published in *Proceedings of the American Philosophical Society* (2008) called "Benjamin Franklin's Savage Eloquence."

Her work has appeared in many venues, including the *William and Mary Quarterly* and the *New England Quarterly*. Among her published volumes is *The Cambridge Companion to Benjamin Franklin*.

Simon P. Newman is Sir Denis Brogan Professor of American History at the University of Glasgow and has been the recipient of numerous awards including from the British Academy, Leverhulme Trust, and the Royal Society of Edinburgh. He has published articles in a variety of scholarly venues, including the *Journal of American Studies* and *William and Mary Quarterly* and is the author of *Parades and the Politics of the Street: Festive Culture in the Early American Republic* and *Embodied History: The Lives of the Poor in Early Philadelphia*.

Jürgen Overhoff is professor of history of education at the Westfälische Wilhelms-Universität Münster and has been the recipient of numerous awards including from the British Academy and the Airlift Memorial Fund Berlin. He has published scholarly articles in leading journals (*Historische Zeitschrift, History of Political Thought, Paedagogica Historica*) on early modern political thought and educational theory. Among his books are *Hobbes's Theory of the Will*; *Benjamin Franklin: Erfinder, Freigeist, Staatenlenker*; and *Friedrich der Große und George Washington: Zwei Wege der Aufklärung*.

Lorraine Smith Pangle is professor of government and codirector for the Thomas Jefferson Center for the Study of Core Texts and Ideas at the University of Texas at Austin. She has won numerous awards and fellowships including those of the Social Sciences and Humanities Research Council of Canada and the National Endowment for the Humanities. Her publications include *Virtue is Knowledge: The Socratic Paradox and the Problem of Moral Responsibility* (forthcoming); *The Political Philosophy of Benjamin Franklin*; *Aristotle and the Philosophy of Friendship*; *The Learning of Liberty: The Educational Ideas of the American Founders* (coauthored with Thomas L. Pangle); and articles on Plato, Aristotle, the American founders, and the philosophy of education.

Benjamin E. Park is a PhD candidate in history at the University of Cambridge. He has an MPhil in political thought and intellectual history from the University of Cambridge and an MSc in theology in history from the University of Edinburgh.

Lady Joan Reid was a longtime trustee of the Benjamin Franklin House in Craven Street, London, where she is the house historian and conserving the only house left in which Franklin spent sixteen years of his life. She has lectured on Franklin in many places, including the United States. She was awarded a Fulbright Scholarship and is a graduate MA of the University of St. Andrews, where she lectured in social economics. Lady Reid served as a governor of Canterbury Christ Church University and had leading roles with a number of charities, including chairing the British Federation of Women

Graduates Charitable Trust. She was also a director of the Urban Learning Foundation in London, which exists to promote teacher training for inner-city schools.

Douglas B. Thomas is a designer at Brigham Young University and an adjunct instructor in graphic design. He received his MA degree in social science with an emphasis in the history of typography and graphic design from the University of Chicago.

Jerry Weinberger is University Distinguished Professor of Political Science at Michigan State University, served as chair of the department, and was awarded the university's Distinguished Faculty Award. He has published scholarly articles in leading journals, including in the *American Political Science Review*, and has edited scholarly volumes. He has also edited several editions of the works of Francis Bacon, including *Francis Bacon's History of the Reign of Henry VII: A New Edition with Introduction, Annotation, and Interpretive Essay*. He is the author of *Science, Faith, and Politics: Francis Bacon and the Utopian Roots of the Modern Age*; *A Commentary on Bacon's Advancement of Learning*; and *Benjamin Franklin Unmasked: On the Unity of His Moral, Religious, and Political Thought*.

Neil L. York is professor of history at Brigham Young University, served as chair of the department, and was awarded the university's Maeser Professorship. Among his books are *Henry Hulton and the American Revolution: An Outsider's Inside View*; *The Boston Massacre: A History with Documents*; *Turning the World Upside Down: The War of American Independence and the Problem of Empire*; and *Neither Kingdom nor Nation: The Irish Quest for Constitutional Rights, 1698–1800*. He and Professor Dan Coquillette of Harvard Law School edited the Josiah Quincy papers, a five-volume collection published by the Colonial Society of Massachusetts, of which he is a nonresident member. He is also a fellow of the Massachusetts Historical Society.

Michael Zuckerman is professor of history at the University of Pennsylvania. He has had fellowships from SSRC, NEH, Guggenheim, ACLS, Rockefeller, Fulbright, Bellagio, and the Netherlands Institute for Advanced Studies. His first book, *Peaceable Kingdoms: New England Towns in the Eighteenth Century*, helped inaugurate the (no-longer-so-) New Social History. His subsequent works—three more books and more than a hundred articles—have ranged over subjects such as American identity, popular culture, and the history of childhood and the family. He has presented lectures and scholarly papers on five continents, and his writings have been published in Brazil, China, France, Great Britain, Italy, Japan, the Netherlands, Poland, and Russia.